To S{

(handwritten)

People Call Ya Crazy when Ya Talk Like That...
(No Turn Unstoned)

up ya Bum

(handwritten)

by

Steve [Speed Machine aka Bastados] Redman

Sex, Drag2
mt Rock and Soul
"cos i Like Fish!!
Steve
F.T.W,

(handwritten inscription)

This book is published by
Grosvenor House Publishing Ltd
28-30 High Street, Guildford, Surrey, GU1 3HY.
www.grosvenorhousepublishing.co.uk

A CIP record for this book
is available from the British Library

ISBN 1-905529-79-1

INTRODUCTION

GREETINGS... and welcome to a tribute to counterculture through the eyes of a young impressionable boy ...who dared look... heroes, heroin(e)s, whores, health freaks, poets, Artie, and Farty, junkies, bikers, punks, skins, gays, casuals, rastas, rude boys, hippies, yippies, dippies, jokers, dopers, cockers, croakers and tokers, smack-heads, crack-heads, fick-heads, big heads and shit-heads. Geeks to Speed freaks, oil sheiks, writers in dypers, nibblers and scribblers, dibblers and dabblers, dabbers, spray paint graffiti wall dribblers, boozers, shmoozers, losers, cruisers, blown fuses, drunks, jerks, hangers on, hangers off, uppers, downers, all arounders, the highs, the lows, the musos and the shows. The tribes and the vibes, tripping, stripping, skipping, running and jumping. Love and hate young and old, rich or poor, black or white, wrong or right, weak and might not need to fight, when all is right. No rules, no laws, no one leader, no set morals, and no morals, no judgment, no regrets, no respect, and respect, respectful and respectable... A VORTEX IN TIME...

CHILDENSTEIN

THE CHILDENSTEINE ...

I was born, kicking, screaming, farting, and burping [not a lot has changed] an ugly little brat according to mother, she say's that when I was taken out from the hospital [or asked to leave] ha, ha, ha fuckin ha, that I was in fact so skinny and long with a shrivelled up little rat face that she was too embarrassed to let other mothers see this 'orrible childensteine scary type creation that she had produced from her womb from the past whole nine months and so kept a sun shade over my pram as often as she could, so as not to scare old ladies, children, small dogs or put any expectant mothers off the very idea of giving birth to anything as freakish as her potato headed breast suckling beast resembling that of a human prune in babies clothing!

So, raised in the darkest parts of West London known as North Acton, on the west way or as it is known to the locals Gypsy corner.

Star sign, Taurus THE BULL, born on the second day of may 1960 [the day of human observation] - or THAT WHICH SHATTERS THE SILENCE WE CALL NOISE. THAT WHICH ENHANCES THE SILENCE WE CALL MUSIC.

Extremely poignant and a vastly typical observation of my nature and being at that, as I think you will discover as I proceed to stumble my way through life, relationships, the odd job [or working for da man] with some of the most bizarre if not wacky good (and bad) stories, fables and also tales of fancy, fantasy foolhardy and in some cases outright verging on the blooming ridicule arse at times adventures…So hold on to ya knickers! open a bottle of bourbon skin up a big fat joint [I have] put the kids to bed feed the bloody dog send the misses out for a girlie night out on the town [turn that porn film off ? Sit tight as I will be you're captain taking you on a helter skelter ride packed full of blood, violence, dark tales of sex and sin!

Add that to an unhealthy fascination with all things freakish of nature mixed together with a dusting of chaos then subjected to a sickly sweet but necessary topping off with an un-healthy sprinkling of luuuve interest [for the girls] so enter if you DARE into a CAKE! (no, stop it) journey where you too can read for yourself about someone rushing in blindly, coming out fighting, if not always knowing why…STUBBORN, LOYAL, ROMANTIC..

FUCKING SEXY!! [Oh, did I add that]

SO HEAR WE

AVE IT …. FUCKIN LARGE!

In a time of change in a world where the rules were being challenged from all angles, the Vietnam war had come to a non conclusive and very much brushed under the carpet state of affairs, man had landed on the moon we were now in the middle of the so called cold war that was inherited from our fathers and a new vision of a very different type was starting to surface a new 'subculture' where the original hippie dream was dying and the engine of a new 'phenomena' was manifesting itself in all shapes and sizes. Where older rockers were seen now as warlords, straddled on near science-fiction, gleaming, over the top gnarling monstrous steeds… AND hippies fast became the new alternative oracles of knowledge, New Age gurus, many of whom were returning from the Far East and other far flung and exotic places, telling stories of alternative lifestyles, newly found wisdom and a new hedonistic way of life trying to establish a collective to the 'squat culture'.

In the middle of all this there was a new rumbling of young initiates within the now near dead 'flower power' love-ins of the 1960's... As in the past music was the main focus on Youth Culture and I will turn our attentions to all but a few of the up and coming bands of the time and such (which I feel were but most relevant to the times) and people of a near-forgotten generation..i.e the so called Punk Explosion of 1977 was highlighted in the press and media as the King's Road, Chelsea phenomena... but as reflected in this book, by myself a (true Actonian).. Most of the righteous people were doin' it in Acton, Holland Park, and Notting Hill Gate and never ventured to the King's fuckin' Road... unknown to ourselves at the time, right in the thick of it. The fashion conscious and posers (as they would be known) could be found in the King's Road (and a good place for 'em) on Saturdays, adorned in their new fashionable clothes, army fatigues, bondage trousers, and all that silly stuff (later I would be wearing a mixture of that stuff myself, NEVER CUT ME HAIR THOUGH..).

Meanwhile the drug-crazed, 'couldn't give a shit' attitude (blank generation), future 'kings of the wild frontier' who were actually living the true, seven days a week, signing on, dropping out, became of 'no fixed abode'. We got thrown out by our parents when Garry and I got 'nicked on our way home from a Motorhead gig with a bag of grass...mmm...that we shared with Motorhead and everyone agreed it was a truly 'different' smoke...that it was, mixed herbs from bloody Woolworths or some such place...(more about that later). Never mind, this served as enough fuel for my Dad, with his son at the tender age of seventeen, to proclaim to the said plod SEND HIM TO THE ARMY...THAT'LL SORT HIM OUT... and thus kicked my arse out the door...but I digress, we will get back to this later I'm sure, as Garry has fond memories of our squat in Askew Road.

So, having no fixed abode, myself and Garry would congregate en masse with other travellers of the Saturday afternoon jaunt down Portobello Road...with amphetamine fuelled passion (proper speed too, methadrine... AH METHADRINE... you could buy it in one-pound lines and it would blow ya fuckin' head off....you'd find yourself talking to complete strangers, drunks, small inoffensive animals, even your parents weren't safe. Drinking establishments on offer were Heneikeys (the Earl of Lonsdale - more on that place later...), the Princess Alexandra, the Elgin, the Colville, etc...

This book is not about the death of a trend but the re-charging of the old batteries and 'more, harder, faster' in my case, living a disposable and chemically-induced and influenced youth. 1976 was one of those moments in time, a lull or short breathing space for 'alternative' sub-culture to take stock of past and present trends, allowing new blood to emerge from the dying embers of a (soon to be) past. Re-inventing it, the old values and motivations, our predecessors still having time to recapture some of their youth and jump on a new bandwagon.

Younger 'space cadets' like Gaz and myself through a series of crazy circumstances eventually sampling the bizarre world of Space Rock...Hawkwind, Gong and the then newer Planet Gong (same hippie ideals, but more of a punk edge) giving Garry the inspiration to find his own small corner of success playing mushroom-flavoured music in a similar vein (no doubt he'll be telling you about it in his own book if he ever gets out of bed long enough to get it together man). Me, I'm a Motor-head.

Both of us adorning leather jackets, white scarves, drain-pipe Levi's, long hair, offensive t-shirt's...with a new freak flag flying and a new slogan, as in the 'anarchy' sign (now replacing the over-commercialised 'peace' sign]...The punk/new wave/space rock movement was beginning to pump up its muscles, grow some teeth, stick a sock down the front of its trousers.. (Stop it)...throw all our toys out of the pram and come out kicking and screaming. Asserting ourselves on an unsuspecting public... or even growing up in public...LEAVING a self-doubting hippie 'Utopia' behind, while grasping with both hands the original purveyors of hedonism, free love, new literature (IT, OZ etc.). the arts in all manor of shapes and sizes, plus adding an alternative subculture created by the self-appointed 20th Century gurus, but showing all the signs of past trends and becoming accepted in the establishment, while most of the, now middle-aged, only in it for a youth thing, now settled down with mortgages (sounds a bit like one of your two heroes)...oops... sorry gaz! (Funny how life gets up and bites ya in the booboo...) well, at least we didn't sell out completely and we didn't 'diebefore we got old'... (I always knew that would come back and haunt them, the Who that is. Not 'our genera-tion' ya see, .hee, hee, hee...)
MANY of those old schools where now household names and worst scenario still? were now selling themselves on TV, talk fuckin' shows with Parkinson and the ilk reminiscing about the past, with even older farts of stage and screen, making a complete mockery of all the good work that was done not that long ago...bastards! YOU KNOW WHO YOU ARE...

Thus leaving the non sell-outs still waving a freak flag at anybody that would listen in a sort of limbo.

UNFORTUNATELY the rest could be found rotting in prisons, rehabs, pubs, clubs, communes, squats or at their Mum's...others found themselves in far-flung-not so-exotic places that they found to their expense while on hippie trails looking for knowledge, enlightenment, instant karma, gurus, teachers and a whole bunch of things that this book is not about...

SO with a few, older leaders of unconformity at the helm, a new recruitment began of young and impressionable rebellious teenagers with a healthy re-arming of drug culture, back to basics three-chord crank it up, who gives a fuck if ya cant sing a note, or if ya Dad's bought you a p.a fuckin' system because he owns a pet shop.

THIS WAS GARAGE MUSIC, [I know this because I used to play in my garage] THIS WAS STREET CRED, THIS WAS OURS...and no fucker on Top of the Pops sporting a bloody ridicule-arse hairdo while wearing some watered down high street flower power type esque flowery dress [and that's just the boys! right] could understand it and we liked it that way... SO THERE...

'All other characters in this book shall be mentioned by their Christian names, street names, or made up by me either to protect or to make them sound silly? unless used in stories with no libel attachment [fingers crossed]

Or when a nickname is best served if not only to protect the guilty and on occasion innocent,

And even more prevalent to yours truly, prevent me from getting a law suit or even worse a good kick in the pants....

p.s. I would like to say though, if you send a postal order, cheque or money order to my p.o. box to lets say in the region of eeerm £100.00 or so.
I will indeed grass every body up and gladly give you on receipt of hard cash all their real names......

Mmmmmmmm......... Well maybe NOT!

THE WERE-TEEN...

Born and raised in North Acton, 1960, the youngest of three (an older brother John, sister Anna and her son making four who was to become my adopted brother and cuckoo in the nest Tony. Raised by my Mum and Dad, Rena and Lou Redman. Mum was a typical Italian woman, short, fat, obsessed with pasta, singing, cuddles, filthy jokes, her very own version of the English language naive to the ridiculous but shrewd as fuck, could always be found acting the fool or dum foreigner but sharp as a button while loving and rejoicing in all things food orientated, bizarre with a totally 'off the wall' sense of humour. Always happy and always feeding anybody or anything that would sit down at her table. Her English was vague, but she had a way of clarifying a situation (that I found quite useful in later years) that with a trusty frying pan, broom, saucepan or any other household utensil that would come to hand.

My Mum…now there's a whole book that could be written about this fish out of water. Brought up in a small village outside of Rome (Villa Santo Stepheno) St.Stevens village. Really fucking poor like 'WE' wouldn't believe. She was youngest of four with three sisters, her being, Rena then Lena and finally Zena and a brother Aroldo. As she was youngest and not the brightest cookie in the jar, Mum earned the rewarding job of house 'skivvie' (bit of a Cinderella). She was however, pretty and that only managed to get her pregnant at a real young age. According to her, none of the kids in the entire village ever talked about or got spoken to about sex, being that they were brought up Roman Catholic and so, with this, came the overbearing strict oppressive devout bible bashing bollocks of hell and damnation! (They even got beaten when they had there first period etc.) So getting preggers was a sin nobody in the village tolerated.

To put a setting to the times, ITALY back then was not anything like the fashion capital it is now able to boast, but a third world country with unclean drinking water, famine, poverty and a Catholic religion bent on keeping a very repressive hold over the whole country, plus a dictator about to lead it's country and the army into a war it really didn't need to be in, as we now know.

With this in mind, you should keep an open and focused view on how things were done.

MY GRAN...

Her mum, who could always be seen dressed in the fashionable colour of the day, 'black' and scared the shit out of me as a small boy when we used to visit her in the village, as she could be found catching birds that got caught in the loft and then frying them up for a quick snack or forever scurrying around the floors of her house with her trusty broom in hand searching like a deranged storm trooper on a recognisance mission for rodents that lived in the nooks and crannies of the old house. Then she would wait in silence for one to bravely face the gauntlet of poking it's twitchy little nose out of one of the many holes and if all seemed clear make a dash for the biscuit barrel or larder whereupon granny would be waiting with broom in gnarled hand nervously and cautiously ready to pounce and splatter the dirty little critter's head all over the stony floor, (small piece of fact, she had a tattoo of the Virgin Mary on her forearm and carried a blade, the Madonna was quite obvious and the blade was to put off any unwanted advances from the male quarter. All the girls back then did and also some had the name of their village tattooed on too). Nan was as I said a very scary lady and resembled at that age only what I can say to was, a witch. So as I had no idea of the Italian language and she had no patience and lets face it was fucking well old, well in fact even she didn't know how old she was but everyone reckoned that when she finally kicked the pasta bowl she must have been one hundred or thereabouts.

I remember one or two stories of my time on holiday with Mum in the village, I've always been fascinated by reptiles [yeah, yeah too easy to go for the cheap joke about wives and certain girlfriends...... oop's I have.] Anyway...

So as a small boy of say, eight, I loved running about the mountains and foraging about in the stone walls which divided the farm lands from each other, looking for lizards of which there were plenty, not that I could ever catch one of the little bastards, but on one occasion I did and was so pleased with my hunting and gathering skills that I took my trophy and new friend come pet back to the village to show my mum. Now Mum wasn't best pleased as she's always thought of such things as horrible wriggly things you stamp you're size nine shoe on but she did have the motherly foresight to see that I, her weird son loved the multicoloured jewel in my eyes and at that age replicating a dinosaur more than that of just a stinking lizard so she let me keep it,

But lizards being lizards wasn't having any of this and I very nearly lost him [or her] so my Uncle had an idea and tied a length of string to it's tail thus stopping the reptile from doin a runner, cool, now I could take it for walks and stuff. It was on one of these walks that a small crowd of the local children gathered to see what I had found and to my surprise and bewilderment they thought I was out of my head and proceeded to tease and taunt me to the extent of killing the small lovable creature. Well with this I ran to my Mother, tears in eyes she unloving brushed it off with a joke and a very unconvincing, "Oh well Stevie you can catch another one". Bollocks to that, so I waited until the next day for the killers to come home from school.

When they got to a break in the road I struck, with my, not so well thought out, plan.

I had gathered a large amount of rocks and when they passed by I was waiting above them behind a wall. I waited for the right moment and then I struck reeking my revenge on the murderous mob of lizard killing scum and stoned them for all I was worth, ha, ha, ha how do you like it now I thought as I pelted them with rocks and as it turned out, not very much, as to my cost, because a farmer had been watching and saw the whole thing. I was dragged by the hair and arse back home. I got a sharp kick up the bum hole from Mum, loads of abuse in Italian [just as well I had no idea what they were saying, but I sort of guessed.]

Another horrible little story of life in the Italian mountains about farmers and such as seen through a boy's eyes from Acton, was on one such day I was once again on a lizard safari and while searching through the undergrowth I was shouted at by one of the local farmers to stop it as I was tearing down his farm dividing walls. I hadn't realized the implications of my actions but was made clear of it by the helpful use of a couple of words I'd picked up and a hand gesture that I recognised, so with this I stopped for a while [as I wasn't getting very far anyway] and sat on a wall to see just what the two old buggers were up to.

Well, there was this lovely old bull in the field, real huge strong with a great mane of matted hair round his neck and a huge ring through his wet and shiny nostril. He looked every bit King of the farm and I remember thinking what a strong powerful image he was. Oh boy was I in for a shock!

The two farmers strolled over to him all nonchalant like, one I remember was carrying a sledge hammer and the other had an axe and a pick axe. I sat watching not having the least idea of the oncoming slaughter that was to take place before me, so as from out of nowhere the farmers looked at me one of them smiled at me I remember that like it was a second ago while the other grabbed hold of the bull's rope that was tied round the giant beast's neck. Then I sat and watched in disbelief and horror as they slammed the sledge hammer into the bull's skull, [thaaaaackkk] then again [wallop], followed by a few more. I sat and stared transfixed to the spot as this god of an animal dropped to his knees then laid motionless waiting for the final blows to the head to finish him off.

I was to say the least, stunned. I ran back to my Mum and told her the whole story as if I had just witnessed a murder but unfortunately this was how things were done and I had learned a harsh lesson that day. I still think of that bull and it's one of those things you witness as a child that never leaves your mind and glad to say my soul.

As we're in Italy still and I'm reminiscing things that happened then and stuff, herc's a story for ya......

It was in the middle of the second world war, so let's set the scene Mum was a skivvy in some rich cunt's house in her village and soldiers were always driving through as there was a war on, so the normally quiet village would get quite full and rowdy as the troops were travelling through, when she met a young and according to her, dashing young soldier. They courted in private and as these things happen she got pregnant. Her Mum tried all the usual things to rid her of the problem e.g. Throwing her down the stairs (that's a good one!), bathing her in boiling water (that's a blinder...) I also think the old coat-hanger trick may have been used... all of which remarkably didn't work, so off she was bundled to Rome, where she worked for the local mayor (as a slave). Basically all her wages went back to her Mum, she slept in the basement and was fed the scraps after dinner and subjected to a whole bunch of crap including beatings and molestation plus she had a new born Son to look after and this became to much of a burden for her and all concerned so they packed my Brother off to an orphanage so as my Mum could go on serving the fuckin' mayor and his shit arse family. According to Mum as I remember it, she couldn't bare leaving her new born and got very ill and so was hospitalized. Now, while in the hospital she was visited by a gypsy woman who read her cards and palm and told her to rescue her Son and that she would meet a man and live abroad [now who can tell if this is a load of bollocks] but she apparently took the advice and under the cover of a bombing raid she done a runner from the hospital and broke into the orphanage and kidnapped [ha, that's where that saying comes from] her Son.

Anyway Mum looked after him best as she could until the war ended [small point of fact, while in Rome she apparently witnessed the hanging of Mussolini in the square, cool eh!] then I suppose she went on to meet my Dad Lou. TOO MANY STORIES ABOUT HER, anyway, she married me Dad after the war and he, like loads of others brought their 'war brides' home to England, where it all started again but this time round the abuse was racism (out of the frying pan into another frying pan). Apparently she was not made welcome here in great stinking Britain and as she was an Italian war bride couldn't speak any English at all and so was totally dependent on my Dad and his fuckin' half Irish and half Scottish with bits of allsorts in their mixed up family [you'd think they would have had a bit of compassion being as they were not true blue themselves].

But hey that's the way we do things here aint it!

She was married, kept her religion ROMAN CATHOLIC and Dad kept his CHURCH OF ENGLAND and so it went on, apparently she used to get spat at in the street on a regular basis, kicked and punched and the family weren't much better either.

Poor mum, I get pretty fuckin' annoyed when I hear these half arsed stories from refugees that we're so used to nowadays, of being made unwelcome in England and all the second and third generation West Indian kid's and Pakistani and the fuckin' rest whingeing on about racism...... FUCK OFF!

I'm not a racist, well a bit, as I have listened to my old Mum's stories and witnessed it myself at home with my Dad always putting her down even up until he died at the age of eighty five, still moaning on about her never understanding anything [Tosspot].

So when I hear of these people that get housed, fed and looked after by our country at the drop of any given fuckin old hat well, then, [deep breath, let it out slowwwwwly and relax] get pampered and still have the gall to moan, it gets my back up !!!

P.S. I'm not sorry if you don't like what I have said and if you wish to take the matter up with me I'm open to any form of discussion on the matter ......

Enough said.

DAD, he was forty years my senior already and the age gap left him seeming a bit of a wanker in my eyes and totally out of touch, maybe as he was. Also there was a lot of physical and mental abuse going on at home and me being the youngest got pushed aside [in more ways than one] I was, in my eyes always looking for some kind of acceptance and never felt part of the family unit really, funny that, because as time has gone by that's just as it was and still is, my Brother and Sister, Mum, Dad, Tony and me! Well just as I was getting to know my Dad as a son should and plus being the youngest, trying to bond with him, along came my Step-brother from an unwanted pregnancy that my Sister who was still at school at the time never wanted and neither did my Mum but never the less, it was to be that Tony would join our family, driving me as the legitimate youngest Son to now second fiddle to a bleeding cuckoo.

I never thought of Tony as nothing more than my Brother until in later life when it became clear that he had reservations on the whole matter and my Sister never took to him and still to this day has no wish to have any part of him nor should I say he with her (wot a fuckin' mess).

Well DAD, now he was half Irish, half Scottish, brought up in Battersea (proper cockney); apparently our Great Granddad was a famous magician who went by the name of THE GREAT ALBINI. I don't know any more on him as my Dad told me just before he died and I can't for the life of me remember the rest of the story. Another story I can't recall and wish I could was one of his cousins or someone emigrated to America and on a return trip used to leave his gun with my Dad's Mum as he was a bit of a gangster apparently in BUGSY SEGALS mob, back in the day, [cool eh]. I can however, remember my Dad telling me that they were very poor, cardboard in the linings of their shoes, five in a bed, you know the sort of thing. Well it turned out that my Dad got a job in the Houses of Parliament as tea boy and would on occasion serve tea to the leading members of parliament and also on the odd occasion to the Prime Minister of the day [bloody name alludes me, I've got a memory like a sieve]. He also told stories of how there wasn't hardly any cars in those days and he could get around London by hitching lifts on the backs of horse and carts. He would also go swimming in the river Thames, and the Serpentine in Hyde Park, where it turns out, is where he went to school in a large tent according to him. Anyway, after the war he made good for himself with a series of self owned businesses that ultimately ended with him owning his very own fish 'n' chip shop on Gypsy Corner in North Acton. DAD played the piano, harmonica and unfortunately thought that everything his Son did was shit...or at least never gave me the push to follow a dream or even allow me to have one. He didn't get anything, as with a lot of people in those days he was a child of pre-war Britain, served in the army after lying about his age (something everyone used to do apparently back then) so getting his wish got packed off to do whatever they do with young boys willing to die for their cunt tree !!!

Well I suppose he got a hair cut, something he used to go on and on about till right up until his death on his eighty-fifth year [kind of thought it made you a man or something]. They gave him a uniform and off he went to fight in the front line in Africa. I REMEMBER MY DAD TELLING ME THAT IT DIDN'T TAKE LONG FOR HIM TO REALISE THAT THE ARMY THING WASN'T QUITE AS GLAMOROUS AS HE HAD ONCE THOUGHT AND SO HE WENT ABOUT TRYING EVERY TRICK IN THE BOOK TO GET A CUSHY RIDE [IF ONE COULD BE HAD WITH GERMANS TRYING TO KILL YOU AT ANY GIVEN MOMENT].

He told me he lied about being able to play the trumpet and they made him bugle player for a time, until one day he played the wrong tune and nearly sent a whole battalion into sure shit! [Cooool]. He then tried out as the camp's cook where he stayed for a while learning the basics of cooking which would come in very handy in later life, anyway, apparently Dad had not got on with a sergeant or something and was put in the firing line as a front line runner [one of those guy's that run the gauntlet with a piece of fuckin' paper from one trench hole to another trying not to get ya bloody noggin blown off], luckily for him in a round about way he managed to get shot in the foot, so having got shot in the foot and managing to fall victim to shell shock, so was brought back to Britain where he spent some time in hospital re-living the whole nasty experience.

After a while I think they sent him back to the war but this time the war was now coming to an end so he was packed off to Italy where he met my Mum.

After marrying my Mum and bringing her back with him. So while his musical tastes consisted of a mind-bending chorus of Max fuckin' Bygraves, Andy Williams and a long and not very impressive collection of proper crapola crooners and warblers how did I expect him to understand the musical revolution that was taking place in his very own front room, yes me. Long hair? NO FUCKIN' WAY!! ..Real men keep their hair short (prat). Guitar music was rubbish and you can't understand any of the words (well here's two…FUCK OFF).

I suppose unlike the deep and meaningful words of old maxy boy (you need hands) yes a song about needing you're fucking hands wot a cunt! Well I suppose I should have pitied him really but bollocks to that. [FUCK OFF YOU BORING OLD FART]. This sort of language went on to become a whole generation's answer to the post - Second World War values that we were supposed to follow…

Funny thing was you would have thought he might have started getting the jist of things as the whole thing had started long before with rock n roll [teds and the like] then a small band that came out of Liverpool the BEETLES they did it all before my time had ever even started, so why was he still bleating on and on about long fuckin hair!

So when a band named HAWKWIND squatted a house on our street and I saw shiny, smiley, 'freaked out' hippies with coloured hair, colourful clothes and outrageous girls… I was eleven and certain things were stirring…mmmmmm.

Their single 'SILVER MACHINE' had just been released but at that time and age I didn't make the connection between band and song... But I had just made enough noise to get my parents to purchase a Chopper bicycle (the first down my road)... and promptly laid it to ground on Mother's 'Keep off the Grass' lawn...

I stole a can of silver spray, and proceeded to customise said bike... It looked great and I even wrote ' Silver Machine' down the side, oh and I sprayed most of the lawn silver too (they should have seen the artist in me then). Oh yeah... then a sharp thud was felt to the rear and over the noggin, a loud doing could also be heard courtesy of your hero's head. So, now the customising was done I set out, on the mean streets (outside my house). I remember riding down the road passing said band's house, just as they were leaving to go out somewhere or indeed, board the mother ship? When somebody noticed my handi-work and said in a laidback hippy drawl [a bit like Dillon the fuckin rabbit on the MAGIC ROUNDAKRAUT] "Cool bike maaaaan".
I was filled with joy and pleasantly surprised and flattered at the recognition. I at once cycled as fast as my scrawny little legs would physically take me back home to pronounce my joy by enlightening my Mum with the words WHEN I GROW UP I WANT TO BE JUST LIKE THAT. Then a familiar warm glow seemed to cover my entire body, a sharp flick round the old bonce, and a claim that if I was ever caught hanging around or looking in the general direction of those sort of people. WELL.

Dad had an Mk2 (I think) Jag, like the one in 'The Sweeney', it was cherry red. He bought it cash and it was his crowning glory. I remember we all drove to Italy in it around 1965 through the

Swiss Alps. I've got vivid memories of standing on the edge of the mountain road side holding my Dad's hand looking down for wot seemed like miles over the pine trees. Back home me and my Dad used to go for long Sunday drives down the A40, it was only a two lane road in them days. He used to open the Jag up, and we'd get up to 130mph+ sometimes, no Old Bill, no traffic. I feel I should say at this point that even though my Dad often didn't see eye to eye, he did let me move back home on numerous occasions, even if it only lasted 'til the next argument. Plus he did strange, secretly caring things like moving my belongings from squat to squat and always putting a fifty in my pocket (I always spent it on dope). My Son's doing the same to me at the moment; he thinks I haven't got a clue where the money's going...nothing changes.

I remember, wot, remember... (Oh yes) I remember me and Gaz bunking off school going to my Mum's, 'cos she didn't mind me taking afternoons off. I kept her company, playing cards, watching 'Little House on the fuckin' Prairie' and translating the soaps to her, or sometimes she'd make her own story up, phew.

And yeah, the teachers my first real confrontation with teachers happened when I was around nine years old at the Acton Wells primary school. [Not there now] well there was this teacher, name alludes me but he was very old school, not old but strict old school.
I was once caught fighting with another lad and we got sent to this bloke for punishment, this is quite bizarre to write actually, coz if this ever happened now it would make front page news.
There were two incidents actually, the first is how I've stated we got caught fighting and the punishment was to have us both make a fist and the teacher would hold both our wrists and wrap

them together knuckle to knuckle, [boy did that hurt]. Then we also got the cane, and it bloody well hurt from this sadistic prick!

The second time the school self appointed Gestapo had his sweet revenge on my playful fighting was when once again I was brought up in front of the jerk but this time he really wanted to teach me a lesson!

How he thought he could get away with this is remarkable but any way, he had a CAT OF NINE TAILS, if you don't know wot this is I'll tells ya. The cat of nine tails was a short hand held leather strap or whip, not very long around two foot with a long laced up handle and nine pieces of leather like thick boot laces hanging off it, the nine laces also had knots tied into them and so when ya got a whipping it would really do the biz. The bastard made me stand in front of him and hold my hand out stretched, and then he came down hard on me THWACK...

This happened a few times on each hand and not only did it hurt like hell but it drew blood and I couldn't hold anything for fuckin ages after. I ran home straight after this incident crying my little sore heart out while holding my hand in pain, and promptly showed my Mum.

Mum was like a bleeding white knight, come screaming banshee from hell, a rabid pit bull bent on revenge, all out war was declared.

WOT DID HE DO I WILL FUCK KEEEEEEL HIM!
NO FUCKER TOUCHES MY STEVIE....

She grabbed old faithful, [the frying pan] and marched me and herself down to the school, oh dear, MR billy big bollocks thought he was a real fuckin dude beating up on us kids but he hadn't felt the full fury of an irate five foot four red blooded mad as a rabid dog on a comedown from speed and smack and with all her teeth gnarling didn't even wait to hear his version of thing's.

SPLATT, WACK, BING, BANG, BONG...

YOU HIT MY STEVE...

I keel you,

Yeah! Go on Mum, she bashed the granny out him and it took quite a few teachers to pull her off. I'm not sure exactly wot happened to that piece of shit but I'm sure I must have been one of the last kids to get the CAT in Britain.

...MR BEETLE (asking for trouble). He taught classes in one of two 'prefab' huts. A tall, skinny bloke, really inoffensive, I liked him but I just couldn't stop myself fuckin' about and messin' with his head. I felt drawn to making his life a misery, but genuinely liked him very much... (Sorry). (Me too). Well, I brought this Gat Gun into school one day, because we were having shoot-outs at dinner-time in the playground... by ' Paki Corner', (yes that's right, Paki Corner). Everyone was so racist, but it didn't feel like that (I suppose that's how bad it was). Oh well, I'm not here to justify rights and wrongs; I'm just telling you how it was. So, back to me gun...there was this other kid who kept shooting me and had some brill hiding places, so when I saw him casually walking over to the hut, a 'Social Science' class or summit, (Garry was in that class too), I had a master plan ... when he opened the door, I'd let him 'ave it...well he did, so I did, only problem was he went to the class next fuckin' door and as Beetle came waltzin' in I shot the old bugger straight in the boat race (he was not best pleased with me I can tell ya..). Another trick would be to glue all our test papers to the desk. While I'm here, another good one is put glue on the blackboard so that when your teacher tries to write with his chalk it slides everywhere... (Snigger snigger).

Another teacher [I'm using the word teacher descriptively, not actually as the job they were doing. Never actually taught me anything of any use], well getting back, the teachers name was WEIR and although I never had him as a [teacher] he did however loom over us all as a strict, not to be messed with authoritarian and you could find this out quite easily by getting into trouble with, or by being sent to, him for punishment.

Punishment was delivered in an array of fiendishly well thought out and proven over years of trial and tribulation obviously tested and tested once again for good measure and with the best possible results in mind [severe pain].

His best law enforcement act was the well thought out simple but very effective if not a bit obvious and lacking in inspiration but making up with inventiveness was the old favourite, the SLIPPER.

I think a round of applause should be given here as the slipper was a bit crap really unless you had the misfortune of having MR WEIR unleash his uncanny way of making a pretty girlie arsed punishment into something of a masterpiece.

Now MR WEIR looked every bit the NAZI law enforcer, sporting a low personal height with those horrible little eyes that were too close together, round John Lennon glasses, a hair cut from a comic nazi book complete with side parting (very adolf) and a small 'tash with no side effect to his hair, cut straight above the ear.

His way of turning the old slipper slap on the bum into a frightening trip to the godfather of punishers was to keep his stature very stern and aggressive, NO talking, no facial expression and just the hint of commands such as here BOY! Bend over BOY! Then he would walk away leaving you in the hallway so that he could get a good run up!

Oh yes! He would give himself a real good run after a real long pause, slow as he dared go as to keep you in suspension, then he would turn take a deep breath and run at you with slipper in hand, wot a bastard!

A jump into the air was the last hurdle in this SADO-MASACHISTIC like act as he would come crashing down hard as his slight but taught, rigid frame would allow THWWWWAKKK!! Bastard...

Then he would walk off and do it again, and then repeat it again normally the standard six of the best would be order of the day but on occasion eight or more could be had.

WOT A CUNT...

Sometimes we'd go to Gaz's house where we'd play Cheech and Chong records over and over (no videos or DVD's then kids). How we'd laugh, if not quite getting all the jokes, but we knew that they knew something our parents didn't, AND WE WANTED IN... Gaz was already proficient in the art of string-ing more than three chords together (and knew the names to 'em), I still don't... He'd played the local pubs and working men's clubs with his Dad, brill training ground... as I recall he knew all the Beatles stuff, I didn't (still don't) but back then it seemed cooler (or easier) to say I didn't want to play 'em..(I did really).

Garry was playing in various bands at school etc. I was playing in a band we formed over the 'park' (North Acton Playing Fields). We moved our new-found venture and girl puller to the local West Acton youth club. The name of the band was ELMIT and our logo was a German helmet in the shape of a penis...'ELMIT, geddit? (Come on, we were fifteen). Our songs sounded very much like the only chords we could play (funny that). Incidentally, one of the songs I wrote sounded spookily like Silver Machine, as I'd spent the last year and a half perfect-ing the chord changes, trashing my fave guitar in frustration,

driving my family 'round the bend, discovering the COLOUR-
SOUND fuzz wa-wa.. oh wot joy (if you kept your foot on the
back of the pedal and gradually moved it down, while playing
the chords to Silver Machine you'd get a feedback type whistle
that sounded very much like the record) So I applied this to my
song and was an instant hit with my friends.

We then went on to record a demo in St Johns Wood. Mmm,
well it was being squatted by some hippies, one of them was the
brother of one of the girls from the park, Sue Stewart was her
name and she was apart of our little gang of mindless yobbery
and harmless funsters although we sometimes thought that we
were a tuff street wise gang of renegades chilling out over the
pavilion in the north acton playing fields.
As Julie Sage recalls we would all chip in for a packet of number
6 fags and a bottle of cheap sherry or wotever and while passing
it round about six or more youths we would all get a few mouthfuls of the rancid grape juice of our parents liking [still cant
stand that shit] well we would only have these small mouthfuls
but this alone was enough to make us act like the scary old
drunk in the woods and start making complete arses of
ourselves, ha, ha.
As we're talking of making arses of ourselves, Julie Sage has a
recollection that she felt needed documenting and I agree!
Julie as it turns out was the first girl I snogged properly and as it
happens I was the first boy she had snogged, ah.
FARADAY HIGH SCHOOL situated in the East of Acton.
After the last bell had been rung we would make our way to the
105 bus stop next to the western pub [where it turns out Gary
used to play with his Dad "in their duo", playing music, you dirty
minded childish readers. Ha, ha!
Anyway it was there that we used to wait and catch the bus
home, this particular day in question there was to be a more

adventurous time to be had and as Julie calls it the first kiss in a girls life is something you never forget ahhhhhh.

Well I'm not a girl but I do recall this momentum happening.

I do not remember this but it does sound like the sort of thing I would've done as it's still the sort of thing I bloody do?

I ran about the school apparently telling all that would hear or give a shit that I was to kiss, no snog Julie Sage after school at the 105 bus stop (plonker).

So after school we met up outside the pub and had a rather large gathering of teenage witnesses giggling and shuffling themselves into positions of how best to see the awkward couple make it school legal.

We approached each other hesitantly and she recalls (in her words) standing there like a stunned mullet our teeth and noses clashing together in an embrace of teenage clueless lust and we kissed, phew the deed was done and to my saviour the 105 bus had arrived thus leaving me with a get out clause as I ran like the fuckin' wind as I hadn't a clue wot to do after that.

So there ya go Julie, not too romantic but hey I always fancied you and never got up the courage to ask you out properly.

Now getting back to Sue cat scratch fever Stewart, well her and Deana Jean burden's sister went to Twyford and were the class of 78, Jean and I were in the same class since we were four in primary school and then in high school.

Anyway me and Sue used to fight like cat and dog, all hair pulling and claws that would penetrate skin draw blood and make a right mess of me.

Oh boy where are you now!

o.k.

Sue would also like it known that she too had a passionate snog with yours truly at some god-awful disco or something, (wot the hell fuck was I doin' there).

Apparently we met up at a pub one night and were both worse for wear and I can only imagine that after all the hair pulling, biting and scratching, ahhh the scratching, the inevitable had to happen.

We screwed each other senseless for hours then cascaded in a sweaty skin drenched torn and bleeding heap onto the car park floor.

Naaa not really.

I was a bit more experienced at the art of snogging so I imagine a healthy amount of slurping and dancing of tongues were in order and not much else.

Although as Sue tells it we never spoke of this again…

DEANA wasn't much better too much testosterone and a unhealthy amount of confused hormones, luckily for our parents it was all a case of too much play fighting and not shagging like bunnies on Viagra and cocaine [not a bad mixture].

Anyway Sue's brother moved to America and Sue followed, later Julie would get married and move to Australia and has two lovely kids.

So hi to ya.

Getting back to the digressed story.

Sue's brother in law had this proper, full up and running studio in the basement.

When we had finished the demo, we had a problem getting my stuff home until some bright spark (I hope it wasn't me) thought up the idea of pushing my four-by -fifteen watt speaker cab and Marshall one hundred watt amp home to North Acton, some —
———- miles walk. Deke and myself set off and Adrian the bassist went missing I think [refer to Adrian] Adrian remembers it like this.

"Steve I didn't help push the amp and cab back 'cause you lot got me so out of it on paki black". [This is a non politically correct name for black hash]. Ha, ha "I was wandering around outside of there fuckin' house for ages trying to find my way back in, eventually I gave it all up as a lost cause and finally found the tube station and fucked off home".

Well there you have it, back to my recollections.

At one point we were pulled by the police, they searched and questioned us then realising our predicament were now laughing, needless to say we were sent on our way and given an 'escort' of sorts, well in fact each watch radioed ahead and then would proceed to beep us on our long and embarrassing walk home.

By now the name of the band had changed to FIREBIRD. This was named after my guitar which was called a 'Ned Callan', which was the guitar builder Peter Cook's pseudonym. He made all of John Entwhistle's basses and a whole lot of other rock celebs of the time and was a bit of a guitarist guru, he later would fix Lemmy's after-tour stuff.

Anywho, we recorded about four songs in a week or so, really good fun jamming with real musicians and just being able to hang out in a totally groovy house. The hippies there went on to move to the States and worked with Earth, Wind and Fire.

The band Firebird was around for a year or so. We played all the usual places, the youth club, Acton Town Hall, some other town halls, I do remember though supporting Gary bleeding Numan at some hall type thing place, well I had just bought one of those new fangled marshall integrated [transistor] 100 watt amplifiers that had just come out and was gagging to plug it in turn it up and let ripp!

No such chance, as the fuckin' over rated radio receiver was proper crapola, and as soon as I plugged it in turned up the volume, it went pop and died. Luckily Adrian's Dad was at hand and he drove us back to the guitar shop we purchased it from and he had a few choice words of persuasion and off we went with another converted radio. This did exactly the same thing so off we trundled back to the shop and demanded two this time and ventured back to the gig where we wired the both of them up together and it worked.

Well the amp worked but as usual the main man's band were arseholes and it all got luverly and horrible and we trashed the fuckin' place.

Anyway, this was 1975 and punk was just rearing its ugly head. The movement hadn't got a name as such then, but there was a buzz around but nobody was quite sure wot. We were still into Deep Purple, Led Zeppelin and the big rock thang, but a friend kept pestering me with Underground music which I didn't really get, but it was more in tune with us than I realised (The Stooges, Ramones, and Johnny Thunders etc.). On reflection we played and was actually one of the first ever Punk bands in West London, WE JUST DIDN'T KNOW IT plus we had the added factor that we were a gang more than a band and would gladly join any hecklers that wanted to throw stuff at us (and usually did) by disregarding our instruments and diving into the crowd..

FIREBIRD came to an end at the beginning of 1976, when we played a gig at the Questors theatre in Ealing. This was a very well established venue of the 'Arts', mmm and once a year they would have a 'Battle of the Bands' (poor choice of phrasing by them). When we arrived all the local talent was there, Pete Townshend's brother Paul, strutting around like he'd actually contributed something to rock 'n roll (oh, he had his own p.a) and in true 'Bad News' spoof rock reality, he wouldn't let anyone use it... WOT A PLONKER. Then there was the musical young geniuses of the time with their GENESIS, YES E.L. fucking P...type shit... and a couple of new bands, some of which were bloody good and some went on to become very eloquent in the

New Wave movement a couple of years later... BUT that night we rocked...we bullied our way from bottom of the bill to second, to top (ha). We had our own following by then, a right old mixture of local thugs, skinheads, or suede heads as they were known by then, all box tops and Crombies, some young bikers, us...Still trying to grow our hair and still wearing flares we'd made at home by cutting out triangles and sewing them into the seam's of our jeans. I remember doing the sound check in the afternoon, and then we went our different ways (a rock band).

I went to the pub with the other guitarist and the bass player but the others had a different plan. When we finally got to go on stage the other half of our band was missing. NOT FOR LONG.... [BASTARDS]. They'd gone down the fuckin' barbers (yes, the barbers!), the place your Mum would make you go to...traitors... only one place worse in my book and that's the dentist (o.k. I'll calm down). Yes, the singer (I say 'singer') had got a crop and had it dyed some daft colour, a Swastika drawn on the side of his face and wearing ladies knickers (no he wasn't but he might as well have).

Our drugs of choice had changed as well, I had my standard three joints on top of my now new valve 100 watt Marshall amp and a bottle of John Smith's beer next to 'em (the bottle was also a good crowd pacifier, if needed) they came on sniffing glue, totally pissed and all hell broke loose. We actually got about four songs in when another gang started throwing stuff at us and calling us names, shouting out 'Fuckin' punks get off!', this I was sort of into myself but mates are mates and the next thing that happened was we all jumped in the audience and the fire hoses were put on us...brilliant... didn't think so at the time. When it was all calmed down the headline band came on, Paul fuckin'

Townshend…we set fire to the theatre curtains, ha! that put an end to his ' I've got a p.a and you can't use it'…

This particular gig did actually make a small but memorable exit. A young journalist by the name of Carol Clerk who worked for the Acton Gazette gave us an interview and a write-up (she later went on to be one of the foremost, cool, 'tell it as it is' media writers for the Melody Maker).

After that, the rest of that band went off to become the SATEL-LITES… Well known West London punk band and their first single were released by Rat Scabies of the Damned and I wrote it. It was the first song I ever wrote on one string (bloody awful).

Derek Gibbs, singer and front man with the Satellites later went on to form the LONDON LOSERS with me. Frenchy (of Flick-nife records infamy) would later pick up on us and try unsuc-cessfully to release a record, the 'Losers' would go on in many forms and line-ups some of which you'll read about later…

It was after the Firebird fiasco that I found myself hanging around with Garry more (Gary Moore?) and more, and less time was spent with the local Herberts over at the park and in my general neighbourhood. At that age you, the reader should be aware, things were at an accelerated speed. One day, Garry was doin' wot he was doin' with his mates, I was in Firebird. We had the connection but needed a push (or shove). So when Firebird went down in flames (so to speak), I asked Gaz 'round for a jam. After we had jam and a nice cup of tea, and some biscuits, I asked wot he had in the guitar bag. He said it was his brand new (to him) Fender Stratocaster.

I remember purchasing Motorhead's first record, and I would play it to anyone that would listen, o.k you didn't have to listen,

I played it anyway. Even my Mum was beginning to know the words (monkey bed?). You could see she had a puzzled look ' Ey Steve your blood' music doesn't make a bloody sense innit?' she would say. But luckily I found that Garry had an uncanny way with music and he figured out the true meaning behind the new 'can you tell wot the fuck this bloke's on about?' music that I was playing...so now there were two of us. This enabled us to share common ground and a friendship that continues to this day (cool, ha!).

As if by overnight my old friends were gone, I can't remember where they went, they just weren't in the picture anymore. I think it was the same for Gaz... Many had done their 'year' or so of drugs, music and mayhem, so they got jobs instead (losers...we did too but hey it's my book and we only worked to further our cause). Most became taxi drivers, funnily enough, as time passed they'd pick me up over the years, falling out of nightclubs at 4 in the morning and take me and my 'little something to warm the sheets' home (and no, it wasn't a hot water-bottle) or a getting a cup of hot chocolate from the all-night takeaway. Anyway, they were stuck at home with Sharon from 2Y at school, or whoever. They'd married 'cos she got preggers and now they've got a mortgage at the age of 20, two ugly kids and a holiday once a year to Spain. And yes, you know it; as soon as the mortgage is paid up off she'll go with Carlos from the local Wimpy. Everyone told US 'You're on a spiral to nowhere, sex, drugs, rock n 'roll...' they were right (would never have changed a thing). At least I have a book to write about the shady, disgusting, all-night parties, threesomes, luvly... that was a good 25 years that was... well getting back to the story.

We started jamming in me Dad's garage, yes the garage; we were a garage band we come from garage land. It overlooked the

North Acton cemetery. I remember the police being called to the house, as somebody was being buried and we were playing the funeral march (in a Black Sabbath style), fuzz boxes at full bore. I had by then gone all 'Lemmy' on myself and got a Rickenbacker bass, fuck trying to learn all those fuckin' chords, especially as I had Garry there (all solos and Beatles). Anyway, I was becoming a bit of a neighbourhood threat; cats were being aurally castrated at one hundred yards from my house with the noise I was getting out the stupid guitar, SO I bought a bass. I had a trust fund or something for when I reached seventeen, so after screaming and shouting, kicking my legs in the air (not a pretty sight) they gave in. ha. Well off I went with me 400 pounds in me bin, Tottenham Court Road or bust. Shaftesbury Avenue, if I recall rightly, was great. Me and Gaz would spend all day there while speeding like two frogs in a blender.

The shops would let you play any instrument you'd like and we did. They would plug you in and leave you alone, we'd be there for hours...sometimes a famous face would turn up and that would impress the shit out of us. They're all gone now but a few, shame Anyway I purchased my 'Rickie' and swiftly took it home. I also bought a Marshall 200 watt amp the last of a kind, (jeez). It had valves like milk bottles and ya could make toast on the heat that would come out of it. I had an Orange 200 watt cab and a Simms-Watt 200 watt cab, I stacked them up together (wooowhoo) wot a noise! I had four hundred watts of speaker and 200 watts of amp (come on, if ya think you're 'ard enough) and not a clue how to use it...

One day at home all on my lonesome I indulged in a little amphetamine and promptly plugged the beast in (then I turned on the amp...) I closed the curtains, turned off the lights, put the fuzz box on 'full' and let rip... there I was at Hammersmith

Odeon on stage and everyone loved me... after an hour or so I stopped playing, but there was the sound of door bells ringing, people shouting, walls being banged, I thought 'Hang on, wot's all the fuss?', I opened the front door to be greeted by the old bill, my neighbours, they weren't best pleased. Apparently you could hear me for a mile down the road, they thought a whole band was rehearsing, but it was just me...oh yeah, my front room had small french windows and I managed to blow a few of those out too.. Plus my Mum's ornaments had given up and committed Hari Kari onto the living room floor. Wot fun.

PORTOBELLO
SHUFFLE

GIVE ME 'HEAD 'TIL I'M DEAD

I remember us going to the Roundhouse in Chalk Farm in 1976 or thereabouts and seeing Motorhead.... We'd take paper and pens and Gaz would call out the chords and I would write them down. He'd then translate them back into guitar music and teach me...at that particular gig, I recall Lemmy staring at us down the front, writing down the chords. He shouted to us 'THIS ONE'S IN "A"!!' which later could be heard on their live album 'What's Words Worth?'...

THE PORTOBELLO ROAD SHUFFLE

We'd catch a bus on the Saturday morning, or maybe jump the fence at North Acton train station and sneak on a train or sometimes we even just walked there (we only lived about 3 miles away) and we always took the same route once we got there....

1) Arrive at Notting Hill Station on the Bayswater Road, if by train then work out plan for getting past the guard without tickets (usually involving barging our way through the crowd or jumping over a secluded fence/barrier).

2) Due to my ability to piss like a horse, Gary would have to wait outside the toilets there while I 'siphoned the python' trying not to look like some sort of gay pick-up as Gary patiently waited for me. It was well dodgy in those bogs and very difficult to piss without an audience (you know, people who stand at the urinal with their dick out but not actually pissing...er...Not that I looked or anything...).

3) First stop, the big 'Record & Tape Exchange' store on the Bayswater road there. That one had a rare, collectors bit upstairs with loads of albums we wanted but couldn't afford, stuff like the 'Glastonbury Fayre' album which had previously unreleased tracks by The Pink Fairies, Hawkwind, Gong and the Grateful Dead (I eventually got a mint copy and have it in a sealed lead container at an undisclosed location). They were mean bastards when you were hard up and had to sell some L.P's to them, you hardly got anything for 'em...but they did sell their records relatively cheap, plus if you timed it right you could get 'preview copies' of new albums that the music journalists had reviewed (or not) and promptly sold down the Record & Tape Exchange for beer money.

4) On to the Virgin record store (as in THE only Virgin record store - pre global-domination, you've got Mike Oldfield to thank for that). It was cool in there, it was the only record shop around that had headphones, you had to bloody queue up to have a go tho'...the place was always full of freaks listening to 'Tubular Bells' shouting 'Adolf Hitler on Vibes!!' at the appropriate moment.. I loved that original 'Virgin' record logo tho'...the one with the naked twins.

5) 'Round the corner and over the road to the other, lesser 'Record & Tape Exchange' searching for old MC5, Deviants and

Stooges albums. I also had a really bad habit of buying obscure albums if they had interesting covers. Album cover art by then had started to get a little bland, ya know, boring photo of the artiste(s) on the front, track listing on the back...we liked the big, fuck off fold-out jobbies with the psychedelic art and booklets and shit, like Hawkwind's 'Space Ritual'. Unfortunately, most of the albums that I bought by cover alone turned out to be in that shop for a very good reason. They were shit. They were either baaaaaad pseudo Psychedelic bands made up to cash in on the 'scene' (man), or they were dodgy disco 'Can you Feel the Force?' type bands whose cover had a 'Sci-Fi' theme.

6) Back over to the top of Portobello Road, sniggering and smirking in deep, manly voices, pushing each other in the arm as we passed the window of the 'Gay' shop with its leather underpants and Freddie Mercury leather hats and onwards into the merry throng. There always seemed to be more people coming up the road towards us as opposed to tackling it from our perspective, so if there was anybody we knew down the 'Road' we'd eventually bump 'bullet belts' with them.

7) Past the expensive Antique stalls and shops with their rocking horses in the windows and brass gramaphones frequented by curious American tourists who would snap up anything if they were told that the Queen herself brushed by but a few feet from or had farted on said ornament. I knew a woman who worked in one of those antique shops, she had a really posh accent but was originally a prostitute in her native Liverpool! Now the pearl necklaces were real...

8) Arrive at Heinekey's pub, stare in awe at the pack of Hell's Angels, Road Rats and the just starting out 'Sons of Satan' (I would later hang out with them so much I eventually joined 'em)

standing proudly by their choppers, (that's motorcycles, mmm) with us secretly wishing we were that cool and that we had chopped motorbikes too.

Gaz and I both had to sacrifice getting motorbikes at an early age when so many of our friends were getting into them, we had to focus on the music and decent guitars and amps didn't come cheap...so it was one or the other. Gary's sister Paula's boyfriend at the time was a 'Rocker' in the true sense, y'know, the leather jacket covered in studs, turned up drainpipes, quiff etc. and he rode a BSA Gold Star. He'd let Gary ride it 'round the block and occasionally gaz would go pillion as they would shoot up the A40 onto the North Circular Road and awaaaaay... (Of course, me and Gaz have both made up for that lack of bikes since then). In we'd go into said establishment, survey the scene and look for familiar faces, pull up a coupla chairs (checking they didn't have any 'one-percenters' sitting on them at the time) and enjoy a few bevvies, catching up with all the bullshit.

9) Exit pub and stagger drunkenly onwards down the road, taking time out to praise/abuse any buskers in the vicinity. One of the regulars was this old guy who had a parrot and a music box; he'd be swamped by tourists fighting for a chance to be photographed with this parrot, as if it was the only one on the planet. Enter nearby Army Surplus shop and admire collection of Nazi regalia and muskets. Exit shop and snigger and snicker at the bald guy in the t-shirt with the large swastika who resembled Adolf Hitler who could always be found goose-stepping up and down the road all day, much to the disgust of passers-by.

10) Swaggering onwards until finally reaching Finch's pub, catching up with more fellow deviants and playing 'spot the undercover cop'. There was a lot of it about at the time... (See

the Smokey Bear's Picnic section further on). We'd often see Lemmy at Finch's, occasionally Fast Eddie and Philthy too. Mick Farren was often with them pissed out of his skull and it'd be no surprise at all to see someone hugely famous there I remember seeing Roger Taylor, the drummer from Queen hanging out there all dressed in white desperately trying to be noticed so he could ignore them. Maybe Freddie was up at the Gay shop getting a 'fitting'...eh?

11) Out of the pub eventually, shouting 'Hi' to blind Bob the accordion player and singer who were always there in the same spot come rain or shine. He was amazing, I'm sure people did things like put bottle tops and ring pulls into his hat but I never did it, just in case the blind thing was an act!
Stop off at comix shop to add to collection while gaz checks out the bongs and eventually arrive at the Mountain Grill restaurant for greasy cholesterol input and large cup of tea.

12) Around the inner market bit under the flyover, stop off to see Rory the electric guitarin' busker play the lead guitar solo that had started at 9:00 that morning. He had this little practise amp that he would have cranked up to maximum and be twiddly diddly lead guitarin' from dusk 'til dawn...he must have had fingers like leather that guy...I remember he eventually put a band together called The Invisible Band...I'd like to say that 'I didn't see them' (geddit?) for humorous purposes...but I did.

13) Get pulled over (as usual) by a group of cops usually containing at least one young 'trainee cadet', we were convinced that this was part of their training (unwilling volunteers that we were) with the same ol' repertoire...'Where ya been? Where ya goin'? What ya got?' On one occassion we'd bought some punk stuff to listen to and there was a single in the bag by a new band

called 'The Police'. We remarked as they searched our bags that this time it was a 'fair cop' seeing as we had a Police record...gee...no sense of humour those guys...

14) Out and away from those boys in blue, under the flyover and over the 'Road' to the music store on the corner where we'd check out guitars and amps and effects pedals (but we never played 'Stairway to Heaven' or 'Paranoid'...ok, maybe we did on occasion). The staff in the music shops were tryin' real hard to be cool and let us play for as long as we liked but they were always edgy...maybe because we liked to play loud?

15) Give our regards to little (another) Bob who was always around there. He was this wee fella, but he had the coolest leather jacket and he'd spend most of the day profilin', ya know, hangin' out with his tassels swinging and studs gleaming in the hazy, winter sunshine. His cool added a couple of feet to his stature, kinda like the Fonz...he was a short arse too...we'd hang out with him, chattin' for hours about nothing in particular (secretly plotting in our heads how we could relieve him of said awesome piece of apparel..), wonder if he's still got that jacket...

16) Past the rastas and their Dub sound systems pumping out over the street and the smell of senseemeeelia wafting over you...as dey wood biddy deng deng all de day...rite??? There'd be a queue of 'em, dressed in their finest army surplus and red, gold & green bobble hats patiently waiting for a chance to grab the 'mic and biddy biddy deng demselves'..Gaz never minded a bit of the ol' Heavy Dub, the real 'roots' stuff...it drove me fucking crazy. Next to them was the old 'Frendz' shop, it was a left-over from the ol' Underground Press days and seemed somehow frozen in time, a relic of those rose-tinted, innocent

(and deprived) times. There were dusty old books like 'The Politics of Ecstasy' by Timothy Leary and the 'I-Ching', all types of incense and best of all a huuuge pile of old, yellowing leftover and forgotten Underground papers, rendz, International Times, OZ etc. and I think over the passage of time I eventually bought most of them...no-one else seemed interested, but to me it was like catching up on the last nine years of the type of news I was interested in, better late than never! (I never got into the habit of buying the tabloids...don't trust 'em as far as I can spit).

Sometimes we'd go further along past the convent with it's high, stark grey walls (some of the things they must have heard over those walls) and through the junky, old crap on the stalls at the 'poorer' end and other times that'd be as far as we got before we turned around and did it all again...this time uphill.

HIGH FRIENDS IN PLACES
(LEST WE FORGET)

There was another Steve kicking around, he'd been a friend of mine for longer than I'd known Gary, we had grown up not far from each other. He was part of the posse from the beginning; he looked like a cross between Steve Marriott and some kind of dodgy, hippy car salesman. Long, stringy hair, a tatty old velvet jacket and a George Cole (the spiv in the St Trinians movies) pencil moustache. Boy, he could pack it away too and sometimes we'd end up at the West End not even knowing how we got there…we'd just started talking and walking..From Park Royal…

Gary adds…

"There was also a guy we knew on the West End scene called Colin who sort of, if you half closed your eyes and looked in a fairground mirror at his reflection, bore a mild resemblance to Robert Plant. He had the long, blonde cork screwy hair thing going with his leather jacket and loons but he also had this great big beer gut hanging over his bullet belt. He was a bit of an arsehole on reflection but ok in a crowd. I know that Steve'll have no truck with him now"…

COLIN——yes, I remember that piece of shit…very well… the son of a whore (I mean Guardsman at Buckingham Palace - which is what he actually was!). I would go on to share a couple of squats with him, one being a Fire Station in Old Street, the other in King's fuckin' Cross, where pimps smashed my head in once with hammers. I'd evicted three of their slimy little gang from my squat and thought I was hard and righteous but they came 'round when I was sleeping and stuck a large and very painful hammer over me noggin, I will be going in depth with this story later, anyway back to the 'living mucus' Colin...

The Fire Station was undoubtedly the dirtiest, smelliest shit hole I've ever lived in. It was so remote that nobody ever came 'round and it was huge so most of the time it was freezing, cold and damp (like Colin's Mum). I could wake most mornings to find large 'E.T' type mushrooms growing on the ceiling and if your bed linen wasn't put in a washing machine every two days or so it would take on a life all of its very own...There was however a large rehearsal room where I would spend much of my time. Local bands could be found rehearsing there e.g. Bitch and a drummer who played in The Adverts at the time called Rod (nice bloke). All-night jams were often the order of the day, as it was a) bloody good fun and b) so fucking cold outside, plus this was the only room that anyone kept clean.

Getting back to Colin, WE FELL OUT. He had a habit of going out with my ex's, then parading about like he was 'top cock' or sommit. Now talking of small cocks (and I have to tread very carefully here) HE HAD A FRIGHTENINGLY SMALL DICK...oh my God...now I'm no Pork God, in fact one girl-friend used to call me Justin (get it? just - in), oh yeah, that reminds me...how do ya make five inches feel like a foot? (Fuck her in the arse) well, as I said I'm not scaring any schoolgirls or making middle-aged women wince at the thought of...Oh dear , BUT HEY anyway the tosser pushed his luck once too many and basically I bashed the Granny out of him. Prat... (Oh yeah, and if I see ya in the street I'll do it again).

Then there was ol' Scruff (Scruffus Bruttanicus) we met at a Motorhead gig, he did the occasional roadie stint with the 'Head'. I think it was at the Roundhouse where we met him (at the previously mentioned 'What's Wordsworth' gig) and we became The Three Amigos for a quite a while. We all shared the same ridiculous sense of humour and laughs would be many and often. He suffered from Asthma which gave him a snigger much akin to that of Muttley, Dick Dastardly's dog in Wacky Races. From that it'd develop into a kind of breathy chuckle eventually followed by a howling guffaw…by then all present would just be laughing at his laugh having forgotten what the original joke (if any) was about.

We also had someone else to hang out with relatively nearby (although his room was only bearable for short stints at a time). He didn't live too far from us and when you're walking home from the West End to North Acton at some godforsaken hour of the morning (as we often did, boy we covered some miles eh Gaz?) an extra dude for company never goes amiss. Especially when he looks like Neanderthal man and smells bad (his face would always relax into a miserable expression too, so he didn't look the 'cuddly' type).

One night a whole posse of us were crashed out on a floor after a particularly good party and we'd all slept real bad due to a) our age b) speed and c) Scruff's incessant laughter but by the time we'd woken up the next morning, he was nowhere to be found, or so we thought. All that was there was his smelly old boots…we pondered the reason behind his abduction when I shouted out 'Maybe his Odour Eaters ate 'im!!!' to which we all produced a mighty roar of laughter which far surpassed any attempt made by Scruff the previous night/morning.

He also played bass and he liked a bit of dub reggae as well as Hawkwind and was to eventually be Gary's bassist for The

Magic Mushroom Band Mk1 (I was otherwise distracted). Last time I heard from Scruff, he'd gone on to do sound-engineering for Youth (from Killing Joke, but by then a Dance Music Guru) and played in a Reggae Dub band called 'The Herb' (Speed Machine? Magic Mushroom Band? The Herb? Is it me or do I sense a theme running through this?).

As for Youth, I stole his girlfriend and thought I was really clever at the time, then after a moment of madness I married her (TAKE ME NOW LORD!). Lynne gave birth to my children SONNY and ZIGGY. I later would find myself dragging them up alone as a one-parent family. My daughter is now 23 and has made me a Grandfather twice and the BOY has made me old before my time. Kidz aaahhh can't live with em can't barter with Arab white slavers...

OUR FIRST BUST (MaaaN…)

Through our formative years and beyond (and still) we've had our fair share of run-ins with the law. It's not that we went out of our way to get pulled, but we just looked guilty anyway. I've lost count of the amount of times we used to get pulled by young police recruits down the Portobello Road for a quick search. I guess we were a safer bet then the IRA terrorists.

Anyway, there we were, still wet behind the ears and living life to the max and we had a problem, big time. We were due to go to a Motorhead gig that night but we had no dope. We searched and searched for someone with a bit to spare but nix, nada. So we committed the ultimate sin, we did something we swore we'd never do, we bought a bag of grass from a Rasta under the flyover at Portobello Road. He knew we were desperate so he charged us for the privilege. They were desperate times tho' and we didn't want to turn up at the gig with nothing to smoke. Off we went to the gig that night and we met up with loadsa people and had our usual riotous Saturday night shenanigans…we drank, we toked, we rolled up, they rolled up and eventually I and Gary decided to make our way home, bleary-eyed and wasted but happy.

We were only a coupla miles from our homes when this plain clothes police car screeches to a halt beside us just as we crossed over the Uxbridge Road. Out jumped two police officers, one male, and one female. I'd never witnessed this combination before and me and Gaz looked at each other with confident smirks as the male officer politely asked us where we'd been, where we were going and why we were smirking...He wasn't having much luck and suddenly the female one launched into us with a barrage of threats (must have been the wrong time of the month) and had us with our hands on the bonnet as they started searching us. We'd shared out the rest of the weed and had a bag each stashed but seeing as we didn't fancy having this sort of drama after such a good night and knowing they'd find it anyway, we gave them our grass. We figured they'd confiscate our weed, slap us on the wrist for being young, first timers and send us on our way under a cloud of shame. But...OH NOOO...they wanted to make a meal of it and were intent on making an example of us. We were arrested, bundled into the car and taken immediately to Acton Police Station.

They put us in a cell and we were individually searched again...but a bit more thoroughly. Earlier that night we never would have imagined that we'd be in a cell, pants 'round our ankles with policemen looking up our bums. S'funny how things turn out, innit?

Anyway, we weren't allowed to call home, but they did inform us that they'd sent officers 'round to our parents' house to let them know that we'd been arrested, they wouldn't tell them what for though...as you can imagine we had a nice, warm reception waiting for us at home. The police eventually let us out early the next morning and told us to report back in a week when the cannabis would be back from the forensic lab and they'd have the results and could charge us.

The week that followed was a long and painful one, we'd had our asses whupped by our respective parents and we dreaded the outcome. Major bummer all 'round.

When the Saturday finally arrived we walked down to the police station ('dead man walking' style…) and through to the desk sergeant. He got us to sit down and looked up from his paperwork with a sullen face (our sphincters by then were going nine to the dozen) "Well? Do you want the good news or the bad news?" We looked at each other and thought we'd go for the happy bit first… "The good news, I regret to say, is that we won't be charging you for the offence". We couldn't believe our ears, whoo hoo!

We'd beaten the system, yay! Take that ya fascist bastards…but then it dawned on us, what was the bad news?? "The bad news is that you didn't actually purchase marijuana, you bought a bag of mixed herbs"…upon hearing that we just burst into laughter and patted each other on the back, we couldn't work out if the Sergeant was pissed off because he couldn't get us, or if they'd been laughing about it all week. He even asked us if we wanted it back?! We declined and hightailed it out of there while the going was good. It turned out that because we were all smoking each others dope at the gig we didn't know we'd been ripped off, but that was one time when we were actually glad it happened….go figure.

TUNING THE SPEED MACHINE

SPEED MACHINE...my nickname... Speed Machine, let's set the record straight. A complete misunderstanding really. When Garry and myself decided to form a band, we agreed on a name (who thought of it, or where it came from I don't know...)

(Garry)
"SPEED MACHINE? Pretty bloody obvious I reckon..?! We didn't eat or sleep for years..."
(Steve)
"Well Gaz at least six months in your case, I thought ya gave it up".
Bitchy I know, but I tells it like I remembers it dude!

The logo that accompanied the band was a cannabis leaf emerging from a broken hypo syringe (full of deep meaning about how marijuana was the way and 'just say no' to fixing). Pretty deep for two sixteen year olds, full of righteous views. In fact, Gaz kept clean and true, steering clear of the needle, never straying into the 'darkside'. I was always pushing boundaries and one day I was introduced to MR BROWNSTONE (but a few years down the road I should add) who being the obliging kind of guy that he is (don't poke the bear if you don't wanna get bit) placed a rather large and ugly monkey on my back..I've managed to shake him off these days, but hey, that's a whole different story, book, life, even person. That fuckin' monkeys got one hell of a grip kids, so don't let anyone tell ya different (moral speech over, let's get back to the good, innocent stuff).

Anyway I made some stickers, I think it cost 50 quid, from a company found in 'Sounds' music paper, a brill paper, the only one to keep street music up and running (unlike Melody Maker and NME, college student's crapola) well I still have some of those stickers somewhere, I think I made 200. As this went so well I decided to paint said logo on the back of my leather jacket... (Real cool)...IN BIKER ROCKERS!! (Not one of my best ideas...) This caused a bit of controversy among the biker fraternity as there were a lot of second division biker gangs with shit 'colours', matching my artwork and unfortunately I fell into this bracket... but being thick of skin and of head I managed to keep my colours and never got 'em busted off me. In fact I kept that jacket for around four years or so. It finally gave up the ghost in Acklam Hall, under the Westway flyover, in Portobello Road one night. IT WAS NEW YEAR'S EVE...And bitterly cold. Myself and a friend were on our way to the Acklam Hall as Hawkwind's Nik Turner was headlining a New Year's Eve party there with his band Inner City Unit.

Talking of Inner City Unit, I actually joined the band later and got slung out after we played at the Music Machine now known as the Camden Palace). The firing was mainly due to me getting my 'script' that morning of Nembutal and Fillon (the little oooo-range ones). After swallowing around four bombers and a couple of Mandies, we set off to the gig only for me to destroy the whole event with a series of 'unfortunate' catastrophes. I forgot the whole set, I had to have a chair to sit on (as my legs were off on their own somewhere), and I'd also managed to send a roadie off to hospital! As the lead kept falling from my bass, he tried the 'old roadie trick', that's tucking the lead under the guitar through the strap... ha ha ha! I foiled his plan though... I thought he tried to touch my arse, so I bashed him over the nut with me bass.

Halfway through the set the band had a short break or inter-mission. I can't recall why exactly, but I used those seconds sensibly and went for a piss...on route I heard a banging and crashing from the backstage fire-exit door, I opened it and to my fiendishly 'Dennis the Menace' type glee and fondness to cause as much upset and confusion as physically possible, I found stood in the street twenty or so skinheads and punk-rockers who obviously couldn't get in for whatever reason. I knew a few of them and offered to sneak them in. I tried to find the way to where the audience were but to no avail, so we went back the way I came and promptly walked all twenty or so skins and punks onto the stage.

Nik at the time was doing his 'epitaph to the hippies' stint, bull-shit-ego thing which consisted of him throwing red roses into the audience as a gesture to the demise of the hippie thing or wot ever 'Hippies are dead!' (Not from where I was standing they weren't, but hey). Well I took this quite literally and started a flower fight with some of the skinheads on stage, wot a laugh! (I think). It was at this point I was ushered backstage for a "band meeting" main, that mainly consisted of me being quizzed on whether I could 1) stand up straight 2) finish the set 3) stop waving that stiletto knife about and threatening the reggae band.. after the pep talk I was allowed back on stage only now wearing the customary doctor's face mask on top of my head like a fuckin bonnet (nobody told me either), bastards. I did however have my leather jacket on even though it was over the long doctor's coat as I wasn't going on stage dressed like a dick-head...mamma.

I did manage to do one thing right though, as I had forgotten all their set I had a brainwave and suggested we play a couple of songs we all knew like some all-singing, all-dancing cabaret 'show'. Songs of choice were 'Brainstorm' NOT THE SHITY REGGAE VERSION EITHER. and 'Master of the Universe'. Then this bloody spaceman was hired to walk about the stage, he kept getting in my way so I kicked him off the stage, ta ta... twenty foot up in the air it was then.. Ooh! That must've hurt. When I spotted friends at the "star bar' holding up a pint for me, I completely forgot I was supposed to be in a band playing bass and wandered off to claim my drink, forgetting about the gap between stage and bar. Let's just say that I came a cropper and joined the spaceman in the audience (best place for me at the time)...but I digress. There's more but even I won't go into it as it's a bit embarrassing for me and said people.

OH YEAH,

I must add a little reference to a certain STEVE STUPID POND... while I've been researching for this book I have come across a biographical look back over the members of said INNER CITY UNIT and I did actually make the biog if only to be made fun of!

Well thanks for that Steve. [CUNT] I REMEMBER YOU TO MAAAN, always running scared and creeping up everybody's arsehole, and how dare you say in reference to my one ever gig with i.c.u. that, (that put an end to any credibility that I might have had). Cheers mate!!!

I've since emailed him asking him to be a little kinder of my short stay in that particular band, and as I have now mentioned him I would like it known that he was a little git and fuck him and his backstabbing dig at my good self.

I WILL OF COURSE BE KICKING HIM STRAIGHT IN THE BOLLOCKS WHEN AND IF WE EVER MEET.

O.K.

BACK IN PORTABELLO ROAD
ACKLAM HALL XMAS.... INNER CITY UNIT.

It was cold, we were hungry, there was a closed fruit and veg shop. We went in through the window, liberated four bags of assorted fruit and veg...And off we trotted to da gig. We got very drunk, made our way to the front and had a flash of inspiration. I got a handful of fruit, got Nik straight in the boat race...got a laugh and a food fight going. The band joined in too, no malice intended, just good fun. Everyone seemed to enjoy the festive spirit of the fracas, but then some self-righteous arse took it upon himself to become law enforcer and started a punch up with yours truly...I was kicking the shit out of him when I was grabbed from behind (never get grabbed from behind.. ooh err) and both my arms were being held, so putting all my strength into one almighty jerk, I broke free.. Yeah free, free to kick arse. The only trouble was, the two blokes holding my arms were now holding just my arms, well, the sleeves anyway and hey presto I had a brand new cut-off. So there we have it. I kept it as a cut-off for a while, but it disintegrated, a bit like one of those old Dracula films, when the sun comes up in the morning and he turns to dust. Thus that was the way of my SPEED MACHINE.

Well, the jacket died but the stupid name didn't...stuck like a hippy bogarting the last joint. I've never called myself by that name, but people still call me it now, although as I don't keep the name an everyday name some people who think they know ya get it all wrong ... The Machine, Snake Machine, Steve Machine is a good one, or a reverse Machine Steve. Wot a lot of bollocks! My name's Steve...or at least let me choose, ah let me think...IRON THIGH, ah no...BIGUS DICKUS...that's bin done. SUPER STEVE will never happen my friend...

It all came together for Gary when he got his Fender Strato-caster. A 1969 maple neck job Hendrix played a maple neck Stratocaster. At this point I'd like to mention that Jimi Hendrix was and still is 'ma main man', he was such an inspiration, watchin' him gyrating, fucking his guitar as it screamed it's pain through those cranked up amps. He taught me how to use the guitar as an extension of your soul (and dick). Even now if I hear his music, I have to pick up that guitar and play, just like yester-day, and then I'd get on my knees and pray.

Around the same time (or so it seems now...) I switched to bass and purchased a rather bitchin' Rickenbacker...Black as night and twice as...er...Dark. I remember we went into the army surplus store down Portobello Road and got some WW2 Nazi stickers and stuck 'em on our guitars (they were a bastard to get off when I had my guitar custom painted). We were baaad muthafuckers I tell ya, hanging around with our guitars and amps out on the street waiting for our Dads to pick us up... We used to jam at each other's houses but the complaints were getting louder than the music so for the sake of home cooking, fresh socks an 'undies (and an easy life) we booked some rehearsals at a studio in Churchfield Road behind Acton High Street. It was deep in the bowels of the building and we could make as much noise as we liked...and we did. We would try to get the Marshalls as cranked up as we were...ya know, so that the mains hum is as loud as the music (they weren't our amps). We'd written a couple of tunes and we had a stack of favourite songs that we liked doing...the only trouble we had at first been getting a drummer.

Try as we might, we couldn't find a single drummer willing to play the sort of stuff that we liked. We asked so many people, we were desperate. At the time, bands like Motorhead were in this sort of 'Netherworld'...they couldn't be classed as Heavy Rock or Progressive and they were too old and ugly to be Punks. We were fully into getting our hair as long as physically possible, loving that freaked out, spun out, wasted 'Mummy, I want you to meet my boyfriend' look and we wanted a drummer that reflected the same. We were almost down to asking people in the street, in fact, we'd go up to any long hair at a gig and say 'Oy mate...do you play drums? No? Do ya know anyone who does?' But no, the drummers would flick their hair back in an important manner and say that Motorhead/Fairies/MC5 were 'way too heavy man' and they were in much too much of a 'Progressive' state of mind for all that and anyway they were waiting for Phil Collins to drop dead so they could get his gig. You see lots of his albums in Oxfam, so I guess he must be doing alright...

Salvation eventually came in the lanky, gangly freaked out metal fork in the toaster hair explosion that was Deso. He was perfect, he had the huge fuckoff Hendrix afro going, all dressed in black velvet, with bells and rings hanging off him and he played like a demon possessed. His hair would be thrashing about, narrowly missing getting caught up with his sticks as he thumped the bejaysus out of his ratty old kit. He was the first drummer I ever saw who had a pair of bongos next to his top tom-toms, a sort of 'shoestring' precursor to the roto-tom thing I guess.

Deso also had a weird, spaced-out hippy chick called Sam, I think, she was an Olympic hippy I would say...by that I mean if there ever was a championship for most hippiest hippy chick, she would have been in the running. She lived in Surrey, her parents had this huge Victorian house and her attic room was bigger than the whole top half of my family's house. It was all decked out with droopy nets, old candles melted on bottles, incredibly pungent incense, velvet ethnic cushions, ultra-violet lighting the lot. It made me want to do my bedroom up a bit more, I just had a large Budgie poster (that we liberated from the Roundhouse), a 'Land that Time Forgot' Raquel Welch poster, a stack of records and comics (and my neighbour's son's 'Easy Rider' magazines which he never got back), a mural of Hawkwind's 'Space Ritual' cover on my ceiling and a very stiff leather jacket standing in the corner...But then we weren't coming home very often by that time...

I still have a recording of our first 'session' together (and I mean that in all respects), we couldn't wait to get in and set up; this had been a long time coming. We were that excited we decided to go hell for leather ('scuse the pun, it was actually unintentional) and shoved excessive amounts of sulphate up our noses and blues into our gullets. It was a good job that we set up so quickly because in no time at all we transformed into gibbering, electrified epileptics (it's all on tape officer...I'll burn ya a CD). UP went the volume and the tempo, you know when you're playing so loud that you get taxi cab messages coming through*****...The first thing we did was to launch straight into an epic jam, faster than the speed of complaint. I think I started the whole thing by suddenly launching into this humungous guitar solo, I was just getting used to the Fender by then and it was hitting that sweet note that Strats and Marshalls make when they orgasm together, the feedback was in tune and I was up up and away, twiddly-diddlying away like there was no tomorrow...as far as I was concerned I was up on top of some fiery mountain, wind blowing my hair, lightning shooting from my guitar at dragons as they chased sweet, young maidens up my leather studded thigh....

When it eventually dawned on me that I may have been doing this for quite a while, I looked over at Gary and Deso as they thundered in with an earthquake of an intro to, we didn't have a clue what but in it came anyway and we were just cooking on gas baby for the rest of the session. Even speeding our nuts off it seemed like it lasted a long time and in fact it did.

We had some great sessions like that, in squats, at parties etc. But unfortunately, due to our excessive nature and our full diary of ligging and parties we never got to the gigging stage. By then though, we were legendary. We were possibly one of the first ever bands to get by on reputation alone, sort of the Paris Hiltons of our day!

Poor ol' Deso died just a couple of years later, it was really weird. Apparently he'd gone to visit some family in Ireland with his girlfriend and on their way back they'd been separated at the train station. The girlfriend made it home but he never did. They eventually found his body by the train tracks somewhere and no-one ever found out what happened, did he jump or was he pushed? He always seemed a pretty, happy go lucky chap to us.

LIGGIN' IN THE RIGGIN'

We went to the Music Machine on one particular night to see a band called 'Kittyhawks', it was basically all the people who weren't in Hawkwind anymore (Lemmy, Nik Turner, Dik Mik etc.) and we were really excited about it...we did our usual early arrival and hung out outside the venue and waited and waited and waited...eventually somebody came out of the building and announced that it'd been cancelled...major bummer!! The only consolation was, because we'd been waiting for so long and being the social types that we are, we'd got to know pretty much everyone in the queue pretty well by then and by the time we got to 'disperse' we all headed off for drinks at the nearest pub and I think most of us ended up at some bizarre party hosted by a druid or wizard, I forget which (witch?).....

We loved the Roundhouse. It was the best venue we had ever been to and 30 years on still the best, reverberating memories of a simpler time. The sights, smells all that 70's hippie shit that I loved to death and if it was still like that I'd still be there, I think? The Roundhouse had these quaint little alcoves where if you looked in you were met by freaks banging away on a bong or passing 'round the duchie on the left-hand side (sounds like a song). You could at a squeeze fit around three, maybe four people into one of these ports of pot heaven, me and Gaz would get there real early so as to make the day as long as possible. Sometimes there would be an all-dayer and you could find us there, yes, all day...Absorbing as much of the atmosphere as we could. I suppose you could best describe it as if the whole venue was like one giant backstage party and we all got v.i.p. passes.

Best bits about Budgie for meeee, Burke Shelley played a Fender Precision bass, had four Vox speaker cabs all stacked together and four Marshall 100 watt amps on top. I used to get a buzz just looking at them on stage, with the orange standby light on, warming up for the onslaught that was to come. Shelley's bass was the main driving force and myself and Gaz would make our way down the front (as Garry says so rightly) yapping to anyone that looked like they'd care...and head banging insanely, from beginning to end...SUCH FUN...

I first started to frequent the roundhouse at the tender age of fifteen, this in fact was to be a momentous night for all, with a dead [no nonsense] guaranteed certain bet ya last fifty pence on [fifty pence was quite a lot of money back then I hasn't to say] night of hard rockin' adult fun with a feeling of adolescent acceptance in the wanting and hopefully making that had been long and very impatiently awaited for by us young wannabie part of the big rock n roll world of wasted demy gods, sex kittens, scantly dressed sirens of the night, so whilst wishfully and hopingly to by the grace of God, Allah, Vishnu or that canteen lady at school, the one with those big motherly come to mamma and loose yourself in my big, fleshy, soft and bountiful breast's of luuurv, making you feel safe in her bosom of experience and womanly lust.

Yet voyeuristically infatuated with the very thought of those vast caverns of well explored sensual deep and out of touch by such a mere boy as myself who spends every waking minute of the day and the night in a fantasy of wondrous thoughts and illusions of a hundred and one scenarios where I could claim a right of way to those gorgeous, mouth-watering, nipples like small pointed hard yet irresistibly chewable and sensual rubber bullets surrounded by mounds of mammary flesh resembling two fuckin' massive hanging and dangling clouds of fluffy, fleshy marshmallows.

Older yet far more mysterious and Freudian than all them silly giggling, mocking, childish girls in school. But with her, her lady perfume with the cheap scent, so very seductive and unobtainable unlike cosmetics counter at Woolworths, who you know secretly, wants you, to come across that one wanton lust filled older and yes not wiser but willing to take to hand or anything else that comes to mind mature maiden of finding that loose morals with a liking for young boys that we had by our very own admissions were adhering to, while scouring the planet or anybody that had found ourselves being drawn into like a swarm of teenage mutant moth men attracted to the heady, oreconsuming shining ray of rock elitism that seemed to be taking our very souls over.

SO with a much anticipated and sizing up of minds for quite some time, so all us lads were all really looking forward to, when a load of us NORTH ACTON PLAYING FIELDS, Desperado's descended on mass for a show headlined by Steve Marriot's all stars, STEVE MARRIOT actually was the first proper gig I ever went to at the Hammersmith Odeon.

When he was still in HUMBLE PIE. That too turned out to be one of the most memorable gig's I ever attended.

STEVE MARRIOT was in my book the epitome of a true rock n roller, lived it as he talked it.

I remember at the Odeon the well old and farty security didn't want any standing at the gig and when this was put into action by them manhandling a couple of guys down the front for [wait for it] bastards... standing up ?

Steve stopped the song they were playing and started a conversation with the old buggers, this was done from the stage and when they dictated to him that they in their infinite wisdom and righteous old fashioned and totally ridiculous within their rights as Odeon staff and security to enforce a no standing policy stab at ruining it for everyone attitude to a good night out and every bugger was to do as they were told and sit down Steve in his own imitable way responded by grabbing the mike and requesting that if everyone in the hole fuckin' place stood up and ran down the front of the venue that there would be nothing the wankers could do.

So in response to the request, every fucker stood up and made haste for the stage.

The Roundhouse gig however turned out to be a totally different affair, as the Roundhouse welcomed such behaviour, thus soon as the band had took to the stage, joints in hand accompanied by bottles of Bourbon oh yeah and a couple of guitars thrown in for good measure the place erupted, the band handed their dope and booze into the audience as if to state a common ground of a good night was to be had by all and there was no place on that stage for any pre-madonnas as they too were there to party just as, if not harder than the rest of us.

Funny thing with the Roundhouse, even though I only got there towards the end of that era I never witnessed any violence ever not inside nor out, funny to think that why should it be that when people are left to their own devices and saved the humiliation of being treated like a delinquent and not capable of having a good time unless it's at somebody's expense that in fact them very same freaks and they must be deranged psychos that must be kept under no uncertain terms and with no exceptions SAT STILL IN THEIR SEAT'S OF BONDAGE, AT ALL TIMES for who knows wot could and would happen, [Point in question] Maybe, have a good time, God forbid!

And may my eye's be taken out of their sockets and placed up my proverbial arse holyoe so as I might see myself as I get my arse kicked for thinking such radical and totally rebellious thoughts as to maybe being seen in public to unashamedly start to fuckin' dance sing or in fact do that which comes naturally to any red blooded tanked up and going for it young wild, rebellious, self mutilating, chicken head eating, goat worrying and granny scaring youth of a man acting as if this was indeed going to be the very last ever rock n roll show on earth rocker, and do that very thing that they paid good honest [well sold the kids xmas pressies actually] money for. That's wot they came for.

And that's wot we want to enjoy, a mega all balls to the wall turn it up so loud so that when ya start to sing all the words to your favourite heavy rock, punk, metal or infact any old shit that gets ya by the booboo feelgood anthem, as if by magic you like everybody else scream it so loud and indecipherable that all the stinking bloody words completely come out wrong whilst as not to mention warbling the larynx with a rendition of unrehearsed on the spot made up bollocks lyrics that at a stretch might in some Icelandic or some other far flung place where unrecognisable speech is the order of the day and the whole place has a bizarre case of severe speech impediment.

AAAAAAHHHHHHRRRR......

MY BRAIN IS FRYING?! ? !

SO.

Anyway, wot I'm trying to get at .....IS...

I've been up for ages writing this piece, now as you may have guessed I am not an author in any religious shape or form but I do like to tell it as it is and as it happens I spent a whole day on this piece getting it right only to have pressed the wrong button on my computer spell checker and promptly sent the whole piece into fuckin space! Gggrrr

AND SO.

I've since resorted to indulging myself in a little pick me up and for ARTS SAKE ONLY, had a couple of GRAMMES of BILLY

WIZZ, and well as you've just read it's a bit messy, I suppose all that needed to be said was, ROUNDHOUSE - GOOD. STEVE MARRIOT- GOOD. FUCKIN COMPUTER – BAD, AMPHETAMINE SULPHATE – NEEDED, EVEN AT THE EXPENCE OF THE DRIBBLINGS THAT YOU THE READER HAVE JUST GONE THROUGH.
So in the words of one HOMER SIMPSON.
HA, HA.
Now I'm off to bed...
Nighty, night.

THE MUSIC MACHINE aka CAMDEN PALACE. How many good times were had there, me and Gaz and (as Garry reminded me earlier) Steve Williams. He was a troubled boy, one year older than myself, used to have long straggly hair, skinny sod. I really liked him but he had his own problems in life like the rest of us and could be hard work in his own way. Steve got right into car theft and would disappear for days on his own, I never asked him wot he done nor where he went as I was not too sure I wanted to know. He used to take drugs, mainly speed on his own and get in some weird situations. But when out with us everything was ok and he would drive, a real treat, better than missing the last train and walking which seemed to be the way it used to go much of the time.

Anyway the Music Machine had started to make a name for itself by booking all the bands that were now getting a name for themselves and outgrowing the smaller venues, punk bands like U.K Subs, Angelic Upstarts, Adverts and metal bands such as Motorhead, Iron Maiden, Angelwitch, Samson, Judas Priest, UFO... and countless others were on the up while the Marquee in Wardour Street, Red Lion in Fulham and the Greyhound in Hammersmith were concentrating on newer bands (I later went on to play the last shows at the Marquee, the last shows at the Red Lion and the last show at the Thomas a Beckett theatre, a pattern is starting to form...was somebody trying to tell me something?).

The Music Machine was great as the stage was a good 20 foot off the floor (see the Nik Turner part in the Speed Machine story) and the p.a. system went to the ceiling (or looked like it to me), it was great for the bands that had more voltage than the national grid, I could often be found in my favourite place, up the p.a. system and crammed into a bass bin where I'd drop a couple of black bombers, a bottle of Newcastle Brown and hang on tight....buzzzzzzzzzz. Motorhead gigs were best, as at the end they would fill the whole place with dry ice, there would be zero visibility, so running amuck was the order of the day, grop-ing, kicking and punching, wooowhoo, nobody knew who it was, so fuck 'em, LETS SPOIL IT FOR EVERYONE. GREAT FUN...

(Garry remembers....)
"With Acton being very close to Hammersmith, we got to frequent the Hammersmith Odeon on a regular basis. They had all the 'big league' (to us) bands there like Black Sabbath, Blue Oyster Cult, Lou Reed, The Tubes (little white punks on dope) Humble Pie, Hawkwind, Rush etc. and we saw them all...or it felt like we did. They had drum solos and dry ice and huge, tribal chants for more at the end. Best of it all, it was great to be out there among so many fellow 'freaks'...thousands of them, all pretty much into (and on) the same things. Yet our parents made us feel like we were the only ones like this in the world and tried oh, so hard to bring us back from the edge of depravity... (We were really pleased for Motorhead when they finally got to do a

show there that was worthy of their talents, their first attempt was a little bit too much, too soon).

We'd all hang out afterwards at a chippy around the corner in Fulham Palace Road steam billowing into the cold night from our sweaty, hairy heads and boots. The Fulham Palace Road was also home to The Greyhound, one of a few really good live venues at the time which featured bands in a lower league to the Odeon but in a league of their own, sort of 'pub rock' but that title doesn't really do it justice".

NEVER SAY THE EMERGENCY EXIT IS THE SAFEST PLACE TO BE...

1978, BLACK SABBATH... Hammersmith Odeon...the 'Never Say Die' tour... Here's a short story of three lads (myself, Garry and Steve) getting very excited at the thought of seeing one of the best bands on Earth, then and now. We had bought the tickets ages before and were waiting impatiently for the night of the 'Sabbs', well the night had come and so we stocked up on alternative refreshments, spent most of the day playing all our Sabbath records, drinking cider and generally getting all revved up for the gig. Around six o' clock we decided to start the madness by getting all dressed down, best patchwork jeans, heavy eye-liner, polished the gun belt, drug of choice was a rather large lump of red seal dope. I think I had a few valium 10's, a line or two of the old white-line fever, leather jacket on...sorted. Off to the Hammersmith Odeon, gggrrreat.

We arrive real early so's we can say our "hellos" to the heavy throng of the 'troops of tomorrow' all gathered in the pub across the road (the name eludes me), it's not there now anyway, in fact none of it is there now, except the Odeon and a fucking big shopping centre. So up to the main entrance we go, showing our tickets to the self-important prick on the door, then taking ourselves to the upstairs bar and lounge area...where we start scanning the area for likely looking lovelies, try knocking out a line or two of the white stuff (beer money), we usually cut a half gram into three times its size with a bit of glucose. After a while we took to our seats ready for the show.

Well, earlier I had taken a large chunk of the red seal and munched it down and this was now starting to perform a rather scary, trippy sort of heavy dopey effect on me, a little bit wooo a little bit waaay, trouble with eating dope is that some people (me) get very paranoid, which is a pretty cool choice of words considering the event. Anyway, I was shit scared of getting caught by the house security that were patrolling the aisles flashing torches at anyone that looked as if they might be skinning up a joint or swigging smuggled-in booze (perish the thought) so up we got and went in search of a less obvious place to roll 'em up. Somebody had the bright idea of going through the emergency exit that led down to the street, so closing the door behind us we sat down on the staircase, safe in the knowledge that nobody knew we were there.

After a while we could hear the crowd beginning to get restless, coool. The Sabbs were close to coming on stage but I was now not feeling too well as all the dope I had smoked and eaten were having a not so pleasant effect on me, I think I threw up. Then there was a loud cheer and the band ripped into the first number, we stood up and pushed the exit door, nothing...so we pushed again...still nothing... BOLLOCKS!!! The door locked from the other side duuuuuuuur... bloody obvious really, anyway we kicked, punched, shouted, screamed, made little scratching noises on the door of doom, but no-one could hear and probably wouldn't care either so we accepted our defeat and sat on the fucking staircase and waited for a song to end where we could do the shouting and kicking thing again.

Unfortunately we spent most of the gig sitting there on the bloody stairs, eventually somebody heard our pleas of help and we got to see the last couple of songs. I've got the video now and it always makes me laugh when I watch it (wot a plonker). While I'm at it, I did the same thing a few years later with Ozzy's BLIZ-ZARD OF OZZ....I got there with my bird, we had taken around four or five mandies each, sat at our seats and the lights came on the band and there was Ozzy, I shut my eyes for a second then when I opened them I was greeted with Ozzy saying 'Thank you and goodnight'. And it was, but not for me.

I'M DREAMING OF A WHITE MARQUEE

Then there was the Marquee, at its original site in Wardour Street, West London. We went there A LOT, punk had just reared its ugly (but necessary) head and we'd go and check some of those bands too. There were odd, quirky bands like Albertos Y Los Trios Paranoias doing punky stuff like 'I'm gonna cut yer liver out an' nail it on the door!!' (we used to sing that one to each other all the time, just that line that is...never could remember the rest of it) and they also did a reggae version of 'Where have all the Flowers Gone?' with the singer bobbing around on stage with a huge, woolly bobble hat with old, curly telephone cables dangling down from it.

We were so cranked in those days; the whole evening would just turn into some kind of weird, circus freak show in which we were major players. Sometimes we'd go down there and our posse would grow from just us two to twenty or thirty people and we'd end up trogging off somewhere else after-wards...maybe a pub, or a party, or a party at a pub, or just in the middle of a park or piece of common somewhere...where we'd yak some more until sunrise (Old Bill permitting)...then maybe go for a coffee at somewhere like the all-night KFC on Shep-herds Bush Green with all the tramps and winos.

One Xmas Eve....can't remember which year (help, Gary? who am I kidding...) The Enid were headlining, there was a late bar and our Christmas had so far been well and truly white. We met a few people we knew there and a lot more we didn't, including the guitarist and singer/front man of The Enid. Most of the evening became pretty much a blur after that, but I do remember noticing the singer getting rather over-friendly towards me, and Gary was panicking as to whether, 'he should warn me that he's a ravin' poofter or he should sit back and watch the fun begin?'. We managed to shake him off eventually (eeeyew, that's sounds weeeell dodgy dunnit?) and then apparently I spent a large portion of the post-performance piss up verbally abusing the guitarist whose birthday was on Xmas Day. He had long parted hair and a full beard and a long, white kaftan and he just looked a little too much like The Messiah to try and fool me that he was a mere guitarist in a poncy, pompy, Rule Britannia rock band like The Enid. I reminded him that he would be reborn the next day right up until midnight, and then I reminded him that he was thereafter. I think I drove the poor bugger mad. We also managed to pull a couple of schoolteachers (female) which was a real coup for us and we hoped that they still believed in corporal punishment.

We also went there on one particular New Year's Eve and although I can't remember who played, I do remember being rather out of my tree and wishing everybody individually a Happy New Year. This was no mean feat, the place was packed but there I was shaking everybody's hands and hugging all the women, the bar staff, the bouncers (good job The Enid weren't there). We went on after that to a party at a pub, we were just strolling past the pub and the doors were still open so we went in, kicked around for a while and then headed off down to Trafalgar Square. It was pretty full on that year, loads and loads of people and I vaguely remember going around and around the roundabout there on the bonnet of someone's car. I wasn't the only one; a few others had decided to join me. We wished each other a Happy New Year as we hung on for dear life. We spent the rest of the night trying to get some shuteye in an underpass at Marble Arch with the icy, winter wind blowing through our leathers and the cold metal of our bullet belts as they touched skin. I tell ya what, we weren't alone down there...it was hard to get a spot!! Of course we OUT! Didn't get any sleep.....

WATCH WATCH OUT. DEM DER DASTARDLY PUNKIES ARE ABOUTIE !

One night we'd decided to go and check out this new 'hot' punk band called The Ruts at a pub in Acton High Street (I think The Satellites might have been supporting them or vice versa). I knew most of the punks there as a lot of them had been in or hung around my band. In a moment of madness Gary asked his Mum to plait his hair while it was wet and put it all in little rubber bands...I didn't know what the Hell he was doing, but he wanted to 'punk out' in some strange way, maybe to try and blend in a bit better, kinda..As it turned out he couldn't have stood out more if he'd tried. When his hair had dried, and Gary took all the 'bands' off and POOOFFF!!! Gary your fuckin hair had poofed out in wispy, spirally big girly punk style...it was BIG HAIR. He tried wetting it again, but to no avail and time was running out. Once my incessant chortling had died down we made our way to the gig and if there'd been a prize for biggest hair (or top wanker) he'd've been a contender I can tell ya...The Ruts were a great band actually and had a biggish hit with 'Babylon's Burning' a bit later (I think it's original title was 'Who's that knob with the Crystal Tips hair?').

By day we'd hang out at the markets, Portobello Road, Kensington Market, Petticoat lane, Carnaby Street. Our local High Streets in Acton were just so plain and boring and didn't cater for Space Warriors on the edge of Reality like us. Kensington Market was really good in those days a twisty, multi-levelled cornucopia of weird and wonderful stuff and people. At that time 'Biba' the iconic swingin' sixties fashion store for foxy chicks was still operational and the quality of female talent was unequalled. Real hotties from their braless 'shot in the back by two missiles' shirts to their skimpy mini skirts or hot pants (otherwise known as 'mumble pants' because you saw the lips move but you couldn't hear what the cunt was sayin'..). The best part of the place was the cafe where the freaks would gather topping up their caffeine quota and discreetly passing around the Jamaican Woodbines in preparation for another jaunt around the place. It was still a Hippy market I guess, loadsa bongs, pipes, beads bells & incense but I remember when Punk arrived and suddenly there were t-shirts and trousers for sale that had been purposely ripped with a blade and pinned back together again with safety pins. We'd spent most of our life trying to avoid having to do that. But our flares did eventually go, at least with the straight legged jeans we weren't getting so drenched on our many long, wet meanders around the City.

AND JESUS WAS HIS NAME...

(Garry)...
"At this point in the story, I'd like to make mention of a certain character who never really got any credit for being a very familiar face at many freaky happenings/gigs/festivals etc.

Steve and I (and countless others) knew him only as Jesus. Now THERE was a real hippy, he always wore a sort of kaftanesque, cassock type shirts and robes, with beads, shoulder (hand)bag and sandals and a kind of strange, monk-like hair style which was very long at the back, somewhat resembling one of those hippies that Kirk and Spock found, squatting a desolate planet in the t.v series of the '60's...he also reminded me of how Brian Eno would have looked if he'd taken too much brown acid in the '60's. Sometimes he had a little 'entourage' with him of pretty, young, stoned girls and strange, sweaty fat dudes in 'Demis Roussos' proportion kaftans.

I swear he was at almost EVERY gig/festival we ever went to, be it heavy rock, R&B, metal, even punk...there he'd be, right up at the front swaying and gyrating, bashing his little tambourine and blowing his little indian flute, to no avail, because he'd be drowned out by the bands and constantly pelted with glasses and bottles by people who wanted him to sit down and let them watch the show. Fair play to 'im though. He stood his ground and did his own thing, I used to feel a bit sorry for him at times, he either had a lot of guts or was just plain dumb. Some gigs would feel a bit strange if he wasn't there, that's how much of a feature he was...

When the Magic mushroom Band finally got to play at the Marquee, I was very pleased that he made an appearance, so much so, I impulsively did what I'd always wanted to do to reward him for his constant determination to have a good time, and I invited him up on stage. His eyes widened like saucers and he was up there in a flash before you could say 'Careful with that Tambourine, Eugene', of course I later realised why many bands hadn't previously done the same...it took a fair amount of persuasion to get him back off again".

[STEVE'S COMMENT]
"I always thought he was a cunt
In the fuckin' way, stupid hippie fuck wad" ...

JUST HANGING AROUND.

Ah, the Clarendon Hotel in Hammersmith, this was before it turned into the Club Foot [punk day's, and stuff I'll go into later]. It was a rock venue for a long time and I would go with the usual crowd from Ealing and have an average night of listening to watered down hard rock with the occasional splat of something worth hearing, then back to the old "tied down with battle ship chains" remember that piece of garbage, and Bon fuckin Jovy, who else! Oh yeah, all them hairstyle bands, wot a bunch of cunts they were, bloody meatloaf, with his fuckin' bat out of his ars' and forginer oh let's see.

Fuck it; you know who I mean I'm not going on and on so let's get back to the story. So on this particular night of mind numbingly boring fuckin hard rock and no women to shag, they all seemed to look the part but they very rarely opened their bleeding legs not even for a quick knee trembler in the bogs so it was always get drunk try ya luck at the end of the night if that was a wash out then have a crap fight with some prat so at least the night wasn't a complete waste of time and then walk off to the Shepherds Bush night bus stop and their we would hang about until the bus came and off to bed unless some one would have a do on but that was rare so I used to go back to me squat and party there if there was anyone up for it [not usually]. Well on this one night as we left the Clarenden Hotel we were walking up the road to Shepherds Bush and me and a couple of other geezers went for a piss down an ally way, when we got to the end I pulled out me knob and was having a piss when I noticed a man hanging from a large iron gate at the end of this ally?

Cool I thought! So I walked over to him and gave him a prod, but nothing so I called out to him, still nothing. By now the other two blokes with me were taking notice and started to ask what was going on. I told them I think the geezer's climbed over the fence and hung himself on the railing, well wot a bunch of nancies they all turned out to be, jeezuz. I mean he was dead so fuckin' wot they were all wearing their heavy metal t .shirts with skulls and devils and wot ave you's on them all looking very frightening [a bit of sarcasm there] so what was all the ballywho about? (Like der!)

I thought it was great fun and started to fuck about with him swinging him from left to right and watching his head bounce about, it was very funny, it was, look I was laughing and it was! So piss off all you 'oh that's horrible brigade', he was DEAD. No big deal, so let's have a laugh with him. I wanted to take him down and sit him on the bus with us so when the ticket bloke came round he would find him dead and we could pretend that he was with us but wouldn't pay his fare and see where it would all go. Just for a laugh, but oh NO!, Girls were now crying, one bloke came and saw and when I swung the funny old looking corpse with the bongaling head he ran away! Why, why, why wot a bunch of lefty middle class wankers no sense of fun and certainly no Anarchy in them what so fuckin' ever ... Tossers !

Well then people started to turn there attentions on me and certain people were trying to tell me off and stop it and girls were crying while saying that I was sick [good] then this stupid young plod arrived on the scene wot a cunt he was too. Looked about twelve and was a complete shit case so I played with him for a while [no, not with his dick, come on] he looked quite shocked so I said that maybe he should take his pulse but that didn't seem like the sort of thing this particular cuntstable wanted to do [good] so I goaded him some more while all the while laughing and having such fun, I kept on at him to feel his pulse which he eventually did then I got him to feel his neck and as he did I screamed at him AAAAHHHHH !!!

Coool, he shit himself and started to get well angry with me, plonker as if I was having any of that from a prick no older than me, well unfortunately it all came to an end when the cavalry arrived in the shape of a couple of meat wagons filled with more plod and a couple of sergeants who knew wot they were doin. So I made a hasty exit, all on my own by now as everybody had got the hump with me and was not talking to me, boo fuckin' who ...

Bleedin heavy metal fans, typists with make up on, and that's just the blokes!

PACK YA BAGS AND GET
THE FUCK OUT [SON]

When it came time for us to leave school (legally), my Dad god bless him, in his infinite wisdom tried to put his Son on the right road and get me out of the 'phase' I was going through (bloody long phase that, Dad) and righteously got me a job working as a warehouse boy in Camden (cheers Dad!). Nice to see your parents having great expectations for ya, ha. Actually it was ok really and I learnt a lot about packing boxes, stacking boxes, crushing boxes and also folding them up and stacking them just right...so they wouldn't tumble and come crashing to the floor. Okay, it was shit, I hated it.

It was getting in the way of my music, girls, partying and as 'blues' pills were all the rage then, French blues, they were best I think, they were prescribed. Then you had just blues, they were made from a concoction of things including strychnine (rat poison) and you could sympathise with rats as they must have died in so much pain, because the comedown from blues was the worst. Going up was the best, you could walk to Brighton talking all the way, completely oblivious to everything around yourself, so intense was the 'up' from blues (although very short lived) and coming down, well you fucking crashed. So the best way of avoiding this was to NEVER COME DOWN. I thought of this ingenious plan all by myself...but the tolerance to blues was quite remarkable. For a novice doin' the weekend stint takin' around 10 or so maybe, that's three to get ya started then another two later on and repeat that the next day. If ya started hitting them more often you could end up like me, buying around fifty to last the day and night. It got really stupid, really quickly.

Fitting a job in there was a real fuckin' nuisance, so I left and signed on for a month or so...Then Garry got this blinding job, in a props warehouse called Pictures (bastard) so of course I got an interview with the same kind of place just a walk away. He's got some really cool stories too, bastard, and he knows why I'm calling him a bastard, I bet ya sniggering as you read this huh, Garry?

Well it's because I ended up working in a 'curtains and pillows' shop.... bollocks! He get's all cool furniture, antiques, good looking babes in and out all flaming day, and I got... GAY MEN...MINCING AROUND, dropping fifty pence pieces and asking me to pick 'em up (not really, but ya get the picture...) I was folding curtains, fluffing cushions, it was crap. Now I've got no prejudice surrounding homosexuals, some of my best friends partake in a little 'uphill gardening' from time to time, hey wot ya do in your bed is your biz) BUT this place was so camp, even the cat had a surprised look it'd mince about like it had just sat on a rusty nail and liked it.. add the fact that I was still a young impressionable (very green) and pretty boy, it seemed as though if I had any homosexual tendencies they were best kept so far back in the proverbial closet they might as well be in Narnia.

Well I stayed there for around a month or so, got caught sleeping off a hard weekend at the John Bull Rock Disco in East Sheen (remember that place, Gaz?) I came into work on the Monday, couldn't keep my eyes open. The front window of the shop was decorated with cushions of every description, and you guessed it, I just lay my head down for a second and I was off, off to the land of 'Iron Dreams' (recall the name Gaz?), the only prob was the whole High Street could walk by and see me splayed out on display for all the world to see. When my boss finally got to work he wasn't best pleased and we called it a gay, ooops, I mean a day...

ASKEW ROAD ADVENTURES

(Garry)

"As mentioned earlier, our drug busts and associated adventures had finally sent our parents off the deep end and while Steve got evicted, I chose just to stay away and avoid the lectures. The next thing I knew, Steve and Scruff had heard about a big, old house in Askew Road that had been recently squatted. Askew Road is in a great location being pretty much on the border of Shepherd's Bush, Acton & Chiswick & Hammersmith in West London. Property there now is just worth silly money but at the time it was really squalid, loads of winos and weirdoes and very much gangster central. There were pubs there that you just didn't go to, period. But like I say, the location was excellent and I was working just around the corner at 'Pictures' too...

The rooms in the house were huuuge so everyone got a room each. One of them had this old Rasta in I remember...he'd make these big spliffs with newspaper instead of rolling papers...kafff!!! Chaaaaa Mon...Got ya stoned but jeez, the smell!! Steve and Scruff moved all their stuff in, but I left mine at home...I'm glad I did now because a lot of good stuff got 'nicked from there...Golden Rule number one, never leave a squat empty......ever... (It might get squatted...)

There were some great parties/jams there. One night after a particularly good one, Jacqui and I collapsed into our bed and after a while we both felt a cat lay down on our legs. It was wriggling about trying to get comfortable and we could feel the

8 0

vibrations of its purring through the blankets. It was pitch black in the room and seeing as we didn't have a 'house' cat we wondered how it'd got in...We lit a candle and lo and behold...there was nothing there! And we could still feel it on our legs!! Freaky deaky...we got up, went back downstairs with the diehards and when we eventually returned it was gone....or was it"???????

Askew Road squat....a string of circumstances led to Gaz and myself living in a squat in Askew Road, Shepherds bush. I was going out with Indrani my first love (her name meant 'Queen of the Clouds'). She was Anglo- Indian, with long black hair, the darkest brown eyes and a curvy, firm young bod... I'd been after her for ages and couldn't believe my luck when she went out with me. Her Dad was Indian and a magistrate at that. He was more English than English and wasn't too well pleased to find his beautiful (and she was) daughter was going out with me. I was all long hair and testosterone. Well, I got thrown out of my parent's house yet again, for dope I think, and she had got thrown out of her house for going out with me. Garry, you had that bird that couldn't handle her speed... Did strange things with her face when she was out of it...

I recall a Rastafarian who lived there, he was upstairs and made a living drying out dope next to an electric fire, he would give us a handful in the morning (to stop us from stealing his, I suppose). He was okay, I don't remember too much about him only that I scared the living shit out of him one morning, as he would never knock on the door, but just come right on in (maybe to get a sneaking glimpse of Indrani naked, or catch us at it..), well one morning his wish came true.

Scruff had lent me his black ultraviolet light ...and myself and Indrani had painted ourselves in fluorescent paint, took some mushies and were going at it like a couple of bunnies. Well, all of a sudden the door burst open, in walks the old boy, all dreads and a fuckin' huge spliff and was greeted by myself and Indrani glowing in the dark, her lovely young nubile, firm, pert (at this point there will be a short intermission, while I reminisce on my own). You the reader should take the chance to make a cup of tea or walk the dog...............O.K I'm back, settled? Then I'll begin. Pert young tits, ahhhh...anyway they were bouncing up and down while I thrust my angry, young, virile, strong, firm, taught (like a rubber chicken).... well, stop it, you get the picture. I let out a groan of ecstasy, she grabbed the sheets to cover her modesty, he just stared and all I could see was eyes and teeth glowing under the ultraviolet light and him saying "Yeah mon, wot freaky t'ing you boat' doin' den"? And he was gone... (Didn't see him for a week or so after that...).

OI! COME BACK 'ERE
WITH ME INNOCENCE!!
(Virgin on the Ridiculous)

..O.k. (deep breath) are you sitting comfortably? Kids out the room? Well I'll begin.... I had been with the usual girlfriends since the age of 14 a whole three years previous, but all my tedious endeavours were crushed and so I ended up 'friends' with most of the bright young things around at the time, so the 'old in- out in-out' was never consummated. But there were a couple of girls that everyone used to lose their boyhood too (or at least they said they did) but alas, I only got as far as a fumble in the park or a squeeze in the dark at some crapola party where every-one would come running in just at the crucial moment, laughing at the site of ya with your blooming trunks down with Shirley with the fat arse (a girl resembling a cross between Godzilla and Jo Brand) that I always laughed at and said 'How could any of you ever do THAT?' but they were only doin' the very same thing as me (TRYING TO LOSE THEIR VIRGINITY). Anyway, with only a couple of fishy fingers to show my mates, funny how at that age you find the need to share your 'encounter' with your friends by sticking your fingers up their nose... I suppose a) to see if everything's o.k and it should smell like that and b) a sign of validity thus proving and quashing any doubt that said finger had ventured inside and had a good old rummage around the slimy slug-hole of love......

SO WHEN I MET INDRANI (oh, she'll love me for this) who was Deso's girlfriend Sam's friend, we got it together and I found myself in the perfect opportunity to lose, throw away, leave if I could at a bus stop, give to a stranger, my virginity. BECAUSE YOU SEE I didn't want it, never asked for it, did not order it, so please waiter take it away. NOW the only problem I was having at this time is the fact that she didn't know I was as virgin as Mary... so I had to make a bloody good impression or pull some magic trick out of the hat so she wouldn't tumble (so confusing, so much pressure ,so little confidence, SO FUCKIN' SCARED).

LUCKILY we had both been slung out of our respective homes, mainly for being disrespectful little bastards and sleeping around taking loads of drugs, horrible delinquents that our parents couldn't stand any longer (not that we had actually done half of wot we were being accused of) and they threw us out..(Let that be a warning to all you parents out there)...SO here I was now living with a girly, oooh. A girly who'd had sex already, oo-er, a girly who would want sex again, whoohoo, and this time chummo (get that rubber band tied up tight 'round the old testis) it's gonna be with ME (oh dear).

Well things got off to a good start, we could be found kissing, fondling, touching our naughty bits (having a stroke n' poke), but I just couldn't get the little General in the bunker. Well finally one night we were play-fighting, like ya do, on the bed. We both fell to the ground naked, writhing about on the dirty wooden floorboards, suddenly we found ourselves both wedged under the blooming bed. Yes, under the bloody stupid mocking bed, with me on top and she underneath. So it was now or never, not that there was a lot either of us could do about it... stuck there like a couple of Swan Vestas in a box...AS IF BY MAGIC, doiiiing!!!! The General stood up, straight up son, proud and to attention, one good eye firmly fixed on his target and with no help from my good self, I WAS IN...Yahoo...

I was in the centre of the universe, a crescendo of angelic harps and those annoying violins all mixed up with this squeaky little devilish voice saying 'Fuck her, fuck her'. I really wanted to tell her I was on the verge of losing my cherry... but no, no you fool, you're in and if all goes ok you'll be out having scored, hit the goal, got a bullseye, a hole in one, one-hundred-and-eighty my son and no-one would be the wiser (well you try having your first in-out, in-out experience under the bed). Now I was in, there was no way I was coming out, not until the dirty deed had been done. So we pushed, pulled, groped and slurped, my back was sore and her knees had got somehow stuck and were wedged in tight and my arse was getting caught on the springs under the stinking mattress. Suddenly I came...boy did I; I could feel the boy melting away with every pump of my now 'man sperm' gushing deep, deep (calm down) (no)...deep inside my woman. I was a man now, no more just fish fingers, now it was fur burgers too and I could have it whenever I damn well wanted (and boy did I get a hunger for 'em)...yes siree...wheeewhoo. I think I'll have a cup of tea and calm down after that.......

EATING BLUES A LA
FUR BURGER SURPRISE...

While going out with Indrani I came upon a rather novel and quite exciting way of digesting my little blue amphetamine 'friends', this unfortunately was short lived but fun and exciting and turned into a cute game that would be played out between the two of us. It mainly consisted of Indrani getting naked (always a good idea), opening her lovely soft, light brown, silky-smooth legs wide open and me strategically placing three or four blues in her pretty pink petals of luuurv. I would then have the time-consuming task of retrieving the pills by the use of my tongue, as you can guess this was a long and precision-demand-ing task that needed a whole lot of attention to detail so I took the job in hand (or mouth) with great gusto.

She would giggle and wiggle while I could be heard slapping and a slurping at the naughty little vixen's love-hole, this game came to a disappointing end one day when I lost six blues.....you see I had managed to push them so far up that all of a sudden her pussy sucked in and they were gone...whooosh!! Lost in her vortex of lust. Well, Indrani had eaten hers so she was coming up already and I had nowt as that was the last of our stash, as you can imagine I was gutted. She was speeding like a nympho train out of control having now had something like twelve blues all kicking in at once and as I had got her all juiced up she wanted sex and lots of it, for hours. I wanted blues and a foot back on

the ladder but it wasn't to be...NEVER DONE THAT AGAIN.
Stuck to the old Mick Jagger way of doing it instead, inserting
Mars bars and the like...

While I'm here I'll enlighten you to a few do's and don'ts of
CARPET MUNCHING, FLANGE SLURPING, MUFF
DIVING, FANJEETA QUIFFING, MINGEETA QUIFFING [
the same but make sure she's not on her monthly cycle? no not
riding a fuckin' bike...] PUSSY PUSHING.ECT, ECT..
The list goes on and on.
So hear are a few of my favourite moments,
(Entitled)

PUT IT AWAY LOVE, YOURE SCARING ME RAT!

OR...

MY GIRLFRIEND REMINDS ME OF A FINE MATURE
CHEESE!

WHY?

BLUE, VEINY, AND SMELLING OF SHIT!

1) I found that if your girlfriend is a bit dry down in the old vag,
never under any circumstance use VIC VAPO RUB...I tried this
on one occasion, the ingenious plan was hatched one night
when there was no lube to be found. I was stumbling around in
the dark when I came upon a jar of the said rub; I managed to
get a good two fingers full of the stuff and proceeded to ooze it
in her cooze. Well all seemed ok then it kicked in and she started
to squirm, then a few choice words were said...'ARSEHOLE!!'
that was one...'WOT THE FUCK HAVE YOU PUT UP MY

CUNT?' that was another (she seemed such a pleasant girl..) then came wot I can only describe as a very violent Indian war-dance type thing (very amusing)..Suppose a blow jobs out of the question??

2) PIERCINGS...ok. One little story, the girls will enjoy this little episode...
A lovely girl called Deedee that I used to hang with; she was a stripper and hostess by trade at the time and loved her fetish sex games. Well on this one particular night I was drinking from the furry cup...now I should say at this point that Deedee had her sex lips pierced with a string of various studs and rings and while I was lapping away in the lap of luxury I got me blooming nose-ring caught in one of her bloody rings and I was stuck fast..HA, HA!! Very funny!! I hear you laugh. And it would have been if she hadn't thought it really funny and kept me there for fucking ages, so every time she laughed her fanny would wiggle and my nose would get stuck further up her puss. I was mumbling for help but this just seemed to make the affair more fun... COW.

3) Another girl was a nympho and wouldn't leave her fucking pussy alone, day and night, fuck and more fuck, vibrators, fingers, if it fit it was in. Well one day she wanted her clitoris pierced, fine, so off we went and got a ring put through it (and very fetching it looked too..), she was told however, not to play with it and to leave it alone to settle down, mmmmmmm...no sooner did we get home than she was naked on the bed and flicking away, she just couldn't leave it alone. Well after a couple of days it was getting quite sore, although she said she liked the pain (girls, hah!). One night I was down there pleasuring her with a vibrator and as I slowly eased the rubber dick in and out there was a sudden PING and out it came and shot straight past me head... woooosh!! BLIMEY...she had managed to wank her

piercing right out of her pussy...wot a dirty bitch...lovely...miss her.

4) UNRULY JULIE....OI, IS THAT A FERRET IN YA KNICK-ERS OR ARE YOU JUST PLEASED TO SEE ME ....Yes, you've guessed it, I had a ferret or polecat for a while. Charlie was his name, a *real* party animal, the most insane pet you could ever wish to have. At the time I was going through a collection of pests....oops, I mean pets. Snakes, lizards, a four-foot iguana that lived in the front room and would sit on your shoulder when you watched TV. I actually had a camen crocodile for while, but we're talking sex and pets, so.....Julie, lovely girl, used to have a great sense of humour, boy did she. She liked to play dirty games and yes she played dirty games with Charlie. Once she had a bath and got Charlie in with her, I thought ferrets didn't like water but he seemed quite happy swimming around with her washing him in rose-smelling shampoo, (did nothing for the smell of him though...if you don't know, ferrets have a strong smell of musk) and when she had finished bathing they both smelt of musk, great.

NOW, Charlie lived underneath the bath, so one morning I opened my eyes to see the little fucker making a bee-line for the bed, I hastily wrapped myself up with my side of the duvet because you see ferrets have a thing for sinking their teeth in any loose skin on offer and giving it a good chew. Now Julie thought it was kind of cute to feel his furry little body under the sheets, but I stayed wrapped up, tight. She giggled and paid no heed to my claims of 'It's gonna hurt', well Charlie wriggled his horrible little self right up to her very own furry ferret and was now giving it a sniff and lick. Julie thought it was rude and cool, rude and cool until he gave her 'fanjeeta' a proper nip... Oooch!!! Right in the clit...ooooch!! Well up she got and did the same dance as that other girl, the one like the Indian war-dance...ha!

O.k. while we're here, if there's any girls reading this, well this is just for you.

HER NAME WAS LOLA, SHE WAS A SHOWGIRL, WITH YELLOW FEATHERS IN HER HAIR AND HER DRESS CUT DOWN TO THERE,
SHE DID THE MARANGIE AND THE CHA, CHA. DUM, DEE, DUM, DEE, DEE DUM.

EALING ON BROADWAY

After the Askew Road squat, Indrani and myself had to move back to my parents' house. We were suffering from mild malnutrition mainly due to a diet of ice cream, cake, beans on toast, blues, dope and an unhealthy amount of sex (well I'd got the bugger in finally, now I couldn't keep him out). We would be at it all day and night, no time to go looking for work or for her to go to school, pubs or shops....it was 'Hey ho Silver'! Let's try this, (cool) now let's try it again this time with cream and them little hundreds and thousands, they'd get everywhere...I'm sure you've all been there (not with Indrani, I hasten to add).

Living at my parents...I think I was 17 and Indrani was 15 going on 16, my parents were so straight but did a really strange thing and gave us their bedroom so we stayed holed up like a couple of outlaws on the run, only coming out for supplies then back to bed. After a while me folks got fed up with the continual thumping on the ceiling and gave us our marching orders.
We had made some friends in Ealing and were offered a room in a squat, number 9, Oxford Road. At that time the squat scene was rife and Ealing was proper cool, dude, a happening place.

I think Garry was still in Richmond or maybe in Southall where he eventually met a rather lovely young thing from 'down under' called Kim...Now I had better watch what I say here as they're still together and she knows where I live..... No but honestly, not and never a bad word can be said of the lovely Kim and I mustn't forget their daughter Jasmine (wot a little stunner). Well Kim met him and has been nurturing the old bugger ever since.... (Lucky sod).

Meanwhile back in Ealing, on Broadway, I was green so green. I look back at photos of us both and the people, places and stories don't seem to fit the fresh-faced spotty Herberts that we were then. Hey ho... WOT'S A NICE KID LIKE YOU DOIN' IN A PLACE LIKE THIS? This was to become a phrase an old biker used to sing at me all the bloody time, it really got up my nose too as I thought I was living the dream and commanded a little respect from my peers (I'm watching my Son going through the same thing) because you see in the mirror that you're a man ready to take on the world, I've had sex, I've whipped a male contender older than me, I've taken a handful of drugs, now I live with my women in my room in a squat. I demand respect! (There's that old song again) 'Wot's a nice kid like you doin'... blah, blah, blah oh well...

EALING BROADMOOR

It had its fair share of weirdoes and I met and lived with most of them. Let me see...Mad John, he lived in the basement, must have been aged around sixty. The poor old sod used to get his food out of skips and such; he had loads of stories about being a merchant seaman and stuff, going round the world, etc....

FRITZ... (Remember him, Gaz?) (Yup, a righteous dude!) Wot a character he was, aged at the time around thirty and stood about six foot, he had cropped hair that was long at the sides, the filthiest pair of originals I've ever seen, proper 'old school' biker look. He used to pride himself on the fact that he only bathed once a year. Even though Fritz was a biker I never saw him on a motorbike. Well, Fritz had a beautiful bird called Carol who had a bad drug experience and was left a bit 'slow', thus thinking Fritz was a real catch. He used to get a black bomber and Mandy 'script and she got a Seconal one, Valium I think. Well she always had loads of stuff until Fritz got hold of it, pick-up day was fortnightly I think so you'd never see Fritz for long periods of time, then all of a sudden he was everywhere and I mean everywhere, gardens, houses, ya shed, car...

I went to the toilet once, opened the door and he had climbed the drain pipe and was nicking my toilet... Wot a nightmare. I stayed at his place for a while, well I had gone out somewhere ...and on my return, and Fritz had built me a bunk bed. 'Cheers!' I said, only problem was the bed only left me a foot or so from the ceiling (nice). That night a local girl stayed the night with me, a bed-warming party or something, as I was putting the finishing touches to my love-making with her I arched my back so I could give a big finale and promptly whacked my back on the ceiling thus causing me to roll off her and as luck would have it go tumbling down to the floor, falling six foot or so. Well I made quite a bang and the door came bursting in and I could see Fritz and Carol standing there having a good laugh.

ON another occasion I awoke to find in the middle of our front room, next to a cup of tea, a stack of parking meters, not the whole pole just the heads. You see Fritz had come across a pair of industrial bolt-croppers and proceeded to spend the night stealth-like cutting off all the parking meters in the local area and bringing them home. We couldn't suss out how to get them open so we dumped them. The next day our TV blew up so I went to a friend's house and watched his.

On my arrival home the next morning I found a new TV in the front room, as nobody was in I sat down, rolled a joint, made a cup of tea and was passing the time away when there was a knock at the door, it was our neighbour. He asked if he could come in and watch our TV as the football was on...no problem, he came in and I made a cup of tea for him and we both watched the game (well you've guessed it), all of a sudden Fritz comes in, sees the neighbour, gives me a look of death, mumbles something under his breath and storms upstairs. The bloke from next door feels uncomfortable and leaves, and then Fritz returns and when he's questioned reveals that I had been watching the neighbour's t.v...That Fritz had liberated the night before...

My first proper trip was in Ealing. I was 17 still, going on 18, and living now with Indrani. Our squat at 9 Oxford Road was writhing with hippies all of whom came from Bolton, why? I don't know, but they were young, around 22 years old and really knew their acid and mushrooms while not being afraid to sample and experiment with other hallucinogenics such as belladonna (deadly nightshade). They made a stew one night with it. Fuck! I had a cupful (a real horror-show, don't do it)....

So on a scorcher of a sunny morning we awoke to Rob inviting us to have our first proper mushroom trip and he was going to be our 'guide'. Rob, he was a true hippie, he had really long hair, love beads, flares, home-made jewellery and was the spitting image of 'Neil' from the Young Ones, sounded like him too. Well he opened a carrier bag full to the brim with psilocybin mushies, they were freshly picked and full of those horrible fuckin' maggots. After munching on the mushrooms, maggots, cow shit and wot ever else may have been in the field at harvest time, we sat patiently with bated breath...Nothing was happening, twenty minutes had passed and still nothing, I was getting bored... 'These things are shit and I feel sick!' I said, so off I went to the bog for a piss.

I thought all the stories I'd heard about tripping were blown out of all proportion as every time in the past, me and Gaz either got ripped off or the trip was just a mild one but, oh no, suddenly I was about to shake me willy after having a nice little piss, when ooops! My dick was stretching (cooool!), then like reeeealllly stretching (not so cool), but wow, I started to laugh at my dick, then I apologised to my dick for laughing at him, he didn't seem to mind.... I was nearly having a whole conversation with my dick while stretching and pulling. It was making faces now , faces I recognised, wow, I've got to tell Indrani and Rob (I thought), so I went running into the bedroom to share my new found friend, impersonator, incredible stretching, rubbery, pulling, really soft and nice, dick thing .. On entering the room I saw Indrani making follow-through patterns in the air, wow maaan! I could see them too, cool.

Everything was getting more intense so Rob, being scoutmaster for the day gave the command that we should go forth, into the wild (Ealing Broadway) where everything was beginning to make sense. Bright, everything was so fuckin' bright! Especially us, we were cartoon characters and life was a film and we were the bloody stars...I knew it! I knew this hippie thang had more to it than met the eye...I knew my parents had missed out on a whole load of stuff and I had found it, me all by myself... (Apart from the other couple of million people up and down the country), this was why I dressed like I did; now I get it, now I get it. I couldn't get enough of it either, I tripped all the time after that (it did me head in). Anyway, we had to go forth and discover pastures new, like Arnie Sacnusem in 'Journey to the Centre of the Earth' we were off, off, down the 'yellow brick road' of life off to find strange new life and bring it home and stuff, (you know wot I mean) bastard.

ARRIVING AT THE DOLE OFFICE...we met Adolf Hitler. We did. We fuckin' did right, there he was, the bastard never died, he got a job in Ealing Broadway dole office (and we'd found him), wot a bunch of losers in that shit-hole I thought (tripping isn't very forgiving is it?). Well we queued up for ever with the stench of piss and unwashed homeless people, yuck....then Hitler came over and talked to me. I was trying not to laugh at him, after all it was Hitler, and I couldn't believe Hitler was asking me to put my name on this bit of paper, because once I had done this he would give me another piece of paper and I could take it across the road and give it to a person (probably Goring or someone) and that person would give me money, more paper, so..... If I give this paper to other people they in turn would give me stuff. Now there was a problem...I had forgotten how to write, no, I'd forgotten how to spell my name, no I had forgotten my name (panic) wot's my name? wot's my fuckin' name? Hitler was getting pretty pissed off by now because I was laughing at him and panicking all at the same time.....buzzzzzzzzz. Rob stopped the madness, being the most intelligent man in the universe and I knew him, he knew my name and helped me write it down (thank fuck for that).

So having made our great escape out of there we ventured off to the station, got on a train and off we went like some spaced out Enid Blyton book 'Three Go Mad Anywhere'.
While on the train or as it was now the space age rocket ship to another place in time, Hitler's mate walked into our carriage, OH NO...IT'S THE GESTAPO...shit, he must have known we were getting the train and sent him after us, shiit. There he stood all dressed in black with shiny medals and some very important looking paper in his hands. He stared at us for a while then shouted, in a German voice, TICKETS... TICKETS.... HAVE YOU GOT YOUR FUCKIN' TICKETS, YOU HORRI-BLE FUCKIN' HIPPIE SCUM... (he didn't say that but he might as well have), but you see we hadn't bought a ticket, no, because we were horrible hippie scum and we was gonna trick them and not pay...Well as luck would have it, Rob paid, the Gestapo walked off and all was ok......

We went off to Hyde Park and had a really wild time, we talked to little red riding hood, we met the three bears, got some coca cola from Captain Scarlet, all in all we had a fantastic time.. We came home and took more that night and stayed up 'til morning and had a great idea of moving all the furniture out into the garden as it was nice outside. So imagine if you can the expressions on people's faces when they went to work that morning. There was Indrani making tea for everyone, Rob was plugging in the fridge, I had found a vacuum cleaner and was busy vacuuming the grass (well you know how grass gets all muddy)..Wot the fuck.....

EALING...BUSKING IT

An associate at the time named Chas, was squatting with me (by now myself and Indrani had gone our separate ways. I think she went back to school or college), he was older than me, stood around five-eleven, quite skinny with jet black hair and resembled Keith Richards in a punky look-a-likie way. Chas was quite well versed in street life and taught me a lot (unwittingly). He was into The Clash at the time (I wasn't), he liked the street poet-come Bob Dylan retro-anarchy, reds under the bed stuff...he also liked the reggae music, I fuckin' hated that shit, still do, all that 'let my people go maaan...us against them...' never fell for all that rubbish, I just wanted to get laid and stoned.

So it came to be that Chas would get me into busking, seemed a good idea, we could earn a few bob, chat up birds, maybe get spotted by a band or musicians or just have a laugh. We took ourselves off to Oxford Street and Tottenham Court Road station, there you had to write your name on a poster so as to secure your pitch, there were regulars that would object to us nicking their spot and they would get quite violent. We met some real characters down there, they'd been doin' it for years, all gone now of course....

We added our two pence worth of eccentricity with our dress sense, I was getting quite flamboyant by now with the use of eye-liner applied heavily like a watered-down Alice Cooper, black nail varnish, dyed hair (from a box of henna), steel toe-capped boots and occasionally a BRIGHT PINK DRAPE JACKET (jeezus). Wot a sight, but it worked, not a standard punker, definitely not a hippie, miles away from the biker look, pretty weird, trying to be me.

Chas had made a practice amp; they weren't actually invented for a year or so after, so Chas was ahead of it all. He was quite nifty with a soldering iron and wired up a couple of cassette recorders with a jack-plug socket so we could plug our guitars in, wired these up to a big speaker and hey presto we were ready for our two-man onslaught on the unsuspecting Oxford Street station and public.

On a good night we could earn fifty quid for a couple of hours and as we had our piece de resistance e.g. electric guitars, this made us the new kids on the block (crap choice of phrasing). We got some good compliments, some disbelief, I think Steve Jones commented on us when passing by one night, we had a few band members swapping comments.

The best thing though was the amount of alternative currency we gathered...everything from lumps of dope to wraps of speed and smack all got thrown in the hat...cool.

We had some memorable nights down there, one of them being two lovely far eastern looking gals who pulled us and we arranged to meet them later for a drink, well we had a drink and got invited back to their Dad's house as he was out of the country on business, when we got there we found to our joy that it was a massive great place (he must've been a diplomat or something), well the girls had some really good dope and the place was stacked with alcohol and we got pretty well fucked up. After a night of partying we went to bed, I slept in the girl's Dad's bed with her (ha, ha). The next day one of the girls ordered a pizza, so when the door bell rang I answered it wearing nothing but the old man's silk robe and a glass of brandy. To my amazement I was confronted by a giant of a man, Arabian in appearance with two 'minders'...oh shit.

At this time the old fairytale of The Three Bears came to mind...'Who's been sleeping in my bed? Who's been drinking my alcohol? Who's wearing my clothes and been fucking the arse off my daughter? INFIDEL....ENGLEEESH PEEG!!' Needless to say we were allowed to get dressed and leave at lightning speed (something neither of us was going to argue about), as the atmosphere was getting very ugly.

I'LL NAME THAT TUNE IN ONE

Busking was all very well and good and we had some great fun doing it but after a while playing the same old shit over and over began to get a bit tedious and so we used to change the words. Commuters would be coming down the escalators greeted by us singing our very own versions of well known songs, mainly insulting the businessmen and women going home from work. It was such fun as they would never be listening to the words and happily drop a few pence into the hat as we sung about their fat arse or 'here comes an office worker' der dum de dum...wot a fuckin' cunt etc. It didn't get much more meaningful than that either, but hey. Occasionally we'd meet up with other buskers and on a good few occasions had good old knees up and some-times the ticket collectors would come down and join us... mental. We had a 'lock-in' one night, 'til around three in the morning. Busking taught me lots... mainly how to work a crowd (so if you're ever doing a gig and the audience are going up and down on an escalator, I'm your
Man).

AFTER leaving Ealing and staying in St John's wood and the Old Street squat, I moved back to Ealing at Number 2, Windsor Road which was a bit like 'Narnia'. As you entered the house via Number 1, Windsor Road (they were the old Georgian houses, three floors up and a basement) to enter Number 2 you would have to go into Number 1, climb the derelict staircase (booby-trapped....well there were a couple of stair boards missing), up the stairs to the top of the house and then into the back room which had furniture and whole lot of junk in it. Here stood an old wardrobe...now if you ventured in and pushed the back panel it would open out into the house next door. We had made a hole straight through the wall, how cool. I lived there for six months or so, had some great times and some great girls.

I was shagging by now every bunny in the wood, doggie style, and feeling every bit the 'stallion' (enough with the animal references). Sheepishly I retracted my slippery python for one night, as a more urgent matter had arose...as if by magic I had a dream, a master plan.

While pissed and on Tuinol, I thought to myself... 'I know wot...I'M GONNA PAINT MOTORHEAD ON THE FRONT OF MY HOUSE. So while being helped by my two mates (or egged on...hmm...I can hear them now, 'Go on Steve, it's a great idea!), I was lowered by my feet out of the window and there I was hanging upside down with a pot of white gloss paint. I proceeded to scrawl 'Motorhead' all along the front of my house and as a point of fact, it's still there now but very faint (my son, who is now a local tagger, wants to revive it back to it's original glory), it's been there now for twenty six years to date. I should point out that while hanging upside down with a pot of gloss paint isn't a very inspired idea as it took me ages to get the 'white gloss look' out of me Barnet..(I now have the same look; this time though it's all down to good ol' wear and tear...AH, KIDS).

A couple of local pubs were part of the scene. THE QUEEN VICTORIA a well-known druggie pub, local freaks and gangster's hangout for years, had a bloody long run. I had many an adventure at this drinking establishment. Another insane little pub was the ROYAL OAK. It was on the Ealing Broadway but it's all changed now, in fact they knocked the whole Broadway down so it's gone completely. Well this boozer was a mad, mad, mad tiny little affair. They had a duo performing every weekend that were blind, and some nights there would be fights going on there in front of them and they'd carry on regardless.. (Brill). The pub was basically a 'corridor' packed full people all of which were speeding their tits off, or cocked up with the gangsters (when I say gangsters, I mean proper gangsters...not handbag and mobile phone stealing wankers)...

SMOKIE & THE BEARS

AROUND this time, the 'legalize cannabis' brigade was on full throttle disorganising sit-ins, smoke-ins, march-ins and run-outs, oh yeah and the much loved but over-rated picnics (wot a load of bollocks).

I remember one such day, the 'Smoky Bears' picnic in the park, London's Hyde Park actually...more 'old bill' than you could shake a truncheon at, walking about looking so fuckin' obvious with their beads and afghan coats and shit. I can't even remember what exactly they were wearing, just old bill looking like old bill, you know wot I mean. There was a stage for all the usual suspect bands to play on, Inner City Unit were headlining I remember, just after I got slung out. I remember being still pissed off with them as the keyboard player tried to keep my Rickenbacker bass and I had to ask quite firmly to get it back and I was contemplating smashing the fuck out of the arsehole, his name was 'Dead Fred' or was it 'Dick Head'? Something stupid like that, he was a complete git anyway. There was a lot of politics about then too, that entire self-righteous hippie shit that was just an excuse to rip you off.

The crowd consisted of the already stated old Billy boy and friends...the usual freaks, flippy floppy hippies, punks and the newer punks that were turning into hippies and the other lot with dreadlocks (wot were *they* on?) all trying to be black for some reason and listening to reggae music, thinking they had some understanding with the black mans' struggle...well it's not for me to say, but weren't the Rastas just as outcast as the white freaks were and the 'straight' black community disowned them in much the same way as we were being misrepresented...oh dear, here I go getting   political....memo.....must keep my thoughts to my self ..

SO....politics aside, back to nineteen with a bullet (or bottle of pills anyway), there was a small contingent of us left over, the 'don't fit in anywhere' league of the unwashed, unhip and unemployed... oops...unemployed, never been employed apart from that fiasco in the dodgy gay, curtain theatre 'props' place.

WE turned up not for the legalize cannabis bollocks, but to poke fun at anyone who'd be intimidated, because you see some of us could see past their collection buckets with the 'give us money and we'll fight your corner politically and get the laws changed'.....for what? Cannabis? I've always smoked dope wherever and whenever I wanted, never needed the help of some self-righteous middle class summer festival hippie to fight my corner and never will!

AND while I'm on a rant, where did all that money go....??? Ah kids stuffed their joints in Ibiza I reckon, not me...NEVER TRUST A HIPPIE.

So, we now had the inspired task to bring our own crusade to court and to the forefront, we made banners and makeshift flags with the truly inspired words 'LEGALIZE TUINOL' that set the Arabs amongst the Jews like a sackful of drowning puppies, we even drew a picture of a tuinol capsule on one flag just in case nobody got it. It was all a joke really; I just like to stir things up a bit. Sometimes you get too involved in the cause and forget it's supposed to be fun, how can you fuck the system when everybodies preoccupied fucking themselves? Well, it all got ugly as the mixing of downers, strong lager and white lightning finally took hold and we got escorted off the site....but not until we had canned offstage a couple of crapola bands and raided a bucket or two for funds to score cannabis (see kids? there's a moral to this story).

(Garry remembers...)
"Ah yes....the good ol' Smokey Bear's Picnics. Sorta nice idea if not a little naive, the idea of skinning up in broad daylight at such a high-profile site in the safety of a huge crowd seemed like a good 'un at the time...but of course the boys in blue thought differently and hatched a 'cunning plan'...They'd dress their boys up in afghans and sandals and John Lennon glasses while we'd all be standing there in our tatty leathers with our beer-stained/hash-burned tee-shirts and bullet belts wondering what they were on...we used to spot lots of them at those do's.

It was quite a simple plan of attack for the gathered stoners really - turn up with all your mates, sit in a huge, fuckoff circle and skin up. That was it, and thousands made the effort. Suffice to say, us brave freedom fighters would get totally blasted and the pigs couldn't do anything about it. Their answer was to put a crack team together, dress them in fur coats, wigs and bell-bottoms and get them to infiltrate the subordinates. As you can imagine, the first sign of any of them even thinking about revealing their true identity would have us scurrying off, further into the safety of the crowd.

The 'campaign' of course, never succeeded in its aim...it couldn't. How can you rally and organise a campaign for reform, when the subject in question has you mostly off yer tits with the only topic on your mind being how to make it to the nearest pizza takeaway without looking too 'out of it'??? There probably would have been thousands more at those gatherings if not for the fact that they probably got the day wrong, forgot about it completely while watching Dr Who on the TV, saw a TV detector van down the road and hid in a cupboard under the stairs, missed or took the wrong train/bus, saw a rainbow and decided to find it's end, or were standing around, confused as to the lack of amenities and media/police as they gathered at completely the wrong part of Hyde Park.....

I remember that there was a nude 'Be-in' organised for Hampstead Heath too...but I never made it there as the thought of seeing Nick Turner naked, rattling his bones around the heath was too much for me to bear..

The whole pot media thing has turned out pretty much as expected, most people alive today in this 'liberated' society have by now smoked dope or have known somebody who has...no more taboo. It's a generational thang, baby".

NO SLEEP TILL WE GET
THE BOMBER SCRIPT

Back at Hammersmith Odeon, 1980 and Motorhead are climaxing their career with a full-on 'going for broke' gig there. This was a real freak show, as all of a sudden the band that a handful of us had been threatening London with and was and should have been doomed to fail (and we liked it that way) suddenly got big, fucking big and where we used to turn up backstage and Lem would dish out backstage passes a plenty, the place was now filled with paparazzi and celebrities...wot a bunch of cunts they were too, All the types of people we thought Motorhead were against suddenly were there all doin' the 'rock n' roll arse lick' dance outside. Thus I found myself in the unusual position of being at the back of an 'I'm a fucking celebrity, get me in there' queue.

Lemmy seemed distraught as he was being hounded with 'Okay mate, remember me?' types, so to get in there I'd have to use the ol' tried and tested, never let me down before move. Standing about fifteen feet away from the backstage door I shouted out 'Oi Lem!' got his attention and put the plan into action...I simply raised my arm and vigorously shook a bottle of black bombers. On glancing at that most wonderful spectacle Lemmy replied with 'Get that man and his bird backstage passes now!'...ha. Better than an American express card that one...

STONED, INNOCENT, FRANKENSTEIN

STONED INNOCENT FRANKENSTEIN

Stoned innocent Frankenstein...Sutherland Avenue...a nightmare on every street.....Sutherland Avenue is located in Maida Vale, West London, a thirty minute stagger from Portobello Road. Our squat was in a derelict hotel just 'round the corner from the hippie commune road of Bristol Gardens and was coming to the end of its alternative life. It was here that I joined Nick Turner's Inner City Unit, the punks had now started arriving and such bands as the Boys, the Ruts etc. were all living nearby. The whole area was still pretty much a hippie vibe with lots of dope, speed, coke, maybe heroin and our squat.

The doors were never closed, as nobody of sound mind would ever wish to venture inside. It looked dark and black and should have had crows and bats flying around the chimney spires. As you approached the front door with the old, dirty black, flaking paint with brass door knockers you could imagine Lurch standing there with his famous greeting 'YEEEES?' Well you've guessed it; I'd reached one of my rock bottoms. How the hell I managed to go from spotty Herbert (so green, so innocent) to here in just three short years is fucking scary in itself.
This place was the house of TUINOL...oh fuckin' dear...Run, run now while you can....this is a long scary big-dipper of a ride so hold on!

WARNING, ONLY READ THIS IF YOU'RE A SICK FUCK AND LOVE HORRIBLE NASTY STORIES. REMEMBER KIDS, TRUTH IS STRANGER THAN FICTION...

Tuinol (Nembutal, Seconol, and Sodium Amatol), Jacks, Ritalin and many more 'prescribed' drugs were now the drugs of choice. Cheaper than Heroin, totally anti-social, violent, with the power to turn the mildest of men into raving lunatics (and it did), lose all inhibitions, self-worth, respect for yourself or anybody else.....in a word, FUCKIN' GREAT...If ya don't give a shit, have no responsibilities like friends, family, pets etc. and can afford to take the next few years off with no guarantee of getting out alive, then come on down, motherfucker, get that self-destruct button wired into you're psyche and let's dance. It's wot basically killed Hendrix, Sid Vicious and a host of others (not Heroin) and in fact it was barbiturates I think you'll find that were the culprits. I had a fleeting romance with these drugs for a couple of years and then went on to smack (Heroin) for a quieter life.

THE Sutherland Avenue squat must have been the most outrageous house I've ever lived in, we had a room in the attic to store people until the police arrived (if they'd overdosed), it was all made up with a bed, cupboard, carpet, everything but a tenant...so if you looked as if you might not make it through the night, up you'd go. If ya did then down you'd come later and rejoin the party, if not then the police were called. They would arrive with an ambulance and take the deceased person away, more often than not hardly a question was asked of us and the whole thing became rather matter of fact... (I personally helped to hump around four of those people up the stairs, call the police and they'd take them away)..Mad...(My parents would have been so proud of me).

Around this time I recall a bloke called John (Mad John we christened him), he was ok. A small bloke around forty years old, another Northerner, always fighting his room-mate. Well he went missing and after the squat had been closed down we found out the reason for the mysterious, really bad stink in the house....yes, you've guessed it. Dead. In fact buried in one of the rooms that we used to throw all our rubbish in (the rubbish room). One of these could be found on every floor as the dust-bin men never came to our house (funny that). One memorable night I recall I brought home a young girl about the same age as myself, that I'd met in Piccadilly, she had loads of downers and big tits (say no more). I offered her a bed for the night, my girlfriend wasn't best pleased, well we did have an open rela-tionship (basically I did wot the fuck I wanted)...'Wot a wanker!' I hear you girls say...mmmmm...yes. I'd never get away with that sort of behaviour nowadays, oh well... (There's a chauvinistic smirk all over my face as I'm writing this)...anyway, we all got really off our faces and went to bed. Now my girl-friend at the time was bisexual so it wasn't all bad after all (ya see girls? ya like to make a fuss, but when it's your turn to join in, it's 'Oh, okay').

Well she and the well-developed young lady put on a real groovy show, and then I fell asleep. THEN I AWOKE. There was smoke everywhere, SHEEEEIIIT. You know when you're really out of it, pissed or stoned and there's no way ya can do anything, then something really wrong happens and instantly you're WIDE AWAKE. As if on automatic control I woke the 'Doris', oops, me bird (sorry, my girlfriend)]. As I opened the bedroom door, there sat on the floor wrapped in a quilt next to the rubbish room was the girl with big tits. She was naked, asleep with her hand in a position that had suggested she was holding a cigarette... the silly cow must have thrown the whole thing into the rubbish room and it had gone up. Boy did it go up, the next hour or so was totally bizarre, crazy, funny and very scary as we tried to tackle the blazing inferno. Everybody in the house had been summoned, only trouble with that was the fact that everybody was totally fucked up on drugs and all got very sidetracked from our new venture of 'have a go' fire-fighters, (it was like a really bad Three Stooges meet the Keystone Cops on downers').

Imagine trying to find water-carrying utensils like buckets, saucepans, pots, anything to throw on the ever-growing blaze, while most of our efforts were being hampered by the fact that we would throw most of the water on ourselves or directly onto the floor. I recall my girlfriend at this point wandering aimlessly about the place, trying to help by holding a cup of water and limply tossing it in the direction of the blazing room. I screamed at her and my mate screamed at me, so I hit him and he hit me. Now we're fighting on the floor, the fire's still raging, other people are now attending the burning room of doom and eventually it's put out. We all survived the night but that incident was not the last.

In fact this was to become a regular occurrence especially when the electricity was cut off and someone had the bright idea of rigging up the mains straight out of the main supply in the road. It was bright yellow with a hint of white, down in the basement and it hummed. On my floor there was a hole in front of the toilet where the floor had rotted and if you dribbled when having a piss, sometimes it would hit the 'live' wires and make a huge, white flash! We stopped pissing in there after a while when I nearly blew off my dick one night...

BILLY, Mad Billy (there's a pattern starting to emerge if you look closely), now Billy was a Merchant Seaman, short, stocky and Northern with a crazed look in his eye (one of those people who would be about one inch from your nose, staring straight at you..) his idea of fun was taking loads of LSD, getting as pissed as he could and then fight everybody, (wot a nightmare). He moved in a woman in her 'forties' or thereabouts, very haggard, you could see she had once been quite a looker but had traded drink, drugs and a horrible way of life as a trade with the devil. She was on the game and no sooner had she arrived than several punters were being 'served' in our road alone. I became a kind of minder for her, making sure that nobody took any more advantage than was being paid for. All in all I had a few scrapes, but everything went ok...

One particular night Billy was bashing her up and she asked if she could spend the night on our floor to get away from the space cadet. After an hour or so the door came smashing down with Billy stood there like a fucking bull-terrier, all red in the face, well he gave her a swift kick and shouted a load of abuse and when I objected to his behaviour he said he was going to do the same to me. Now Billy was around thirty-five years old, well travelled and very street wise and fuckin' hard. I was 18 going on 19 and not used to fighting hardened men (and not to put a point on it, shit myself). I stood my ground though...well actually; I sat up in bed and told him in no uncertain terms to fuck off back into his room.

He looked at me then lunged forward with both of us now on the bed lying down (here I must explain, squat life meant you never knew who would be in the house and when, so I always had an iron bar, a stiletto knife and an axe handy), so when Billy

115

knocked me to the bed I thrust my stiletto into his back, twice I think, he then got up and said in his gravelly northern voice "Ya bastard, ya stabbed me!".

I said "Yes, now fuck off back into your room", he didn't and we repeated the whole dance again, after which he just got off and quietly walked back to his room. We all settled down, called him a few choice names and went back to sleep.

Next morning the hippies downstairs came up and said that Billy had gone to the hospital and that they'd looked at his back and there were four large-ish holes in him. It turned out I had punctured his lung. He stayed there for a month or so, made a perfect recovery and a month later I met him in Heneikeys and he bought me a drink (very strange). The prossie stayed for a couple of weeks more and one day a mate of mine was getting a 'freebee' when she just gave up and died, poor cow...hey ho.

I had a similar experience with a girl I'd brought home; we got extremely wasted on Tuinol and after a while started indulging in a little in-out in-out action. It then dawned on me that she was either really crap in bed or she'd overdosed, well as luck would have it, it was the latter. I kept going though, but when I noticed her lips were turning blue, I stopped thinking about myself and brought her 'round. Things like this happened all the time around this period, I can't reveal all the stories as many are worse than this and quiet frankly I don't wish to tell (we'll just leave it there).....

It was here that I had my first 'fix'... I had thrown a junkie out of the house for having a fix in my room as this was still a big taboo to me, people who injected themselves with drugs were a different breed...I didn't understand it and didn't want to. This all changed when I fell into the trap that was 'Ya can't knock it until you've tried it....' wot a lot of bollocks that is.

So not paying any attention to my better judgement, a well known dealer who I'll call Stan, a nasty piece of work, a real bully who stood a good six foot, stocky and dressed like a rockabilly. He would lay drugs on anyone knowing they couldn't pay so he then owned a piece of ya.

(THE VIRUS known as Stan became a real pain, he would walk into your crib without an invitation, totally unannounced and if you had a spoon with a 'washout' (leftovers that would be enough to stop withdrawals) and if you owed him money, something everyone in West London seemed to do, he would take his own syringe (ARM SPANNER, a name given to this piece of equipment by a well known ROAD RAT) out of his pocket and suck up the remaining leftovers, then inject himself (dirty arsehole) thus leaving yourself with nowt. NOW, Stan was bigger and extremely more violent than the rest of us, as we only used violence as a defence or just bad-tempered attacks on each other, he on the other hand was a professional bully and used his size to gain an advantage (never been impressed by fat bullies). I'm no fool though and realised a smack in the head was a complete waste of time, so I, with others, concocted a plan, not a great plan, not really thought through with relevance to the outcome or to wot would happen if it worked or if it didn't. (So glad now that it never did).

WELL a spoon was surreptitiously left out on the sideboard with a very appetising looking bit of cotton wool doused in in a generous amount of wot looked cunningly like Smack, in fact it was BATTERY ACID, yep CAR BATTERY ACID. Now I have no idea on the effects of injecting battery acid straight into your veins nor did I at the time care very much, but one thing is for sure...Stan would not be nicking my drugs, I don't suppose he would be nicking anybody's drugs, actually he wouldn't be doin' very much at all, another contender for the room in the loft me thinks. Well we left the bait out for him for a week or so, but he never showed, phew... Lucky really as I would have been done for murder and he wasn't worth that...)

Anyway, he came 'round to our squat one night with some really nice methadrine crystal and everyone started injecting it. I put my case forward as a non-voter to fixing in the house but this was met with much laughter as they were all hardened users (I just didn't realise), so the 'outing' of the guy in my room was a waste of bleeding time...

I was in an experimental mood that night as I had just done a line of the meth and was now coming up rather fast. My girlfriend then decided to tell me that even she had done it before and that I should try it , duuurrrr...o.k., if you have I'd better do it as well (say that line reeeeaaallly slowwwly). Well as luck would have it there was a spare syringe, oh that's lucky, so now I was about to join the fuckin' witches 'coven of the night'.

I don't like telling this story but I feel it's appropriate to the book. Ok, with my shirt sleeve turned up, a tourniquet wrapped tightly around my arm and a slight tap to get my veins to rise to the occasion, then I can't remember who but someone slid gently into my deep blue vein the small orange-tipped needle FUCKIN' HELL.. I've never had nor would I ever again have such a rush, it blew me head off. I could feel the methadrine burning its way up my arm, I was scared and nervous and sweat was shooting out of the pores of my skin. I could feel a sharp tingle at the base of my spine which worked its way up my back to the base of my head making every hair on my body rise up, tingling, and then POW...I was up, really up. So far up I thought I'd explode, I needed me girlfriend to hold me down (hence the expression WOT A RUSH...) I would like to say it was horrible and I wish I had never done it but, maan.

BUT!

Wot a rush. Unfortunately I loved it and couldn't get enough.

We used to recycle our needles by the way on the sides of boxes of matches?

YEP go figure, I actually had the same needle and arm spanner for around a month until somebody said wot the fuck are you trying to do with that, as my arms where sore and bruised from my repeated jabbings trying to pierce the skin and try in vain (no pun) to find a vein and then give it a good old stab...

ORRIBLE...

Or as the STONES once wrote, IT'S ONLY COD AND SOUL BUT I LIKE FISH!

I went on to inject every known detergent known to man. IT NEARLY ALL CAME TO A VERY STICKY END FOR ME... I decided one day that everyone in the house was out to get me, so I was gonna get them first (wot a plan). I tooled up for the job in hand with my trusty stiletto in my boot, my axe was tucked down the front of my trousers and I came bursting into everybody's room in turn, frothing at the mouth and screaming and shouting, lashing out at any and everything I could (wot a nightmare). Somehow everyone had collected themselves into one room, they had barricaded themselves in with a pole against the door, I was outside kicking and smashing an exhaust pipe I'd ripped off a car outside and was charging at the door with it when all of a sudden the bastards opened it just as I got there. So in I ran, fell, tripped over and was met by everyone now holding bits of wood and furniture. A barrage of "let him 'ave it" was hailed to my head and as I went down they managed to kick my arse out the door, where I got myself together and tried walking to the hospital. Luckily someone had called an ambulance which took me to the outpatients where they had to fix a broken nose, two black eyes, a cracked rib, and various bruises... INFAMY, INFAMY, THEY ALL HAD IT IN FOR ME...

LADY "DY" CANOL

Dycanol.....what were they about??
Originally made and prescribed for women to relieve serious
period-pain, Dycanol were small and pink in colour with a plastic silicon ingredient in them so as to stop junkies injecting
themselves (didn't work). There was quite a craze for these little
pink perils back in the eighties that coincidentally led to a
number of amputations and deaths.

Dycanol had a very weird, weird buzz....a bit like Heroin. Even
so, the effect wouldn't last long so you were always chasing
another hit. Junkies would inject themselves, leaving the needle
in the hit spot and use a large syringe so all they had to do once
a hit was made, was to push the plunger in a bit as and when the
effect wore off. Dycanol also had quite a strange side effect
accompanying the buzz, there would be a really weird bout of
hallucinations, not in the L.S.D. or mushroom sense where it
was spiritual, had colourful psychedelics, or bouts of laughing
and a strong sense that you were right off ya fuckin' tits no, no,
no. 'Dykes' were frighteningly subtle, just as you might be
getting used to the fact that the buzz was all over and maybe
you were watching TV or some such, something fucking weird
would happen. A bloody great dragon, all teeth and fish guts
could easily appear from the TV, under the carpet or while
opening a cupboard door to fetch a box of cornflakes...sheeeet...

Now this would not be, as I've explained, anything like a trip. This was REAL man, fucking one hundred percent, in ya face, all teeth and fire, hell and damnation in your very own front room...fuck! Bring me the men in white coats, coz it's in here and it's gonna get me.
Yep, pretty scary stuff wot!?

I will now give you an example....(here we go again) strap your-selves in for another white knuckle, death defying ride on the Speedy Steve rocket ship to ga ga whoopsie fuckin' twiddly bloody doo doo land..
GONE TRIPPIN LE DYCANOL WAY...ooooooooow....

AFTER a typical night of getting pleasantly toasted. Some arse came 'round with a bag of dykes. They weren't cheap and I didn't like them very much either, but there wasn't any 'skag' around and I was getting bored smoking dope, so we raided the wallet, scored a few of these pink 'pissoff' pills and retired to the kitchen to start the long and laborious job of now trying to find a vein, a vein that hadn't been so badly perforated, jabbed and gouged, that I could once again try and inject some drug vaguely resembling a household detergent and having not so dissimilar an effect on me old noggin. Vein 'up', tourniquet tied tight 'round my arm, needle in, push the plunger and in go the dykes, silicon, plastic and fuck knows wot else. If you left the dykes in the spoon for too long, they would congeal and go hard. Yes, this is wot happened in your vein, so you really needed to get them in and rushing 'round the blood stream in double-quick time or the old circulation would get cut off....bollocks to that! On this particular occasion, everything went according to plan and I got stoned, talked the usual shit, ran 'round like a chicken with its beak stuck up its arse and came crashing down only to find myself bored, so with no lack of haste I proceeded to the kitchen where I did it all over again and pissed everybody off in the room, so they left leaving me to watch TV all on my lonesome.

I was now getting used to being straight, when I heard a scuttle under the bed. I didn't think too much about it at first, but when I heard it again, this time my ears pricked up...you know like when you think you can hear someone outside? Well I got all panicky and strained my hearing to trace just where it was coming from, then I heard it again...a scuttle under the bed, it must be a mouse or something, I looked but couldn't see anything, then I heard it again. This time the scurrying was under the sink...this was getting on my nerves now, I wanted to know wot was making all the racket, so armed with my trusty shoe, I lifted the quilt cover that was draped around me off the bed and onto the floor, put my head under the bed and heard a swift scurrying sound as the thing went rushing off (little bastard). I still couldn't make out what exactly I was chasing, but I was going to catch it and most probably bash the fucker's head in, or kindly put the delicate mammal in a box and set him free, free with the other wild animals of the wood ...nnnaaahhh...'course not .I'd simply bash its head in and sling the piece of shit in the bin.

The piece of shit in question was still under the bed so I fetched a box just in case I felt merciful and once again went into the breach (or under the bed). This time I got a glimpse of the little fucker and managed to chase him out, when I noticed I wasn't chasing a mouse, but a crab...yes a CRAB...and not as you might think like the ones on the sea-shore, oh no, this was like what ya get in ya pubes, a friggin' dick crab! Now I must stress this was not only a pube crab, but the biggest pube crab I have ever seen...it measured about seven inches round with all its crabby little legs wriggling around underneath, nasty, bloody ugly thing it was. I promptly shit myself and jumped onto the bed like a big girl (then again it was a big crab...). I called my girlfriend in to see the monster crab, she eventually came in and once I'd told her the story, she had a thought to herself then told me I was a fuckin' nutter and left the room, bastard. So nobody was going to believe me, that's cool.....I'll just catch the fucker, put it in the box and show them disbelieving wankers...then they'll see.

So with shoe in hand, box close by, a new sense of bravery and swashbuckling bravado, I lifted the quilt (or gates to the underworld), in I went, like an S.A.S trooper on a mission from God...I'll catch that friggin' crab from hell if it kills me. Under the bed I could still hear it scuttling around, and then in a flash I caught a fleeting glimpse of it and struck out with my shoe. The crab ran and I positioned the box directly in front of him and he ran in...GOTCH YA!! Ya little fookin' bastard. I then closed the lid of said box and with my new trophy went down the corridor to where the 'non-believers' were watching TV. As I opened the door, a look of 'Wot's the nutter doin' now?' was obvious to see on their mocking faces but hey, here's the proof dickheads, now you'll see.....

I gathered my girlfriend and other 'so called' mates 'round and shook the box at them; they looked at me unimpressed, so I shook the box again, nothing. 'Listen!' I said in a mocking voice....'Listen to the fuckin' crab, I've caught it, it's in the box!' They looked at me as if I had lost my mind, I could hear him running about but no-one else could, so I opened the box reeeeeal slooow, so's not to lose him, as you know he's a flighty little character, isn't he reader? The box opened, I stood back, they looked in, unamused at having to go along with the farce to keep me quiet and every one of them told me in no uncertain terms that there was nothing in the box, not a sausage, let alone a bleeding dick crab, so I sulked off, threw the crab and box outside and went to bed. On going to bed, I opened the wardrobe to get a towel and there hung a city 'gent upside-down in a suit, umbrella and suitcase, he didn't say a word, I didn't say a word, and I just closed the door and got into bed and went straight to sleep...

THE WILD WEST (WAY)

The long trek from the pub to the Green under the West way flyover. The long haul like a pilgrimage of migrating extras in a post-nuclear war 'B' film would take around 30 minutes for any normal bystander to casually walk the half-mile or so distance from the pub to the Green. The pub in question being the Earl of Lonsdale (or Heneikeys Free House as it was known then) at 277-81 Westbourne Grove.

The journey would take in such sights as the antique stalls, the second-hand record stalls, hippie shops; army-surplus stalls etc. Although the army-surplus stall outside the Princess Alexandria pub (95 Portobello Road) wasn't such a well thought-out plan. Complete with all it's shiny knives, second world war bayonets, replica guns, German regalia, 'under the counter' flick-knives and other assorted bits, and let's say, pieces. Bad planning because this was frequently used as a handy pit-stop to stock up on various implements to start or settle any disagreements that may have arisen during the afternoon. Some lesser anti-socials would also use this outlet store to help purchase handbags, cameras, or any other item that a would-be tourist might offer in exchange considering the alternative currency being bran-dished in their face.....

NEXT STOP... on the trek was the Mountain Grill restaurant. The Mountain Grill was a cafe made legendary by Hawkwind. They used the cafe on a regular basis back in the day and had made it well known by using the name as part of an album title 'HALL OF THE MOUNTAIN GRILL'. The cafe was a handy stop-off point to feed the troops and make some last minute wheels, deals and occasional steals, before descending on the 'holy ground' (or the Green under the flyover). Making it to the Green would mean a kind of sanctuary as the police would give us the benefit of the doubt and turn a blind eye... (That must hurt). Once you had found a plot to secure and make your own, one could relax in the sun with a bottle of Thunderbird wine, a well stacked joint, and revel in the fact that you'd made it...(in one piece or several as sometimes was the case).

Depending on that long and sometimes violent walk or stagger from pub to Green, trials and tribulations of said trek would manifest itself in many forms. As I've said, for 99 percent of bystanders the Portobello Road was strewn with market stalls offering an array of pleasantries, one could soak up the sights and sounds of a bustling, heaving, and visually beautiful market. TO OTHERS... it could be a battleground thwart with danger, ambushes, police harassment, clashes of sub cultures, street gangs such as skinheads, mods, some wannabe punks who didn't quite get it or come up to scratch. You see a lot can happen to a boy in a few months of growing up with the underworld. There would be groups of young offenders on corners, like birds of prey, just waiting to catch you off guard, then they'd pounce, all Doctor Marten boots and bald heads (wankers, although most are best mates now..) but usually they'd keep their distance from our elite array of misfits.

THEN THERE WAS THE CAMERA-TOTING BLOODY FUCK TOURISTS. Who in their right mind would wanna come over to a bunch of guys wearing swastikas, obviously carrying weapons, shouting, swearing, falling over, trying to control their dog's girlfriends, holding up motorcycles, trying to look cool with hot dog sauce dripping down their face, flies undone, openly taking drugs, scaring small children (basically a bunch of bastards)...and request a photo?.. A fucking PHOTO! Who would be brave enough or just plain stupid enough to walk straight up to a gang of openly outrageous bastards and take a picture....? DUUUURRR, I mean come on...please. Sometimes it would be the last straw and a fee would be asked... If payment was handed over and it was a sufficient amount then all would be forgiven and said tourist could go on their merry fuckin' way and hassle some other dumb shit. Other times the appropriate use of the English language, words such as 'FUCK OFF!' and 'GO AWAY!' would be enough, but as usual there would be the TOURIST FROM HELL.

This was normally a woman, aged around 40 to 60, very proper, well dressed, normally had a couple of real ugly kids, the sort you'd like to set your dog on, a husband who could see wot was about to happen and was visibly walking 'quickstep' down the road trying hard to pretend he wasn't about to witness the approaching violation his dumb arse wife was about to make.

VIOLATION ONE - do not under any circumstances sit on a biker's chopper... (Ooh err) if not asked.

VIOLATION TWO - do not walk up to a punk rocker, biker or any other misfit and STICK YOUR FUCKIN' CAMERA IN THEIR FACE, especially when they've just told you to "Fuck off and go away, or I'll kick your stupid tourist head in".

On reflection I couldn't then and still can't see what was so hard to understand about that phrase, mainly because it would end with said tourist standing their ground and trying to make a case for themselves. Being tourists they should be able to take your photo, sit on your bike, have their ugly kids, grandmothers, pets, husbands (if they're not already on the bus out of there yet) etc. stand next to you and take a picture like you're some kind of circus attraction. And if you (God forbid) waived your right as an individual not wanting to be photographed like some uncaged animal for tourists to photograph, touch, poke and occasionally laugh at, it was as if it was you yourself that couldn't speak the English language and that's why they didn't understand "Leave me alone motherfuckers!".

WHITE CITY... DARK DAYS

METHADONIA
Methadone (the heroin substitute) was around all the time as junkies became more rife within the squat culture.
Before I begin this section, I think a bit of alternative history is called for...you may find this interesting, you may think it's a load of shit...who cares?

DID YOU KNOW? (1)
That Hitler had to invent a heroin substitute as a large number of his crew were heavily into drugs and especially smack, so when the opium trails were cut off due to the invading of many of the bordering countries, something had to be done. So he put his scientists to work and they come up with Methadone.

DID YOU KNOW? (2)
Methadrine Amphetamine was also invented by the Nazis. The way it worked was, we had purple hearts (crappy little pills that the mods went mad for) made after the second world war for pilots and as an appetite represent. They were ok but not as good as 'bennies' (or Benzedrine) made famous in a hundred films about the American air-force bomber pilots. Then we come to Adolf and the boys, you know it's politically incorrect to compliment the Nazis but hey, they got their shit sorted as far as speed and smack were concerned. Pure meth, pissed all over our shitty purple farts, this is the reason why German troops could go for such a long time on shite rations while their

air-force could stay up longer than any of ours and complete more bombing missions on us (bastards, we should have scored a few kilos), apparently meth helped in the way Hitler delivered his speeches, but also fucked up his judgment in vital decisions, fuckin' paranoid speed freak. It sort of fits tho' coz if you look at Hitler on a rant and look at a speed freak on full throttle...not a lot of difference.

Well, getting back to 1979, in White City. I, in my infinite wisdom had scored a bottle of methadone, now I wasn't a heroin addict as such then but I couldn't find anything else and the girl who sold it to me said it was a good hit so I had to do wot she said...... (I'm the sort of cunt that would've bought magic fuckin' beans if I thought they were going to get me high). So off I went with my 200 mill. bottle of methadone linctus, this I found out later was enough to flatten three junkies, let alone a mere novice at the time, so I drank the lot and consequently lost three days of my life, nearly lost my life.

At that time when I was awake (or speeding so fast I could see myself coming back) I was auditioning for bands and giving guitar lessons to punks. Not that I was that good, but had got the hang of a couple of good licks and had mastered all the chord changes needed to be in a band at that time. Kevin from 'Conflict' used to go to all the Motorhead gigs and I was teaching him at the time. Anyway, while in 'methadonia' I apparently auditioned for some heavy metal band and got the job, I only found this out a few weeks later when they called my parents, for me to go for a rehearsal!

Getting back to the 'done I had drank so much water it looked as if I was nine months pregnant (funny? no. As it hurt like hell), smack and stuff can really be a bastard when it comes to having

131

a piss or shit (constipation etc.) so the more I drank the more it built up...I was at bursting point at one stage, crying in agony, so my girlfriend called an ambulance and off I went to Hammersmith Hospital were I lay on a bed and this lovely young nurse gave me a jar to hold while the Indian night doctor inserted a bloody long tube down the hole in me willy. As soon as it reached wherever it was supposed to reach all hell broke loose from my erupting, volcanic, uncontrollable, throbbing cock.

Piss was now gushing out everywhere. The young nurse was trying in desperation to try and control the situation by asking me to slow down as the jar she had given me filled up in less than a second and she didn't have another to hand. Not my problem, the piss had commeth and I couldn't stop it, even if I had wanted to. Boy, there was piss everywhere, all over me, the bed, my girlfriend and the nurse. We were standing in a small pond I had managed to create on the floor...a flood of golden shower everywhere, I actually started to feel quite turned on as my stomach finally went down and the pain went away. The Indian doctor was cool and sent for an ambulance to take us home.

Well, two days later and the whole scenario repeated itself again as I found I still couldn't piss and had drank yet again gallons of water in vain. So off we went again, this time driven by my Dad. This time though, the doctor on call was a young middle-class prick that seemed determined to make an example of me. He laid me in a bed and took the screen away so as the whole fuckin' ward could see my predicament (not a pun, well they could see my 'dic' too...). I wasn't best pleased as you can imagine and was objecting quite loudly to my treatment. He then went away and left me there for a good ten minutes in agony, then he returned with a small group of student doctors. I was fuming, while he inserted the tube....this time it hurt...and when I started to piss it hurt more, he then walked off.

I had done my piss real quick this time and was waiting for him to take the tube out of my dick, but he was nowhere to be seen and I was left completely unattended in the ward with no screen, raging. It was then that I begged my girlfriend to pull the tube out of my cock. She was quite hesitant but, god bless her, she had a go and managed to get about a foot of thin, rubber tube pulled from my burning dick. She then started freaking out that there was no end in sight (again, no pun intended), so I grabbed the tube and closed my eyes, counted to ten, took a deep breath and yanked it. A bit came out but it was so sore on the inside, anyway, I bit the bullet and gave one last pull and out it came.....phew....I was sweating and crying.

I got my girlfriend to help me out of the bed; I got dressed and was walking towards the ward exit door when the doctor appeared with the students in tow. He started beckoning me back to my bed, but I stood my ground and waited for him to get real close, then I grabbed him by the scruff of the neck and gave him one blinding head butt, knocking the cocky little twat to the floor. We then made our hasty getaway...mmm...'shuffle' away. My legs were so bandy; I was walking like John bloody Wayne-meets-Ozzy Osborne with a hernia. We made it to my Dad's car, he knew nothing of what had happened as he was embarrassed enough with me having to go to the hospital in the first place, and anyway we got in his car and made our getaway....

I lived on the White City estate in Shepherds Bush, West London for a short while with a girlfriend. I was sleeping on the floor previously at a friend Nora's house. NORA was originally from Scotland, a mass of hair, looked tougher than she was and has a son named Zak... (Hi Zak), she was and still is a good friend. At the time Nora was hanging around with a bike club who originated from South London (well, all over really) enter ...SONS OF SATAN. I tip me hat and say hi to Freaky, Haystacks, Kirk, Lee, Joker Pete, a host of others...you know who you are.....

As stated in another piece, I joined them later on, but at the time they were bikers and I was...I don't know wot I was... I'd drifted off the 70's rock-come hippie look and was looking more biker-ish due to the leather jacket and punk thing. Although they were into bikes and I was into guitars there was a common ground that we had......drugs. I've been reminiscing with Freaky while writing this and he's been a wealth of information (much of which I can't put in), but here's a story or two that shouldn't get us into trouble....

ONE HOT, MEMORABLE SUMMER'S DAY...after the pub had closed for the afternoon (yes, the pubs closed for the after-noon in those days), most of the after-party were on foot, a handful of the 'Sons' were on bikes. 'Rat' bikes most of 'em as I recall, twelve inch 'over' forks, ape hangers, straight-through pipes and matt black in colour, with their red and black 'patches' catching the eye of the Saturday afternoon throng, walking not riding, through the crowd but keeping the throttle open just enough so as you knew they were there...as for the rest of 'em, they were on foot with myself and others. Well some bright spark had a good idea and borrowed a wheelbarrow from a neighbouring back garden and was walking down the Porto-bello Road with it. This was too good a situation not to exploit to the full, so we decided to liberate every leather jacket, gun belt and studded wristband that came to pass. The wheelbarrow was full of booty and I can't for the life of me (or Freaky either) remember wot happened to any of it.

There's so many more stories that they really needs their own book...hey, sounds like a plan!
Anyway back to White City, this was quite a shitty time for me as I had my Rickenbacker bass stolen, bastards... I went after the slime that nicked it with two 'prospects' on loan. We kicked in a few doors and found one bloke in the middle of burgling some-one else's flat that we had just kicked the door down to. He was standing on the toilet and we only found him as I went for a piss and there he was , he thought we were the police and when I walked in he said "It's a fair cop" ha, just like the pictures..Dick head, anyway we helped him nick the TV and stuff and move it to his flat three doors down.

Oh well, I loved that guitar and never did get it back. White City was getting worse all the time, I was doin' too many bar-biturates and acid, fighting skinheads, they used to rule the es-tates then before the onslaught of black youth (not my bag). I never had any trouble in those days with blacks anywhere... just a thought... I do however remember making a make-shift cross one night, I had gathered a stack of logs and such, laid them down and preceded to nail them together into a crucifix, seven foot by five let's say, in the front room. I then went to Nora's after a violent argument with the girlfriend; I had man-aged to drag the poor cow across the estate (with no resistance from the public) by her hair, and then into the flat where I was going to nail her up. Apparently I was so exhausted that I fell fast asleep, waking in the morning wondering wot the fuck was a seven foot crucifix doin' in the front room? Phew...soon after, we moved and I HAD had to slow down...you think so too? Yeah right.

ACKLAM HALL...." WHITE RIOT"

SPIKED WHITE LIGHTNING, SKINS, PUNKS, BIKERS A FIGHTING...BABYLONS A BURNING BABY OOPS!!!

U.K. SUBS, CHELSEA and a host of others were headlining an all-dayer punk fest, do, thing, at the Acklam Hall in Westbourne Park, under the flyover, so it was inevitable that everybody went after the Heinekey's and Princess Alexandria 'afternoon experience' had come to yet another eventful drug and alcohol-induced day and as the pubs closed at three o' clock, this stone's throw away, jaunt down the Portobello Road which incidentally was exactly the direction in which we were going to go in anyway as the 'Green' was next to it and this was our regular stop-off point for a couple of hours to mooch about and kill some time, wear off the afternoon's drink or just top up and recharge for the weekend's onslaught on humanity, seemed like a good idea.

Back at the pub earlier, I must say things had gotten a bit lively and a bit of harmless spiking of white lightning with tuinol had come to pass. This was a favourite of mine as I could sip away all through the afternoon getting slowly bombed. On this particular afternoon certain people kept hassling me for a mouthful of my nasty concoction and feeble, yet potent attempt at a cocktail. I was however in a mischievous mood and found it quite a humorous twist in not informing anyone of the contents of the bottle, thus letting nature, strange as it can be, take its unpredictable toll on the drinkers.

I soon found myself tired of the endless hogging of the bottle of booze that I was trying in a vain attempt to keep to myself and liberated it amongst the group of associates while inventing another for myself, thus leaving me to stand back and watch the fireworks. Didn't have to wait too long either, as a couple of bikers that I shall keep nameless were now trying in earnest to straddle their motorcycles, hilariously drifting side to side as though being blown in the wind like a field of leather-bearded marsh grass....Other less experienced of the crowd found a new assertive side and were becoming a bit bolshy, I on the other hand wandered off down the market road with me bird and a couple of mates, laughing at the confusion we had left behind.

ON arriving at the Acklam Hall we went in and found a plot to stand in and secure it as our own, opened another bottle, dropped a few more 'traffic lights' in to give it that familiar kick and started to enjoy the afternoon's music. Everything was going kind of ok, until I went to the bog for a piss and was confronted by three very tall, very foreign looking skinhead-come-punks that had no idea wot the fuck they were doin'. They started jostling me about, asking me why I was kind of made up like a punk but had biker undertones to my dress sense, this did not seem to compute to the gormless giants...good, it wasn't supposed to...it was punk, proper punk, no 'uniform', remember?

Shitheads that they were, I could see no reason why I should explain my image to these wankers, big and ugly as they were. So we had words and one of them swung a punch that luckily missed my head by inches, then I gave him what I can only explain as the bestist head butt I've ever had the pleasure in sharing with another receiving individual.....THWACK! And he went flying. His feet left the ground and no word of a lie, he glided straight through the doors of the shit-hole opposite and landed smack-bang on his foreign, punk, skin, bastard, pick on me ya twat, fat arse onto the toilet seat...fookin cool, great fun. I was so impressed and full of 'that taught him' bravado that I turned to his mates, asking if they'd like the same (dick head that I was) but as luck would have it, they bloody well didn't and pissed off outside leaving their mate unconscious on the bog hole.

I was now feeling quite chuffed with myself and couldn't wait to tell. On my arrival back to our designated spot, things had got a bit serious and a few scuffles were going off here and there. A few of the 'Sons of Satan' had arrived and were accompanied by other bikers and stragglers from the pub. Now, bikers didn't get on too well at the best of times with the punks and skins, but usually everyone knew their place and scape goats would be found to vent drunken abuse at...MODS mainly, if one could be found. Well not that day, the afternoon was taking on a rowdy twist as everyone seemed to have a point to prove, an itch to scratch or a stupid look on their face and to make matters worse the idiots in the toilet were standing only a few feet away and were starting to give me the evil eye again. Well, I personally wasn't going to let my afternoon go by quietly avoiding a punch up nor was I going home early to escape a free-for-all bundle, instead I decided to mingle and pass the bottle of good hope around, making the most I could of the afternoon.

IF I recollect correctly and I am sure that it was about this time, I saw 'Sack' or was it 'Bullshit' from the 'Sons of Satan' on stage, jumping up and down then being harassed by punks, thus forcing him to start kicking the shit out of this bloke on stage. I shouted over to the others to look at the stage and they retorted by steaming down the front, punching and kicking all in their way, their frenzied actions seemed to ignite the already edgy touch-paper tinged atmosphere, so as they kicked off so did the whole place. It seemed as though this was the moment everybody was subconsciously waiting for because the whole place went fuckin' ballistic. The Heinekey's ruling mob that usually got our own way were having it good and proper, maybe it was the vast amount of downers going 'round that day, something I felt I helped fuel in harmless fun, but this was getting quite out of hand and it wasn't just the usual suspects either, everybody wanted in.

I was fighting anybody that came close to me, there didn't seem to be any focal points, the biker thing was getting a little lost now that every other fucker was kicking off. I must say I got a bit concerned for mine and my girlfriend's safety around this point and as I had no allegiance to anyone in particular I grabbed her hand, tried to keep a low profile and got the fuck out of there. We made our exit and hastily went about our speedy retreat to the station calling it a day. The week after, apparently, all went off again, this time though everybody came 'tooled up' with weapons and back-up and a few people got seriously hurt. I heard that when everyone was inside, a convoy of transit vans turned up waiting for people to come out, then pelting them with slabs of concrete, very nasty.

AT A LOSS IN KINGS
(stinking shit hole) CROSS

What a shit hole that was. I had missed most of the good stuff a year or so before, what with the fighting with casuals and teds (ted's wot were they doin'), there used to be some historical fights there with the squatters manning the roof with makeshift Molotov cocktails, bricks, roofing slate and other such fighting materials.. apparently it used to go off big time, lots of rising faces lived there too and of course it had it's own brand of drug culture, bikers and punks, a few hippies trying in vain to legalise everything in sight... and make small non-descript 'utopias' out of council estates.

I left Ealing and Acton only to end up in Kings Cross next to that nightmare estate, by now just full of prostitutes, drug dealers and a few left over hippies and such. The road I lived on was called ...wait for it....Acton Street. Wot's the fuckin' chances of that?? Out of one frying pan straight into another, although Acton seemed more appealing looking back on it. We only moved there as nobody else would give us a roof over our heads, we tried Centre Point but they were only interested in fuckin' northerners. As we lived in London, apparently we could go home and stop misbehaving, grow out of our phase we were going through and live at home, get a job and live happily ever after. Why it was different for northerners I don't know, it seemed to me like they should have been looking after their own Londoners and fucking them northern twats back home...(Sorry if ya come from up north, but you wouldn't like it, now would ya?).

So, getting back to the story, we managed to find a place to live after I saved a hippie from a beating one night outside his squat. I saw he was getting mullered by some straight-looking casual arse so naturally I jumped in and gave the mug a few choice digs and he ran off. The hippie was very grateful and asked us in. He said his "thankyou's" and we told him of our plight, that of being homeless. He told us that the fight was over the fact that they had both opened up the squat, but the other bloke wanted it all to himself. We'll see exactly what the fight was over in a minute or too....Well, as we had liberated him of the nuisance, we asked if we could have his room and he agreed that we would make a better house guest than his last choice, so I grabbed a few things from Ealing and moved in.

Unknown to us, living next door was a really good friend of ours from Henekies....we will call her Val. Val was living with one of the outlaw bikers who we knew as well, he was cool as he let me deal in the pub without buying from or paying tax to the 'club'. I think they just turned a blind eye, probably wasn't making enough to draw attention to myself anyway. Val, like us, was a good friend of Steve Took so when the 'old man' was out we would have little 'stoner' parties behind his back.

One day the club were out on a run, or so we thought, and the five of us got pretty ripped. She lived in a basement flat with a glass door. Well I was sitting on the sofa having a 'fix' when the doorway went really dark, then there was a loud knocking...I could hear the thumping of motorbikes and it was quite obvious they'd come home fuckin' early! We all jumped up and tried hiding all the paraphernalia under the chairs, in the cushions and under the carpet. The door opened and in they walked, pissed off at something or someone....who knows? Or cares any way? I had two geezers, sitting one each side of me asking me if I was okay, as I looked a bit peaky.....mmmmm. One of them was sitting with his foot on my syringe that I had masterly hid under the carpet.

Unfortunately we did still have 'Took' with us then, Mr 'Nondiscretion' himself...even though the bikers and Steve went back years, he could still manage to get them right were it hurts (verbally that is) so as Steve was being quizzed on what drugs he was on, I was trying to make a hasty retreat towards the door saying my goodbyes and edging backwards, trying not to fall over anyone's feet. Then Steve came over all stroppy...why should he lie about what drugs he was on? A valid argument apart from we were in someone else's house and we all knew the bikers' 'zero tolerance' policy towards smack, but Steve kept shouting, they started shouting back, the dog started barking, Val started crying and I started moving closer to the door. Then Steve in his infinite wisdom, decided to call them all a bunch of wankers and to fuck off out of it, a bit hard as it was their house....so Steve got a smack in the mouth and a couple of digs. This was quite common for him though, especially when stoned.

BACK next door, everything seemed to be okay for a short while. We had started painting the place up, fixing a few things...and the place was looking quite homely. A friend of the hippie robbed a chemist one night and didn't have a clue what he had and asked our advice on the bounty. Obviously I agreed to help and spent no time in telling him that, advising him that the bottles of pharmaceutical morphine and coke were out of date and not worth a jot... I also kept the mandies, fillon, tuinol, deckspansuals and other assorted chemicals out of harm's way and said that I would dispose of all the rubbish drugs. All he seemed interested in was the valium, mogadon and bloody tombstones, so we divided up the booty and gave him a few quid for our worthless 'out of date' class fuckin' aaaa's and embarked on a week of total annihilation...

THE squat came to a sticky and violent end when the hippie became friends again with the bloke we met at the start of this story, fighting with him in the road. They had made up and he was coming round with these Scottish guys...turned out they were part of a small firm of dealers and pimps that had just moved down to London and were taking over the squats for their own uses. Well they had a couple of foreign-speaking girls with them and they wanted to move in to our home. I objected straight away, smelling a rat, but the hippie liked the idea of having a couple of birds 'on tap' as it looked to him. I wasn't a happy bunny as the squat had a good chance of becoming legal under new council tenancy rules, they were working with the hippies to give squatters rent books and if you paid your rent on time and didn't cause trouble, you could get a tenancy agreement.

Well it all came to a head one morning when these stinking birds made the place a mess, the hippie wouldn't throw them out and I lost the plot. I acquired a broom handle then made my way into their rooms and made them an offer to move out. Unwanted tenants gone, I made good the day and cleaned up, giving the house a good once over. That night around four in the morning, I awoke to four men standing in my bedroom wearing balaclavas. One had a large bag and placed it on the floor while another opened the bag and took out a rather large hammer, he then gave me a close look at it from the top of my head ....bang, bang ,bang. Boy did that hurt! There was blood everywhere, up the walls, over me, over my girlfriend. They didn't speak much...only to say if that I was still there in the morning they'd kill me. I took the hint and fucked off, fucked off back to sunny Ealing.

IF YA CAN'T TAKE A JOKE... YOU SHOULDN'T HAVE JOINED...

I'd like to explain a bit of a musical 'faux pas' here....well...erm...I actually ended up playing for Screwdriver (not the best idea I've had). Ya see, a couple of my mates at the time were skinheads; this is a bit later on, around 1982... And as I've never really been a racist, I do get peeved when racism goes all one way. I have had a number of friends, girlfriends and two grandchildren of mixed race; in fact my Mum being Italian was treated far worse than any whingeing West Indian, so let's get that straight. POLITICS AINT MY BAG..... but I don't bow down for no man and I'll gladly treat everyone I meet with the same contempt as they individually deserve...so there....ner, ner, nee, ner....back to the story.

Well it all happened as a bit of an accident that turned into a joke that turned into a dare that turned into a mini nightmare that nearly got me shot. Two members of Screwdriver had got into bikes and had built two of the best bad-ass Triumph chops I'd ever seen and as luck would have it there was this gig coming up and a guitarist and bass player were needed. I was at the bass player's house one night when he got a call asking if he would help out, and did he know a guitarist? Well he said "yes" and I said I'd do the guitar playing; it was a joke, a joke that everyone laughed at until I was getting teased as to wot would happen if I dared turn up and actually do the gig... Well this got a bit silly and I got all out of my pram about the whole situation and said 'Bollocks, I'll do it...I want to do it now just to prove a point' (wot point I don't know) but found everybody agreeing and so I was in...CRAP.

So a couple of days later I found myself rehearsing a set with Ian Stewart and Co, getting ready for the annual 'Rock against Communism' gig that took part on a farm in the middle of England somewhere... Well we arrived in the middle of the night and were led to a barn to sleep the night, in the morning I awoke to a barn full of skinheads! (A bit like the scene in Quadrophenia when the mod wakes up with all the bikers). We all got up and went off to the village for a spot of breakfast, JEEZUS! It was amazing; the whole village was full of skin-heads....everywhere you looked there were boots and braces and I was the only fucker there with long hair and leathers. It was now that it started to dawn on me just wot I had let myself in for and I was made to feel that I knew it. Wot they didn't know was that the bloke with the long Barnet was in fact one of the geezers that many had travelled from all over Europe to see! (Oh dear).

It all went well though and I found myself being assigned roadie to the day's events and made a good job of it too. When it came time for Screwdriver to come on stage we were all worse for wear as I'd been drinking and speeding all day...the stage set was impressive too, all swastikas and banners with an audience of around a thousand or so skinheads chanting "Skrewdriv-ah! Skrewdriv-ah! Sieg Heil!" and stuff, then the two with the bikes rode onto stage and it looked fuckin' great (shame nobody else thought so), then Ian came on followed by me, "boooooooo!!!!". We got stuck in to the set and did a few numbers then it got a bit stupid as I noticed some little mook waving a gun about, I was shouting at the bouncer at the side of the stage "Look, he's got a gun!", the bouncer jumped into the crowd, beat seven shades of shit out of the dweeb and promptly got back on stage and asked me if I was ok and pulled out a shotgun and aimed it at the audience. He was then joined at the opposite end of the stage by his mate brandishing yet another gun and doing the same thing there. We played on for a couple of numbers and it all started falling to bits, Ian was now very drunk and I was very scared and had forgotten all their songs. Then I had a brainwave and said we should play something we all know, and yes I did.... I didn't even think of the repercussions of the song but I tore straight into JOHNNY B GOODE...by...the very black CHUCK BERRY...I did all the solos and everything. When I had finished we all got off stage real quick and went off to the pub or something...we had to keep our heads down for a while....

RED, GOLD AND GREEN WITH A HINT OF RED AND BLACK...

On the topic of race and circumstances at the time, I must add that in all them early years I never had any trouble with any of the black community, they did their thing and we did ours. They didn't 'get' our music and personally I couldn't stand and still can't handle all that 'dum dee dum' fucking shite, but all the old Rasta's were cool and we all knew where we stood. There was never a cross word about swastikas and stuff, they had their fair share of it too...black power (clenched fists and all that...cool) looking out for ya own. I used to go to the Acklam Hall a lot and sometimes would drop into the reggae night as it was open all night and you'd get proper toasted on super-Rasta joints. They used to laugh at how quick we'd get stoned and go all silly. I remember one night getting so fucked up I ended up on bloody stage with Aswad...I think they always played with Steel Pulse and Misty. Well it started backstage and I ended up onstage dancing (I never dance, never never) the only thing that should have made it worse was the fact that I was wearing my 'Pistols Anarchy shirt, the one with the the upside- down Jesus and swastika on it and yet no one batted an eyelid! I didn't feel racist and they certainly didn't feel threatened ....where did it all go wrong? A government conspiracy me thinks, divide and conquer. There was no racist shit then, it came later instigated by men in suits......

GET YA TATT'S OUT MOTHERFUCKER...

IT was while living in KING'S FUKKIN' CROSS that I first got bit by the big bad tattoo 'bug'.

'Sailor', an old boy who ran a tattoo emporium opposite the King's Cross station was the first man to DO INK to me. Sailor actually looked like a sailor, short, gnarly-faced old bastard with a sailor's cap.

Well I nervously ventured into the tattoo shop, with my girl-friend holding tight to my hand as I was not feeling my bravest and the thought of hot, searing needles puncturing my flesh was a little off-putting and I'm sure if she hadn't been there I would have made my excuses and bolted for the door. As I recall, it was a hot summer's day and I had the words fixed firmly in my mind of what I wanted, so walking through the door I said what I'd like and Sailor asked me to take a seat....the immortal words that would inevitably lead to a lifetime of unnecessary pain and torture, not to mention a healthy dent in the old wallet, this combined with the most repetitive sayings ever....

1) Does it hurt?
2) Can you remove them?
3) You think you're hard just 'cause you've got tattoos.
4) DO YOU WANT A FIGHT?
5) Little old ladies saying "Oh that looks nice, dear".
6) You'll regret them when you're older.
7) Can you remove them?

Yes, the last one has been repeated just for your benefit, so as you the reader can have a little insight into the moronic babblings of lesser-tattooed people.

A FEW COMEBACK REMARKS!

1) These enhance my already stunningly good looks.
While you have to bare the scars of your inbred cloven hoofed fathers. (Mine)
2) I can get these removed.
While you, arshole will always look like that. (Not mine)
3) My tattoos show the world, my independence.
Your skin shows how boring you are. (mine)
4) I don't have lots of tattoos.
I'm multi-racial. (mine)
5) You laugh at me because I'm different.
I laugh at you because you're all the same. (not mine)
6) Strip a man of his clothes and he'll stand naked as the next man.
Strip me of my clothes and my skin will always show my true colours. (mine)
7) Fuck off
8) ok. swaaak
Now!
Fuck off... (Mine)

Well, the words chosen to be embossed into my flesh for life were 'FUCK THE SYSTEM'. Truly righteous words of momental truths and insighted wisdom. Actually, neither I nor my girlfriend (or Sailor) had a clue how to spell 'system' while knowing that one of the options offered for spelling of said word, would leave me forever telling the toilet wot I thought of it, so we ventured out into the street and had a quick survey on the spelling of said word. This was not to be the last time members of the public have had their literacy skills quizzed, as it seems it's quite a common occurrence with a lot of tattooists (be warned).

SO, armed with my new bad-ass 'ink' I had now to brave the parents...Dad, typical of Dads of their generation "You're marked for life now boy!". Oh, here's a good one "You'll never get a proper job!" (Whoo Hoo!!). "Only sailors and convicts have tattoos!". The list goes on and on, not like nowadays where it seems like every mook has a fuckin' tattoo, thus making a mockery of the whole fuckin' thing in my book anyway, as it used to be 'straights' that would piss you off with their repetitiveness, same ol' sayings...now it seems just as annoying as every wanker and his mate thinks they have some kindred bond with you just 'cos they've got a picture of a butterfly delicately placed on their arse.

Girls...don't get me started with them; my daughter has a pierced tongue, tattoos, and the lot. Wot's the world coming to? (Old man moaning again)
My Mum, on the other hand (as stated at the beginning of the book) had no probs with them at all as her Mum had a fuck-off, big Virgin Mary tattooed on her forearm. All the girls had one with the name of their village underneath, mental eh? This was I must say, in Italy and she's long gone now, but still it puts things into perspective a bit and should shut me up about girls having tattoos and stuff, but, bollocks! It's a geezer thing; keep to the make-up and flower-arranging, girls.... (*That's* put the final nail in my coffin).

MY second venture into getting 'inked' was at one of the Stonehenge do's, where some new-age hippie thing was tattooing anyone that would let him for a couple of joints, that was the man for me!!!

Well he butchered me good. So on my return to Ealing, I sought out the legendary GEORGE BONE in Hanwell, West London, at the time just down the road from me house. George is proper old school, at the time he wasn't, he was just the best in my book.....anyhow, I would start off with a couple of choice pictures and ended up with both arms fully 'sleeved' within a year or so. Boy, did I get the bug good and proper, plus George became quite a good friend and would do 'cheapies' if the shop was dead. We also shared a liking for all things skeletal and we exchanged human skulls, I also got for him the 'ritual' skulls he has in the shop if you ever venture in there (say 'Hi' to him from me too). He went on to tattoo my back, chest and stomach. I remember one day I was to get my chest tattooed and George is well known for having no mercy and digging in. Well today was no exception, as I lay on the bench, George began the onslaught of ink and pain into my chest and I had a thing for jiggling about, so to stop this he had his wife sit at the end of the bench and hold my legs down while George leaned with all his weight on my chest and tattooed away. I recall the pain getting to be quite severe and I made the stupid move of saying to George "IT'S FUCKIN' HURTING, MAN, I THINK I'M GOING!". Well George looked at me and said with an evil grin of self satisfaction "STEVE, YOU JUST GO"... bastard.

MY next adventure in 'Oy, that fuckin' hurts!' world was with my ex-drummer and good friend, Brad Sims of SIM'S TATTOOS in Croydon. Brad was in the 'George Bone Appreciation Society' and styled his work back then on the 'old master'. He's now established his own style and has done and is doin' very well.

I became (with others) one of his early 'crash test dummies' and later on he was responsible (although his apprentice actually did them) for the tattoos on my face. Brad was always apprehensive that I would somehow wake one morning and curse him for letting him tattoo my face, but although the stigma is always there, I love the tribal tatts on me boat and that desk job in the bank is well and truly not gonna be mine now, so wot the fuck?

Although Brad wouldn't tattoo my face, he did however agree to tattoo my penis. The penis tattoo was truly 'great fun' (at my expense...), but fun it was. Brad had never tattooed a dick before and said he would do it just so he could say that he had done it, jeezus! Well, before he put tattoo gun to todger skin, I sneaked off to PATRICKS. Now Patrick had a piercing clinic a few doors down and I was quite a good friend of his and his old lady from the 'fetish' scene, so I asked Patrick to numb my penis as he had a nurse's credentials and could administer a local anaesthetic. Patrick was more than happy to oblige and gave my penis five or six injections, I think, I wasn't counting funnily enough. I then waited for the anaesthetic to kick in and went back to Brad's shop where he was waiting with 'Biker Lee' (or 'Chewy').

It must have taken thirty minutes to an hour before he could begin as my dick was looking real stupid, as the trouble with local anaesthetic is that its liquid and having my todger stabbed frightened the little sod back into his shell, then adding the insult of liquid to the little Nazi helmet, he got all fat in the middle and looked like the fuckin' Michelin Man... BRAD now had the unflattering job of holding my cock in his hand and stretching it out, then rubbing grease into it. This proved too much and we fell about laughing like three giggling schoolgirls. After we had gathered our senses he once again rubbed grease onto my dick and I remember asking Brad if this meant that we were now gay? I don't think he was amused, as he gave my dick a sharp jab and asked me if I could feel anything yet.

I stopped getting tattooed for a few years, but my kids have been having some nice work done and having taken my Son somewhere locally, I've struck up a friendship with the occupants and I'm now having both legs completely covered (not one of my best moves) watch out for the kneecaps! Oooch!!! SPIDER... (PAUL) is responsible and doin' a great job at 'WORLD OF TATTOOS' in Ruislip Manor....

A POEM AND LYRICS TO SONG... [Not released, but I thought you might like it]

CALAFORNIA'S BURNING.

Surgeon's knife, cold, cold steel.
Cut's the flesh, Watch it peel.
Precision cut's, the crack of bone.
A thousand dollars, just pick up the phone.

Verse 2
Tighten the skin, her age it fades.
Suck out the fat.
Now sharpen the blade.
A thousand cut's, a chiselled jaw.
Watch the years, scrape off the floor.

Middle
In the waiting room, her melting flesh it screams.
Waiting for a fix, botox baby – you're melting flesh it screams.

CHORUS.
California, don't ya wanna
Tear it down.
Burn you're, plastic crown...

Verse 3

Tasteless tattoos, on a tightened skin.
Cut out the bone, start again.

A new face for old, cheating age is a sin.
California dreaming, a cancerous din.

Hollywood harpies, a tinsel town tart.
Selling you're soul, cutting out you're heart.
Pruning the skin, tightening the flesh.
Bake in the sun, California you're done.

TALES OF DASTARDLY DEEDS, STRANGE GOING'S ON AND A HEALTHY APPETITE FOR ALL THINGS TABOO.

A few short stories....

THE WITCH, THE BITCH AND THE EX...

Treacherous goings on were underfoot in the Princess Alexandria drinking house in 1980. I was in a relationship with one of the 'now in-crowd' at the 'Alex' called THE WITCH. I was still good friends with an ex, THE EX who was now good friends with my latest fling. This, as I'm sure you know, can be a disastrous affair, but on the whole everything was ok. Then came this girl, well not really a girl, as she must have been at least thirty, old when you're twenty, so we'll call her THE BITCH. Now I was quite happy in my new relationship and things were going steady for once, but I still had an eye for the ladies, so as I was now quite a fixture in the scene, this opened up a lot more doors with the local opposite sex...typical really. Why is it when you're single ya can't get a look in and then as soon as yer hitched they're falling over themselves to show you their knickers, mind you I wasn't complaining and the thirty year old looked as if she could go a few rounds.

Well, one day 'The Bitch' organised a deal and said she could get a load of tuinol cheap, well naturally we all wanted in. She said that it was a bit dodgy where she had to go for them and maybe

I should go as back-up in case of trouble. I said "ok", but my girlfriend wasn't so sure, as she knew this bird was after my dick, but after a long, drawn out talk about how nothing would happen and I only wanted the stuff, no way was I or would I get involved in any way. Besides, I didn't even fancy her (well I didn't) but I still wanted to stick one up her. Let's face it, at that age I wanted to dip me bread in everybody's plate and have a taste of the gravy, just in case they were having something I hadn't tried yet. SO off we set to where the goodies were, we did all the usual stuff, hung around for ages waiting for the man, spent a small fortune on 'cabs to places I had no idea of, then finally we scored, yippie, thank fuck for that, now the only thing on our minds was having a hit.

BITCH plan now in full-throttle mode, as she said her place wasn't too far we could go back there, have a hit and then get back to the others and my girlfriend who by this time was most probably sharpening the cutlery...We eventually arrived back at her place, a squat somewhere in South London, typical of the times, still very hippie with the mattress on the floor, low-hanging tie-died sheets draped from the ceiling, with a hint of punk, e.g. studded belts, chains, the customary pet for dangerous girls, a rat in a cage that had no door and some unusual whips and fetish gear straddled around the living room floor...mmm...I liked the look of them. I thought this bird was a dirty cow and now having been and seen where and how she lived, it turns out I was right. I sat down on the mattress and she joined me with a tourniquet, a spoon and a brand new box full of syringes, boy was she ever well stocked up. We did the deed of mixing up the potion; she then gave me my hit...bloody hell, all I remember is falling back onto the bed.
Flop!

When I awoke I was completely naked and she had somehow managed to get my cock as stiff as a sailor's hornpipe while she was now on top of myself, straddled, with both legs firmly dug into my thighs and was going for it hammer and tongs. JEEZUS was she ever the live one (cripes! I hadn't seen thighs that mighty since Shelly Winters swam underneath the hull of the Poseidon)?

The more I tried to join in, the more I was pushed back down and shagged like a terrier stuck to a small boy's leg! Damn, I was all for being seduced but this Bitch wanted to rape me. The tuinol were still fresh in my blood, while my head was spinning...I couldn't move...did I want to? Is this what it's like to get raped? I was thinking as I never gave any consent, ok with a little prompting maybe we could have had sneaky shag but this Bitch planned the whole thing.

After a while I shot me bolt (180)! And she then fell on top of me and we cuddled for a while. I was still not too sure how to react to the way she manipulated me, I must admit this was a strange to do, so I kept schtum and decided to go with the flow, but if she started anything I didn't like maybe I should gather up the drugs, give her a smack in the chops and fuck off, but she then got up, rolled a joint, had a few puffs then handed it over to me. I lay there smoking the joint while she then went off to the toilet, I thought? But came back a few minutes later with a jar of grease and a vibrator as thick as my arm and she was now dressed in some black, lacy affair and made me do some proper lewd, disgusting and totally outrageous things to her. Dirty cow! That was my first delve into the fetish side of things and I must say, even though she scared the life out of me to start with, I quite liked it (well actually, just thinking of it again has got me old todger stiffening up. Too much information I hear you think... ah well reader, if you've got this far ya must like it?).

And so.
Being used as a human sex toy was bloody good fun.

IF that had been the end of it, all well and good, nobody had to
know a thing. But this nutter had to have a fuckin' weirder side
to her ('don't they all?'). She said and I'm gonna look a fool for
believing her, writing about it too, but she gave her word that
she just fancied the boots off me and now that she had had her
wicked slutty way with me it was all over and no more would be
said (I believed her too). It was about a week later when we all
met up with her down the Alex, everything was ok to start with,
then she started to get drunk, then loud, then abusive, threatening people, all the usual bollocks...I tried to calm her down, then
she let rip and told the whole world what we had got up to.
THE BITCH!! And you know when you're trying to tell your
side of events of how she seduced me by getting me so out of it
I passed out on the bed and then she took advantage of me, you
can sort of hear yourself talking and it just sounds like the
biggest pile of human verbal crap ever, so I shut up and got a real
ear-bashing. The Bitch eventually got a bashing too, not from
me or my girlfriend but from some other fucker she managed to
piss off...

ANOTHER GIRLY FRIEND AT THE TIME WAS
ROSIE...we had quite a long history one way or another, I was
a complete wanker to her actually (sorry) only in the way that
she fancied me rotten (head explodes with shiiiite and ego) or
'wherever egos I go'... ha-ha Dee, ha-ha.
I fancied her too but I was and still am a slut, although I keep it
in me trousers nowadays as I've got me a good women, phew!!!
Well me and Rosie loved our tuinol, nembies and all things
barbiturate and would and could fall asleep with the best of
them, ha.

I remember one incident me and Rosie were on a mission to get on the metropolitan line at Old Street station and all we had to do was go one or two stops, (can't for the life of me think where we were going or for that matter what to get) but I digress, we boarded the train sat down and promptly opened our eyes at the end of the line, fuckin' miles away from our destination. So we got the train back and as if by magic did the same thing. So we got off the train crossed the platform waited patiently for the train to come, got on, and done the whole thing again ? ? ? This went on all stinking day up and down the metropolitan line asleep…

Rosie was a good girl and would put up with me starting fights with anybody that looked at us funny or just looked at us or even just looked like they were gonna look at us. BASTARDS, people were always asking for it, and they got it, sometimes though I got it and boy did I have my fare share of kickings from all sorts of people most of which you wouldn't believe would dare be the sort to have a go, but hey they're out there you just don't know until you rattle that cage .

But on the hole (it's hairy) idiot!…we had a good time but I was forever leaving her for someone else, then I'd phone her up a couple of days later and she would always come down, especially if I had some downers to persuade her, little minx. We had some great sex and fun times and she could always be trusted to hold my knife and drugs down her pants just in case of searches that were constant as the old bill never left you alone. You could expect to be searched at least three times a day and they would make you take ya trousers down in door ways and stuff and girls, they had their own grief from women cunt-stables as they would taunt them while crushing their make up into the ground. They would then be seen to be teasing them about the state they apparently looked and what does your Mother think of you dressing like that! Fuckin cheek! At least they looked cool unlike them, but then again I've always liked a woman in uniform, oooooohh handcuffs and a truncheon, yes..! We all know where we would like to put the old police truncheon in the words of that old cunt in dad's army (THEY DON'T LIKE IT UP EM, MR MANNERING). I bet they did though! And I'd 'ave liked to have been the bloke to slip it up there!

Fuck I'm getting turned on now, shit sorry Rosie I can't even reminisce without going behind ya back and thinking dirty thoughts about shoving a policeman's truncheon in and out of a women cunt-stables soft wet squeaky clean and moist puuuuus-say..

I BET YOU ARE AS WELL NOW....... Fuck I fancy a bloody wank. Erm, I think I'll leave it here for tonight, so I'll catch up with you lot tomorrow, I'm...er...going to...ere...m bed!!! Nighty night......

GOOD MORNING? YES ME AGAIN!

With another story of filth and debauchery... lovely jubberly.

TWO HANDS UP SISTER SARA, or SAY? SAUSAGES!!!

MMMMMM.... Well I'm not to sure where to begin with this short story of sexual speed induced frustration, come dirty rubber glove drug influenced mutterings, but on the whole a very naughty and yet such fun happening. So let me begin with a name change, Sara, that'll do.

I was going out with this lovely and sexually, very liberated and oh yes, bad, bad girl for a while and on this particular night we had been out on the town as she was dressed to kill in a stunning pair of fishnet stockings, low-cut see-through top with, I must say an ample pair of tits, with really nice nipples like two little gnomes dicks, you know the sort that stick right out at ya! then point in ya face when they're set free? And with the longest of legs topped off with a lovely shaved puss. Cooor!

We had been out drinking and she liked to flirt and show off her naughty bits at any given time or be it, moment. Giving a bloke a flash was her bestist thing, so she would mostly be out, without knickers on, so she could give any unsuspecting bystander a quick flash or a good view. So obviously I didn't take her to, too many places where my mates would be 'oggling' her all night, as she could get me into all sorts of shit with other girls or me getting into a fight as I'm prone to getting bloody jealous when pissed.

So on this particular night we had been out partying and were very drunk, and speeding and quite cocked up which as you know makes the girls very itchy in the old fanjeeta garden, plus they do tend to get right horny and up for it! Little minxes.

Nearing the end of the night we caught a cab home and it all started with me being drunk and resting my weary head on the cab window with my eyes closed. After a while I felt the cab was swerving a bit so I opened my eyes a quarter inch or so to see what the commotion was, well, the dirty little mare was giving the cabbie a flash of her pussie by sitting in the middle of the cab with her legs open and so as she had no knickers on he could see right up there (I presume). She on the other hand was pretending to be asleep so as not to make a big deal of it but I noticed, as the cab was all over the road as he was trying to get a good look while trying to keep the car in lane. This was all very exciting and I was by now getting quite horny at the thought of this Pakistani cab driver staring at my bird's fanny. Turned on but sort of wanting to smack him one as well (you know wot I mean! And if you're a Pakistani you'd be thinking the same if the tables were turned, so don't go getting all fuckin' politically correct on me).

On getting home we paid the driver and saw him off (to have a wank, most probably) and went inside where we skinned up a couple of joints, had a couple of lines and went to bed to carry on the night's debauchery. Sara was still in her stockings and I thought it a good idea to cut them off using my bayonet that I just had by chance in my jacket pocket. She used to like stuff like that and so we started to make out on the bed and things got decidedly dirty as she was really going for it. Well this isn't a dirty book and I can't write filthy stories as they should be wrote, so basically SARA was getting really fuckin' turned on and I had managed to get my hand and most of my fuckin' wrist up her fanny and she was loving every moment of it, moaning and groaning. Sara was in another world and I was liking this very much, I was doing this hand puppet thing for wot seemed like hours and she wasn't giving in, in fact she wanted more so I started to wriggle my other hand in, up her bum. I had already lubed her entire body with baby oil so going in wasn't much of a fight, in fact my hand slipped up her arse surprisingly easy I remember thinking to myself   (maybe I should try and clap...STOP IT !)

So now I had both hands in her. One up the fanny and the other in her bum hole, and she was in ecstasy, writhing around while making all them sounds only women make when they reach that place we never get too, (lucky bastards). Anyway by now I was getting a bit bored and she was all over the place, I was up to my elbows it seemed in fanny and arse, wrists deep inside her as I could feel my fingers touching each other she on the other hand (excuse the pun) was in seventh heaven and I was starting to laugh at the whole thing (while thinking to myself, that I was glad I wasn't wearing my rings...ssssnigger). Now I know its not funny but I started to think of stuff I could get her to say while

in this state, and so the whole situation began to feel like I was
in some puppet show so when SOOTY sprung to mind, (yes
SOOTY and SWEEP and remember BUTCH?) well I have as
you are beginning know a rather sick but I think quite funny
(some might say bizarre, some might say weird, some might
want to fuck off and get some themselves instead of judging me)
sense of humour, so the whole Sooty thing started to make me
grin!

A rather devilish grin at that, ha, ha I thought, I know wot I'll do,
and so I started to say to her in a very smarmy but coolish way,
"SAY? SAUSAGES, yes, yes, that's right SAUSAGES, say
SAUSAGES". I repeated this a few times in her ear until it was
quite clear that she was gone dude because the next thing I knew
there she was whispering sausages, sausages just like good old
BUTCH would have enjoyed had he been real and not a puppet!
Wot a laugh, so I'll have to give a big hand, oh dear, big hand,
get it ...To Sara...

NO MORE HEROES ANYMORE

...O.k well here's a strange story, being a young revel (no, that's a chocolate) I mean rebel...if I was a revel I wouldn't be that coffee one, it tastes like shit...I'll start again.....

Being a young rebel (?) in Portobello Road, having only left home a few years earlier and making friends with the subculture of West London, I thought to myself 'You're in, you're hanging around and in sorts been adopted and accepted into this dysfunctional 'family' of losers, misfits and bandits.' O.k, now I was young, but I thought that by hanging out with Tookie and his ilk (the underculture), I might have left the straight, family, do wot I tells ya, behind, because now I could do wot the fuck I wanted. These were people who would accept me for who I was and let me make my own mistakes and stay the hell out of it, as they were doin' it as well..... WRONG! Even amongst the subculture I found that even the most outrageous factions of underground life and lifestyles were still hanging on to the same 'apron strings' of basic morals as my parents, (damn and blast).

Now I must stress here that as I'm writing this, I am forty-four inches 'round the waist...no....years old and trying to describe the way I saw things at the age of nnnnnine-teen. O.k so I thought that once I had injected drugs that I was now in a different class, not that anybody would care but my parents, NO, NO, NO. How wrong can a stupid little kid be? Very wrong. Most of the heroes that I'd tried to befriend were now turning into surrogate parental figures from hell, full of righteous indoctrinations. For example ...having scored one afternoon a lovely bag of brown, and returning to a house with a couple of local babes I knew, we got down to getting pretty fucked up, when a loud thundering sound could be heard outside, a Harley (bollocks, it's Charles).

Now Charlie was a Hell's Angel back in the day and you'd think that they wouldn't have given a toss, o.k, most probably wouldn't, but not Charlie. He was like your own personal 'guardian angel of mercy' on a mission to reform, salvage or save my soul before I would inevitably sell it to Satan for a bag of magic beans, or smack. Well he gave me a roasting (that's not a Hell's Angel torture, nor is it a sign of affection between three bikers), wot can I say? I left my home to be part of this alternative life and they're moaning at me worse than my own family.

Another righteous moaner that I wished at the time would have minded his own business is Lemmy, yes Lemmy. He of 'wasted' infamy, he used to nag, nag, nag me and everybody else. It was a bit like living in a 'B' movie and your family's turned into were-wolves, so just when you think you've found the sheriff and everything's going to be ok, ya find out they're all werewolves. Well, one particular day I found myself with a young lady and as I was walking her home, I bumped into the 'Three Stooges', no sorry, Lem, Mick Farren, and Drunken Sanderson, I mean Duncan Sanderson, he of Pink Fairies fame....They were just leaving Heneikey's pub. I had just bought a new t-shirt (whoopie) that was decorated with pictures of syringes. I thought it was 'fab' and fitted in quite well with the anti-social theme of our little 'community'.....wrong....Lemmy thought it wasn't and promptly ripped it off my good self. I was amazed, I couldn't believe wot he had done as he's not a violent man. I, however, was and I was raging and we exchanged words.

He was trying to tell me that if I kept taking that shit I would end up like all the 'others' etc, etc. I didn't need a speech, I needed a t-shirt and he'd just ripped mine up (bastard). So without a thought (never was any good at those) off I trundled to the army surplus stall and borrowed a bayonet (the owner knew better than to try and stop me). I then began to 'barter' with him and we decided that he should give me all of his change, It was then that Mick Farren decided to say a few choice words somewhere along the lines of 'Cool it maaaan...' or something, my reply was ..'Keep out of it or I'll have no fuckin heroes anymore (The Stranglers went on after that to record a song with a similar title). So the moral of this story is....I don't know. I would like to say on reflection that they were only looking out for me and others like me, but fuck it....ALL YOUR HEROES ARE FUCKIN' HYPOCRITES, SO DON'T TRUST ANY OF THEM ...O.K. KIDS?

THE LIVES AND CRIMES
OF THE EARL OF LONSDALE
(Or....trust no-one, suspect everyone)

The great 'Earl of Lonsdale' (aka Heinekeys) drug busts in 1979 and 1980 were the biggest of their kind and made the history books apparently. I, of course was there and arrested on one occasion for being in possession of an opium substitute (I can't remember the name of it) and some 'decks' or was it a gram of sulphate? I had a long and tedious court case over that, lasting a year and I think it all got thrown out in the death or there was a suspended sentence...who cares? I walked anyway.

HEINEKYS, the pub has been written about a lot over the years, mainly by people who never went there. I think most of the stories I've read have the same quotes by the same people. Well I would like to add some new insight into the 'goings' on in that particular drinking establishment. I tried tracking down the usual suspects, but thought better of it and instead I'll give *my* version of the way it was.
Firstly I would like to dedicate this to all the freaks, zombies, creatures of the night, underworld gangsters, dealers and mustn't forget plain-clothed coppers who frequented the boozer, not in any order of preference.......

DIK MIK (Hawkwind noise-maker and all-round good guy), TANK (Sue) biker bird, and still a fixture in the 'Grove. SCOT-

TISH JIMI (r.i.p) Motorhead's roadie with GRAEME REYNOLDS.

JANETTE (had a crush on her for ages).

GARRY MOONBOTTLE OR SOME SUCH STUPID ARSED HIPPY DIPPY SNIPPY SKIPPY NAMIE on occasionie, when passing through cautiously avoiding eye-contact with the very scary locals who lurked within and were now your hero's bestest friends? (I think he lives in Australia now, sheep rearing, more like worrying or they look pretty fuckin scared to me in the photos he's shown me. Apparently writing a book about his life and the forming of a band based on the growing of mushrooms or something).

CRAZY CHARLIE (now ex-Hell's Angels)].... who still might be adding to this collection of whitterings "if he gets his way ". Or find his bleedin' way.

LEMMY (plays in a popular band, you may have heard of them.

Assorted HELL'S ANGELS .and other OUTLAW bike club's, ANNIE + ROSIE the BARB SISTERS FROM HELL, one's a nurse in a drug re-hab and the others a butterfly.

NORA (SCOTTISH) and son ZACK ...Nora get some sleep! Zack "put it back, it's not yours!".

FREAKY, keeping the freak flag flying.

HAYSTACKS, BULLSHIT, CHEWY LEE, KIRK (too many stories about us ...love ya bro.). Vincent brother of Nev gold whose ex turned into my ex now lives with a Scottish geezer who used to be in the club.

MICHELLE, hi 'Chelle, thanks for helping bring up my two babies when I needed a friend, p.s. she could do with a good night's sleep too.

Vicar, 'EL PRESEDENTE' Triton BILL, KERNAL,

SACK (r, i, p). ROY (Frances Barnet), JOKER PETE (where is my fuckin' log book) and a cast of thousands....SONS OF SATAN (M.C) MOTORCYCLE CLUB.

Jackie (r.i.p) + Anna.

STEVE TOOK (r.i.p) gone but not forgotten (WOT A STAR). Mick Slattery, another Hawk.

VERMILLION, she of vermillion and the ACES, I was a bit younger than her and a watcher from afar.

GERMAN JOHN used to ride some mad bikes and could on occasion be seen riding around dressed in German regalia. Drucilla, Terry the roadie.

ANGEL you lovely slut, Colin (gone and forgotten).

GERT (GERMAN) totally insane biker junkie from White City hell, most famous phrase 'YOU CAN'T KILL ME, I'M ALREADY DEAD!' that used to confuse a lot of people. LONG JOHN we had some fun (in a manly way of course) barbs, speed and fighting, unfortunately with each other mainly.

BRIAN JAMES, Damned guitarist and all-round gent, BUNNY shut up talking shit you fuckin annoying speed freak.

RALPH, THE MOUTH. Wot can I say! It's all in the name?

Marco, (wot a plumb)he tried to copy one of my first tattoos, BORN TO LOSE, but the dipshit miss spelt it and wandered into the pub one Saturday proudly displaying his new piece of needle art and the immortal words BORN TO LOOSE,

PAUL BLACKEN, PLAYED BASS WITH ME IN MY BANDS F.T.W. AND THE LONDON LOSERS,I asked him to contribute to this book but he never got back , oh well, cheers for not getting involved !

GEORGE BUTLER, drummer with ALEX HARVEY, the PINK FAIRIES offshoot band LIGHTNING RAIDERS and anyone else that would have him.

DIM, I mean LYNNE; I married this one, jeezus?

SNUFF, French punk nutter. Never understood a word he was saying.

MOTORCYCLE IRENE, if only I had been older and mmmmm.

TINY wot a cunt.

HAIRDRESSER DAVE, still a good mate, bravest gay bastard ever. The only gay person to get beat up at 'Gay Pride' marches by dykes, once again too many stories to tell, subway four - Piccadilly, old man Steptoe in the toilets in Shepherds Bush. TOM +GARY the tuinol skinhead mental gay contingent (nobody's calling these guys a couple of dirty poofs and getting away with it)...LADY JANE...or JANE THE PAIN you dirty cow, we had some x-rated times. TOOTS + ALLEN (I was aiming for his head and the bastard put his arm up...he once borrowed my replica hand gun and tried to hold some business-man up, when the fool in a moment of enlightenment told Allen that he could see the gun was sealed down the barrel, so he battered him with it instead.)

THESE are the people I remember; only a handful of the guilty can I recall but these were the main characters in an everyday way of life that came to an end when Heinekeys got busted. It took a couple of years after that to really kill it off what with the migrating to the PRINCESS ALEXANDRIA, which came about due to tourists taking over Heinekeys. They even managed to kill that off too by turning it into a fuckin' wine bar. Totally bizarre, as nobody wanted to admit defeat and the opening day was met with a 'no beer' policy that left everybody standing outside with glasses of bloody wine. I wish I had a camera that day...'Angels, gays, junkies, rockers of all description, wandering about with glasses of fucking wine...STOP IT...

THE DAY OF BUST NUMBER ONE.

I can recall standing in the main bar, holding a bottle of Newcastle Brown ale in one hand and the other in the pocket of my newly acquired donkey jacket. This was a new choice of clothing as it would let me have one pocket filled with downers, tuinol, Nembutal, secanol mainly and the other with 'grammed up' sulphate ready for bizziness.

I wasn't the only dealer in the pub though, it seemed around them days that everyone was selling something and things had got completely out of hand on reflection, with hippies returning from India and other places with fuckin' large amounts of hash. In the garden you could score a kilo, it got that blatant and obvious. There would be people sitting at the garden table with fuckin' great scales and weights, pulling out machetes and stuff to cut the hash up...mental. There was no subtlety to any of it.

CHOPPERS would be lined up all along the outside entrance to the pub and it seemed as though a kind of truce was unspokenly held on a Saturday between the different outlaw biker gangs, as everyone was flying their colours. Not too sure how that went, as I wasn't into all that then, being a mere nineteen, although the SONS OF SATAN decided to give the club its first airing in public, I recall once, as I was asked to inform a member of the SONS to have his newly acquired tattoo removed by next week or have it removed for him in an old traditional way! I never asked how, it seemed rude and I wasn't sure I wanted to know the answer.

TALK THE TALK.

A comical piece of none-sense by
Gaz ...
I thought you might like a short interlude from
Drug's and violence ....

ENJOY

EXTENDED FORKS; eating implements for people with short arms.

APEHANGERS; Execution apparatus for bad monkeys.

DIGITAL SPEEDO; Swimwear that shows how fast you're swimming.

PANHEAD; Cookery enthusiast.

SISSY BAR; Plenty of them in London (don't pick coins off the floor)

REAR SHOCKS; you had to pick that coin up, didn't you?

SPRINGER; Someone who gathers dysfunctional families together and gets them to fight live on t.v.

JOCKY SHIFT; to adjust one's genitalia.

IRON HOSE; to remove wrinkles from an aged horse.

PILLION; More than a million.

RE- BORE; To tell the same, dull story again and again.

EVO; To give your girlfriend the flick.

HIGHWAY PEGS; Ideal for drying cloths while riding.

CARBY; Stinging insect that lives in cab of land rovers.

.

BULLET INDICATORS; Guns.

PIKE NUTS; Fish genitalia.

SLASH CUT MUFFLERS; Devices that greatly reduce the sound of a man screaming when he's cut himself shaving.

STROKER; Someone who needs to get a girlfriend …quick!

SADDLEBAGS; Tired eyes from long journeys.

TOLL ROLL; Dick in a bun.

JAP CRUISER; An individual who prowls the streets looking for orientals to have sex with.

GOOSENECK; Common complaint from people who try to take off their helmets without undoing the buckle first.

DUEL FIRE IGNITION; Wiring that enables you to have two fires on your bike simultaneously.

DEGREE OF RAKE; The amount of gardening left to do before you can go for a ride.

Well I hope yee'all enjoyed that …
Now back to the story…

A MEETING OF OTHER CLANS would also congregate on the Saturday excursion after 'TISWAS' the popular t.v. program had finished. HAIRDRESSER DAVE, TOM (Dave's brother) and an assortment of gays would frequent the pub; tuinol being the main allure, musicians to every fucker used to turn up, from the usual locals to bands from abroad would come down. I remember bumping into SAMMY from HANOI ROCKS he played bass with them and we had struck up a friendship of sorts as I helped him out one night in a fight at the 100 CLUB after I'd gotten into a punch up with MENZIE from the ANGELIC UPSTARTS and Sammy had joined in as Menzie was pulling my hair and Sammy stood his ground and was shouting at him to let go and calling him a girl (cool) until Menzie knocked him out but at least he let go of my hair and that gave me the chance to reach for me knife, it all got broke up then and me and Sammy and their guitarist Andy went back to their flat where we got smashed.

Well on this day Sammy once eyeing me, ran over shouting "Hey Steve" much to the surprised look of every one as he did look a bit suspect in his make up and scarves (Johnny Thunders look) but we sat chatting while all the bikers made stupid references to my new girlfriend, slash lady boy friend. Ha, ha, ha. A healthy amount of what on the outside looked very much like straight business men could be found milling around, they always looked out of place and were frequently mistaken for the filth and harassed sometimes questioned but they usually turned out as they too were only there for the drugs, all this with a very small smattering of tourists who never stayed long, once realising where they had stumbled into (ha!).

HEINEKEY'S must have been one of the last bastions, where all were tolerated as we all mainly had one thing in common.....DRUUUGS.

Getting back to the bust.
Just to refresh, I was standing in the main bar, pockets full to the brim of happy pills, when all of a sudden, boy did it go off and

nobody knew what had hit them. Uniformed and plain-clothed police came in from every direction...I was lucky as I could see it from the position I was standing and luckily for me I wasn't one of the dealers that had been 'marked' straight away, with a close-contact copper on hand to bust immediately. So on witnessing the assault I made like a human windmill, all arms and pills, there were pills everywhere...I was simply throwing everything I had into the air as fast and as indiscreetly as I could (fuck it). I wasn't alone, it was raining drugs and it would have been funny had it not been so impulsive, scary, quite violent as people were being ushered out the door to make room for more old bill. When the 'spotted' ones had been led away the police slowed things down a bit and gave out tickets to certain people after they had been searched or not thought worthy of a 'nick.

Outside it wasn't much better, bikers were pulled from bikes, Toots a friend at the time had a baby in a pram and had this searched, plus baby's nappy (aaahhh).
One of the Sons of Satan I recall was being searched in a corner by pulling his trousers down in a not- so-discreet way. This was pushing certain boundaries of decency and on reflection lucky for them that the whole episode didn't turn very ugly. But I must confess they did their job well, as no-one had a fuckin' clue, let's face it, the old bill was renowned for being bloody obvious and *everyone* was caught off guard.

DOWN THE COP SHOP
What a fiasco that was, I've got no information on the whole outcome of that day, or where everyone was taken (try as I did), other than my own memories, so all I can say is that Notting Hill Gate police station was awash with the entire clientele of Heinekey's drinking establishment. The cells were choc-a-

block with every freak worthy of a more in-depth frisking; needless to say it was here that I was rumbled. I thought everything was gone from my jacket, but they managed to find the two incriminating objects in my pockets, buried deep, so as even I had no recollection that they were there, oh well....... A rather nice detective by the name of CUTS asked me if I had anything else on me, I answered "NO" in a stroppy, but not aggressive tone. This led to him whacking me around the head and with a jolt of super-cop strength, the fuckin' neanderthal lifted me of the floor thus pinning my good self to the wall, ooh! That wasn't called for, now was it? After a few questions I was led back to my cell.

Camaraderie set in and we started having a laugh and joke for a while until the inevitable rumour of 'grassing' had started rearing its ugly head. I in fact, was accused by some mook of informing on one of the SONS...can't remember what I was supposed to have said, but it was enough to get certain people all riled up and after we all got released I had a beef with a couple of members until the muck-spreader was confronted and made to tell his story, then confess to being a fuckin' lying cunt, he got a kickin' but I also gave him a quiet talking to on my own one day, with a screwdriver (prick).

GOING TO COURT

We all got bailed and went to court, where I had another encounter with the SONS over more bullshit. This was put to rest there and then and everyone shook hands and that was that. I wasn't dealt with that day and as I said before, went on to go back and forth for a year. I've got no information on the outcome for the others involved with that bust so if you want to know more look it up ya self.

SECOND BUSTING OF YE OLD HEINEKEY'S DRINKING HOUSE OF THE DOOMED AND DANGEROUS...

Much the same as the first this time, they missed me by seconds having just made a deal with an undercover constable for one hundred dexspansuals. The punter looked every bit a righteous dude, all long hair, leather jacket, gun belt, boots, friggin' Motorhead shirt (not so easy to get then either). I made the deal and was just about to pick the pills up from a dealer in the back bar when off it went again and Motorhead fan with a warrant card told me in no uncertain terms that I was 'nicked, my son. Well actually I wasn't! Arse-holeyoh...

THAT whole second bust as stated earlier, was to become the beginning of the end for Heinekey's, West London's shrine to counter culture, an alternative 'school' of sorts for me, a meeting of minds, birthplace of punk rock, biker sanctuary, a breeding ground for us less fortunate travellers in life's weird and wonderful tapestry to meet and greet.

STEVE 'ANARCHY IN WESTBOURNE PARK' TOOK

Brace yourselves kids, this is a bit gory...those of a nervous disposition should skip a couple of pages... I FIRST MET STEVE TOOK or known to his fiends THE PHANTOM SPIKER. (Who together with Marc Bolan formed Tyrannosaurus Rex and had been unceremoniously kicked out when he shortened it to T.Rex). He was also a part of the infamous PINK FAIRIES MOTORCYCLE CLUB and ALL STAR ROCK'N ROLL BAND! Partly formed the pink fairies, had a band much like the ones of my own in being mainly in name rather than actually doing anything called SHAGRAT I was the last to join this band of musical illusions and we spent many an hour in his flat in Westbourne Park getting stoned and jamming? So it was here in the Earl of Lonsdale drinking establishment (Heneikeys) that we both met. Gaz was just putting together his 'Ali Katt and his Baghdad Boogie Band' in Southall and I was hanging out in Heneikeys more often than I should have.

One afternoon I was shmoozing with a couple of local gals from the 'Grove when a short-arsed, long haired bloke who dressed like a late-sixties, early-seventies rock star came staggering over to the table I was sat at AND ASKED THE MAGIC WORDS 'Hey ..Got any downers?' I said no. Then he sat himself down (nice) he was pretty much messed up to tell you the truth and was getting right up my nose.

We got talking and before long Steve decided to tell everyone who he was and how single-handedly he was responsible for forming every cult band in West London (or that's how it seemed) over the last ten years, and actually there was quiet a ring of truth in what he said. After that meeting, I would bump into him on a regular basis (literally) and over the coming months we got quite close. If not because we shared a common ground (mainly anything that would get us out of it). I could always find him either in the pub or Lemmy's squat in Colville Terrace where he was a not-so-welcome unofficial flatmate, sleeping on the settee in the 'video' room (a new and wonderful thing at the time). He wasn't destined to stay there for long, as Steve could be a bit of a handful, a little bitter at not getting the acclaim he thought he deserved (not for me to comment) but he was more rock n' roll lifestyle than playing rock n' roll...

He then moved in with his girlfriend in Westbourne Park. We used to get stoned and jam and he was always on about forming a band but I knew it wouldn't happen (I came along too late). We auditioned a couple of drummers from the area but all that would happen was we would play for an hour or so, then go and score to get inspiration, but that usually meant a lot of bullshit would be spoken, or slurred, with people crawling about on the floor, others trying to find veins in leathery scarred arms... (not a nice sight). Unfortunately a hell of a lot of very talented and beautiful people ended up fucked up at that time and unbeknown to myself I was slowly joining them. SO, one afternoon I got a call from Steve "Come round maaaan and have a jam", so I grabbed my bass and off I went, got to Steve's in the afternoon. We plugged in, made a noise for a while then swiftly set about scoring, once the deed had been done we were on our way back to Steve's pad when I stopped and bought a pound of cherries.

We got back to his place and got wrecked, I hung out for an hour or so then said my 'goodbyes' and left, leaving him the cherries (didn't think nothing of it - WHY SHOULD I?) Later that day I got a phone call from his bird... "STEVE'S DEAD"...shock...we all thought it was an overdose as sometimes you don't have to overindulge to overdose (a warning to anyone thinking of dabbling with the brown stuff).. MR BROWN-STONE DON'T TAKE NO PRISONERS.... But he had CHOKED ON THE BLOOMING CHERRIES AND A PIP HAD WEDGED ITSELF IN HIS THROAT THUS KILLING HIM - How ironic...

The funeral.......WOT a fiasco...what with the way he lived his life, his send-off was just as scarily entertaining (I won't be naming names). We met at Steve's girlfriend's house and like all funerals it was awkward, there were family members, bikers and his close druggie friends of the underworld there. We set of to the cemetery, in Kensal Green and it was raining. Steve was getting buried there. His family were very remorseful, but we had just scored and had our own way of sending him off. With no water to mix up the 'brown' we disappeared into the church, someone produced a spoon and we used the water from the 'holy water' bowl to mix up a cocktail of the the stuff. We kept our seedy little habit away from the family but once we were all standing around the grave it all got a bit bizarre....somebody had brought a crap guitar and threw it in. Other stuff was thrown in and then as if by magic, I slid on the wet grass and now I was in...Sitting on top of his coffin (sorry mate) wot a plonker!

THE PUB... after the burial everyone went back to the Princess Alexandria pub where we had a good old drink up, sharing stories, telling jokes etc. all the usual stuff. Then one more thing happened, THE POLICE decided to bust his sending off, they must have thought they had all the usual suspects in one place (and they were right), so they gave it a spin, bastards. Well they were met with a very angry reception (well I mean) we were getting harassed every day, fair enough, but we couldn't bury someone without the Old Bill breathing down our necks.

XMAS EVE followed Steve's death; I stayed with his bird and young daughter to do the Xmas morning thing. It was the Xmas Eve that was totally bizarre. I had no idea that Steve was quite religious and knew the local vicar well, so when we went to Mass on Xmas Eve, I was very surprised to hear the vicar dedicate the sermon to musicians and to Steve and then he pointed to myself...I was in shock as before we got to the church I'd injected two 'amps' of Physeptone (a heroin substitute) and was all over the place. Well, to add to this the vicar asked me to come to the front of the congregation and lead the small procession around the church with lighted candles (jeez). I obliged, staggering about with his girlfriend holding me up, helped by a lovely old lady who thought I'd had a bit too much of the old Xmas cheer (well I suppose I did).

I THOUGHT A POEM MIGHT FIT IN WELL HERE, ONCE AGAIN LYRICS TO A SONG...
(Not necessarily about Steve Took or anything but I think sort of fits)

FLY ON....
Chromium plated iron horse glistens in the sun
Extension of his ego
Stands proud with the others warrior to the end
Twentieth century black night
Last of a dying breed
His morals are his fortress
Hero to the end
With no damsel to defend

He rides the open road
Wind in his face
Leaves all his cares behind
Exchanging pressures of the city
For rainbows so pretty....

CHORUS.....
Fly on with angels wings
Ride on warrior
Fly on with angels wings
Ride on warrior

Chrome implanted iron horse
Worshipping false gods
But this god won't ever lie
No this can never die
This god can never lie
Stone free in a purple haze
Easy rider in a dream
Feel as free as a bird
Not a sound is heard
Not a sound is heard
Ride hard ride free
From the powers that be
They'll always put you down
Try and drag you to the ground
Cut your wings and hope you'll drown

CHORUS.........

Don't take any prisoners
Never suffer fools gladly

No hostages to be taken
Commandments of the road
Where nothings given and nothings owed
Love always comes second hand
Tears are sparing
Head on down the endless road
Into the night
That never ending light
Travel a thousand miles
Through villages and towns
Through pastures old and new
Leave them all behind
Leave them all behind

CHORUS.........

MEANWHILE, BACK IN THE GARDEN...I have very fond memories of Meanwhile Gardens, situated at the back of Ladbroke Grove British Rail station. It was a purpose-built site provided by the local council for the local community and it was next to the Grand Union canal. There was a skateboard-themed park as well as a large sand pit approximately 50 yards from side to side, a full circle that had angling sides upwards. Weather permitting, there would be some great free gigs that started in the early afternoon with local bands and headlined by Here and Now. At the time they were excellent and used there own equipment to put the events on. At these 'do's' you could spend a really pleasant afternoon free from police harassment, no skinheads, no football thugs or any other idiot, they seemed to miss this spot entirely and none of the insanity of the Green under Portobello Road and the fiascos that went with it.

Here was a more relaxed time for all, my daughter Ziggy was now born and aged nearly one (aahh), while myself and it seemed the whole motley crew, were calming down a bit. I would meet up with Gaz around this period again, his band in Southall I think was coming to an end (I actually tried out on bass, but it wasn't to be - musical differences), I was still getting far too wasted to take it or myself seriously and Gaz had his own dream he was chasing. We were both captains of our own ships in life, and in music, and this was a bit awkward at the time as ya can't see the big picture when it hasn't been painted as yet...Now it's bloody obvious and that's why I'm having so much fun doin' this book .. only took 30 years to see it as it was ...

2005. HEINEKEY'S REKINDLED.

While writing this book, I passed through Portobello Road trying to get a feel of 'days gone past' and I decided to venture into the EARL OF LONSDALE and visit some old ghosts and memories, when shock and horror took a hold of me. The breweries have actually transformed the pub *back* to its original format! ha, ha, ha! All this in a vain attempt to recapture the 'feel' of the place for the newly populated Notting Hill Gate brigade of pretentious middle and upper (these days) class, I don't know wot they're called, it used to be yuppies..... But let's say for arguments sake, CUNTS. Bizarre how the very thing the establishment tried so long and so hard to get rid of is the 'selling point' for this prime piece of London. Everyone it seems wants 'in' on a culture that if still there they would cross the road to avoid. Hypocritical bunch of ... (IN THE WORDS OF PUNKS GONE BY) POSERS.

WELL AS I'VE SPOKEN SO MUCH ON BIKERS AND OUTLAW BIKER CLUBS I FELT IT NECESSARY TO ADD THIS!!!!!

CLUB BASTADOS

F.T.W. INCORPORATED

THE LEGENDARY CLUB BASTADO
GRAND RE-OPENING NITE
90'S ROCK WITH A PUNK ATTITU
FROM HIPPIES TO BIKERS NO BASTARD REFU
WEDNESDAY 24TH APRIL
GOSSIPS, MEARD ST. SOHO
LIVE BAND CALL OF THE WILD
OPPOSITE INTREPID FOX PUB
ADMISSION £2

BASTARD BREW

■ WE PICKED up (
even) interestin' flyer reshently
for new club, Bastade: Bros
Inc. 'Butt-kicking muzi¦, from '76
Punk to '93 Metal', boas¦:s the ad,
to which we're hip an' we can dig
it, etc, but it was the footnute
which intrigued us: 'Gil, wearing
four articles of clothing or less –

half price. Men wearing four
articles of clothing or less – a
severe talking to'.

So get it sussed, boozers –
g¦a¦kers except for five pairs o'
socks, an' yer spared an ear-
bashin'...

BASTARD BROS

*Club Bastardos, Soho Theatre
Club, London
Tuesday, March 2*
WHAT OTHER band would you
expect for the opening night of a
place called Club Bastardos?
And what else would you expect
from their bad but bastardly
behaviour?

They kick off their drunken set
with a pretty good rendition of
'Enter Sandman', much to the
surprise of vocalist Dave, who
obviously knew nothing of the
plan and has never rehearsed it

with them. Actually, it would be
surprising if they'd rehearsed
any of tonight's set they
... even met before?), but it's
2.30am and everyone is drunk, so
what the hell

And funnily enough, they're
really not bad at all. There are a
handful of their own tunes, mixed
in with the occasional bad-tuned
cover, like 'Sweet Jane', that
bears little resemblance to the
original. When they run out of
songs, they simply play a few of
them again.

'Are we F**king Genesis or
what?' slurs the giant frontman.
Thankfully not. Bastard Bros are
more reminiscent of early
Motörhead – and yes, they are
complete BASTARDS!
—MORAY

MANAGEMENT RESERVE THE RIGHT TO PARTY HARDER THAN YOU STEAL YOUR GIRLFRIEND & SELL YOUR MOTORBIKE.
DRUG OFFENDERS WILL BE DELT WITH IN THE USUAL WAY.
NEAR NAKED GIRLS GET VIP TREATMENT–NEAR NAKED MEN WILL GET HOSPITAL TREATMENT.

SINGLE OF THE WEEK

FTW (UNINCORPORATED)
'Club Bastardos' (Bastardos R Us)
EXCELLENT PUNCH-DRUNK Rock from a bunch of yobs also
known as The Bastard Brothers. They look like they sound, and
sound like, well, a bunch of bastards, really thumping guitar wall
of sound with cool Jack Daniels slur vocals.
FTW stands for F**k The World, in case you hadn't guessed!

GLOSSARY
OF
DANGEROUS MOTORCYCLE GANGS
&
TERMINOLOGY USED BY
DANGEROUS MOTORCYCLE GANGS

1%ers – The 1% symbol is derived from
a statement by the American
Motorcycle Association (AMA).
That 99% of the country's
Motorcyclists belong to the
AMA and are law-abiding
individuals. The 1% symbol
has thus become the mark of
the outlaw bike rider and
they display it on their
colours and many have it
tattooed on their person.

13 – Patch worn on an outlaw
member's colours, symbolizing
that the biker either smokes
Marijuana, deals in it, or
have contacts for methamphetamine.

666 – Patch worn on an outlaw member's
colours, or tattoo, symbolizing
the mark of Satan.

69 – Patch worn on an outlaw member's
colours, or tattoo, symbolizing
that the wearer has committed
cunnilingus or fellatio with
witnesses present.

A.M.A. – American Motorcycle Association.
It's composed of average people
who like motorcycles and the
companionship of club activity.

They are seldom intentionally
a problem to police and are
usually willing to cooperate
with law enforcement. According
to the A.M.A., they constitute
99% of the nation's cyclists.

Citizen – A cyclist who belongs to the A.M.A.,
Not a member of the 1% club.

Class – To do something out of the
ordinary, usually an act
which is violent and/or shocking to the public.

Colours – The official uniform of all
Outlaw motorcycle gangs. The
Colors consist of a sleeveless
Levi or leather jacket, with

Club patch on the back, and
Various other patches, pins,
And Nazi metals attached to
The front. Colours belong to
The club, are worn only by
Male members, and are always
Held sacred by outlaw gang
Members.

Crash Truck – A van, panel truck, or converted
school bus that follows the motorcycle gangs runs, and picks
up broken down bikes. Also known to
carry the club's weapons, drugs, supplies, and camping gear.
Usually driven by one of the females.

Cross – An emblem worn by 1%ers, either
as an earring, patch or pin
attached to the colours.

White cross – Earned when a
person digs open a grave,
removes an article from
the deceased with witnesses
present, and wears it on his colours.

Red cross – Earned by committing
homosexual fellatio with
witnesses present.

Cutie – A female picked up off the street
and taken to the clubhouse or
other place for a party. She is
the victim of a gang bang, rape

and beating. Later, she is
released with threats on her
life and family if she talks
to police.

D.F.F.L. – Dope Forever Forever Loaded.

Dresser – Large Harley-Davidson motorcycle
with custom trim, saddle bags;
Used in bike shows.

Eightball – Patch worn on colours, earned by
committing homosexual sodomy
with witnesses present.

Fash Truck - Same as crash truck. This term
comes from Canada.

Fly Colours – to ride on a motorcycle wearing
Colours.

Free Rider – An individual who shares the
same values and enjoys the same
life-style as outlaw gang members
but who prefers to keep a degree
of freedom of choice by not
formally belonging to one specific
Club.

F.T.W. – Standing for "Fuck the World,"
These initials are found on membership cards, as tattoos,
and are patches or pins on colours.

Garbage Wagon – A stock motorcycle with standard
parts intact, loaded with saddle
bags and chrome, as distinct
from a chopper.

Hardtail – A rigid motorcycle frame with
no shock absorbing device on
the rear.

Heat – Law enforcement officer, also
known as the Man.

Hog – Harley-Davidson motorcycle.

Jap-Scrap – Japanese motorcycles or foreign
Made bikes.

Knucklehead – A type of Harley-Davidson engine
manufactured prior to 1948, which
was characterised by large nuts
On the right side of engine above
the cylinders. Appearance is
somewhat similar to knuckles.

Legal Name – Most outlaw motorcycle club
members have nicknames or club
names which are called "Legal
Names" by club members. They
are also called "Street Names."

Loner – See "Free Rider."

Mama – A girl available to all club
members, usually sexually.

M.C. – Patch on colours, meaning
Motorcycle club.

Nomad – They are members of a motorcycle
gang and will wear the club's
colours. The bottom rocker will
Read "Nomad." In some clubs
they are the enforcers. They
do not belong to any one chapter.
He will attend club meetings and
pay required dues to different
Chapters, depending on his travels.

O.F.F.O. – Outlaws Forever Forever Outlaws.

Old Lady – Wife or steady girlfriend of a
Club member.

Originals – A member's first set of colours
Which are never to be cleaned?

Participate – To aid a member in a fight by
ganging up on the opponent.

P.O.B.O.B. – Pissed Off Bastards of Bloomington –
The original gang that
later developed into the Hell's Angels.

P.P.D.S.P.E.M.F.O.B.B.T. – "Pill Popping Dope Smoking Pussy
Eating Mother Fuckin Outlaw

Brothers Bikin Together" found on tattoos, colours, and business cards.

Probate – Club membership hopefuls, who
ride with the gang during their
probationary period. After
this time a unanimous vote must
be cast by the membership for
acceptance, initiations, and awarding of colours.
Prospect – A prospective member.

Pull a Train – For a girl to have sexual intercourse
with each man in the
group, any way he would like it,
one after another.

Run – A club sanctioned outing for a
day, weekend, or week, to a
certain location for a party,
camping, or special event,
sometimes with other chapters
and/or clubs.

Sheep – Same as "Mama."

Sissy Bars – Bars, often high bars, on the
rear of a motorcycle uses as a
back-rest for a passenger.

Static – Trouble or harassment from law
enforcement authorities or other
members of motorcycle clubs.

Striker – A prospective member; term
normally used by Canadian clubs.

Suck to the Bulls – Talk or act friendly towards
policemen.

The Man – Police or Law Enforcement Officer.

Turn Out – When all members come together in
the case of an initiation for a
new member, or for a girl to pull
a train for the first time.

War Wagon – A vehicle used to transport the
Club's arsenal during an outing
when trouble is expected from
other clubs.

White Power Fist – Patch worn on colors which display the
gang's racial ideals and philosophies of
white supremacy.

Wings – emblem worn by 1%ers, as a pin or patch (cloth)
attached to the colours. All wing earning
must be witnessed.

Black Wings –Earned when the wearer performs cunnilingus
on a Black woman.

WELL THERE YA GO!
I HOPE'S I NEVER SCAREDID YA'S ALL TOO MUCH
NOW?
HA, HA, HA…

SAVING PRIVATE REDMAN
(OR) STOP THE MADNESS
I NEED SOME GUIDANCE!

1984, and my daughter ziggy was now four going on five years old. I was now twenty five going on a one way trip to hell, or so it seemed at the time. I do not wish to dwell on this period in time too much as it's fuckin boring and mostly tedious family shit that I don't wanna remember and I am sure you as a reader are not interested in, in the slightest, so let's get it over with quickly ....

One good thing that came out of splitting up with my girlfriend (not yet my wife, I did that a year or so later, but I'm gonna spare us all the boring details and shall definitely not be going there. Phew).
As I was saying, the best thing that came out of my split up with Lynne was meeting LEO, now Leo is fifteen years my senior and lives in Edmonton, he was and still is a jack of all trades builder, artist, animal lover, spiritual in human observation and hardcore Bob Dylan fan. Actually far too many trades to mention and has over the years had his sticky fingers in as many pies as a small boy let loose in a sticky pie factory!

He also has a great sense for open mindedness and the art of seeing through the bullshit things in life and I revelled in this train of thought and attitude as it was one of the things in life that I was striving to be a kin to.

I met him through an add I put in Melody Maker while looking
for a bass player and his son VOMIT (of the band DIRT an of
shoot of CRASS) had phoned and we seemed to get on well so
I ventured to deepest Edmonton where he lived with his Dad,
Leo and his brother FOX who was the drummer in DIRT and
was now married to DONNA also known as HONEY BANE,
she had carved out a bit of a career for herself in the punk world
and had a few singles released and so while on the rebound from
going out with JIMMY PURSEY met FOX, well we all got on
pretty well and I found a kindred spirit in Vim's Dad, Leo, plus
we shared a liking of HAWKWIND so that was cool and groovy
and we would listen to the albums getting blasted on weed and
that friendship still remains to this day ......

Leo was to come to my aid as if by a divine calling it seemed at
the time as I was going through murders (literary) with Lynne as
we were splitting up and she had gone off with some hairy arsed
biker (not giving any names as it's none of any one's business).
This was
mainly down to the fact that I was caught having an affair and
she decided to reap her revenge by getting off with some one
else thus causing a fuckin' great rift in my life, and everyone
else's she came in contact with, socially and still to this day in
some places a FUCKIN' GREAT LOAD OF STEAMING
BITTER AND TWISTED SHIT !!!
Well this and that happened she did something so I did something back and it all ended in court with me getting evicted from
my home for shooting her with a 22 air rifle nine times or so (it
was bloody horrible, could have been a hell of a lot worse, luckily it wasn't) anyway I had to leave and get the fuck out as soon
as possible.
Well as luck would have it I was actually sitting in my flat all
alone, my so called friends had deserted me (something that was

to happen time and time again) I had nowhere to live, no money, no bird, the iguana didn't recognise me, nothing zilch, fuck all... up shit creek without a paddle and no fuckin thoughts of how I was going to get out of this one?

Then the phone rang, riiiing, riiing. That's the phone ringing, and it was Leo, "Hi" he said "what's up with you and how are ya mmmmmmmmmm!?".
Didn't take long to explain the grief and told him it was only a matter of time before I was to be getting a visit from the local motorcycle m.c. club to add to the rest of my problems, well knock me down with a bulldozer, and while ya there smack my arse and call me mary (no don't do that, oh alright go on then you smooth talking fucker you) Leo came up with a plan there and then.
He said, I've got a spare room as Fox had just moved in with Honey Bane and I could rent it for a tenner a week, fuck I was in, but what about my stuff I had all me guitars my hi fi, (yes that's wot we called them back then, so fuck off taking the piss !).

Well wouldn't you know it, Leo said "hang on a minute" and I heard some debating going on and he came back to the phone and said, "where do ya live?". I told him and he said, "Ok. DIRT are here and I've had a chat with GARY BUCKLY and well he say's they have their van with them and wot's more they'll be with you in one hour". FUCK YEAH. I rushed about like a headless Alsatian on methadrine with an elastic band tied round his nutz, packing everything I could or wanted up and was waiting outside my flat when a van painted matt black and well 'ard pulled up, "where's all ya stuff". I showed them and we preceded to pack everything in the back of the van plus everything I didn't got trashed and as my home was now gonna be owned by my now ex and her new live in lovers I thought that they could start

by doing a bit of d.i.y. So I smashed the whole fuckin' place up, even taking the light bulbs and smashing all the windows. Oh yeah I think a couple of interior walls got wot they had coming to em too? (Fuckin interior walls, never liked them!) and off I went to sunny Edmonton.
Cool.

Leo had a studio he had just finished building for his boy's in Dirt so I had a free rehearsal studio and he let me store all me shit in the back of the studio. I in return moved in my t.v. and my video (new things then, so don't scoff). Leo by the way fuckin' hated it as we used to watch THE YOUNG ONES all day long and most of the night plus I had a healthy video collection of music and stuff so it was great .... For me!
I ended up staying there a year or so and while living with Leo it was the best thing I could have done as he taught me to calm down take a look at situations don't go rushing in kicking and screaming. We had some very, very long chats and he I'm sure was sent as a life messenger to steer me from one age and train of thought to another, so all in all it was in a very strange and at times frightening way (maybe the only way for some of us, thick of skin and head to grow up and take stock while learning a few lessons in life and how to manage it).
CHEER'S LEO....
LOVE YA MAAAAAN !!!

STONED HENGE !!

It was while living at Leo's in Edmonton in 1985 that I was to attend the one but last Stonehenge free festival before the old bill smashed the fuck out of everyone and put a stop to the whole event once and for all.

I had just signed on at Ealing dole office and was off on my travels back to Leo's when a van pulled up and a bunch of people I used to hang with from Ealing were in the back all packed and smiley faced and telling tales of going off for two weeks to Stonehenge. Well I had nothing better to do as I had just rescued my Daughter from a bunch of drug addicts and pimps oh yeah and my ex! So she had now gone to stay with my sister in Bromley and there was nothing to do back at Leo's apart from that, I think he was gonna go anyway, turns that he does later on in the story, well I didn't really need much more tempting from my old chums in Ealing so I slung my bones in the back of the van and off we went.

On route we stopped of for refreshments and I hit the chemist as I hadn't had any hard drugs for a while and I was getting to say the least a bit bored with being the straight guy while fighting all these old junkies in Kings fuckin' Cross and laying low from my ex, her new boyfriendz a London m.c. motorcycle club and trying to stay straightish with Leo, listening to Bob Dylan and ZZ Top but I needed a release and this seemed to be the best deal I was getting so off into the chemist I went and righteously scored a carrier bag full of two mill' syringes and a shit load of orange spikes.

So now armed with enough arm spanners to get me a day job as a relief nurse in a Vietnam War zone I felt I was in fact ready to face whatever came to pass at the stoned henge event!

A long two and half hours later and we had arrived. There was one person who decided to get there early, a lot earlier it turns out in fact two weeks early as he had decided to go down with the hippies and cut down trees and build a fuckin' house it seemed. Now I've been to a few of these things even though they're not really my scene. Sitting in fields listening to hippies muttering on and on about how bad and down everything was maaaan, but stony henge was different and had a whole feel of it's own unlike the fuckin' big sell out pile of shit GLASTON-BURY FAIR with it's Ban the Bomb signs everywhere and it was run by C.N.D. Wot a bunch of cunts they were, a bit like and I bet the very same people governing that fuckin' sham as well. You know who I mean them self-righteous bastards getting people to go round collecting for banning the bomb? How? Why? Or collecting for legalize marijuana, once again WHY? I have said this already but I'll say it again I smoked dope wherever and whenever I wanted anyway so why give some middle-class arse wipe my ill gotten gains so they could get high on my supply!

I think time has proved all my misgivings and untrustworthy thoughts of them people as it's still not legal we still have the bomb and they don't exist anymore. mmmmmm

So where is all the money and wot did you hippie fuckin' bastards do with it?

A villa in Ibiza maybe!

Mmmmmmm I think sooooo...

Well getting back, my mate from Ealing had built this makeshift wooden hut come house complete with a double bed, a stove, a settee, a generator and oh yes a harem of naked nubile young girls waiting and willing to succumb to your every wish (nahh- hhhhh) you know that ain't true, but the rest is. Blooming marvellous it was, he had done one hell of a great job and every- body congratulated him on his efforts, only thing was he had been down there for two weeks and had started to go a bit weird, there will be more of this weirdness later.

That afternoon I spent just walking about sussing out wot was wot who was who and where everything was e.g. food stalls, bog holes, and now checking out the local talent! Bloody buck- ets full, great! Shit loads of girls all looking for Mr Right, oh well I wasn't Mr Right but I certainly could be Mr Rightnow!

And so my trek began. I met up with loads of pals and wanted to score by now as I had done most of my surveillance of the site and I had just purchased a fuckin' big machete just in case and I had brought with me a small but sharp and very effective hatchet axe. This I could conceal in my trousers and the machete I just slid down the outside of my boot, cool! Now I looked like a cave man or at least I was armed as good as one. I went about my business asking people if they had any speed or downers and eventually I bumped into CRAZY CHARLIE from the HELLS ANGELS now he knew of my concerns over certain people but he, like most others kept out and only tried to give advice and keep me on the straight and narrow path. Well I say straight and narrow path, the straight and narrow path on this day led to a man in a tent with a rather large dick? (Stop it) I mean bag of amphetamine, cool, I scored a half ounce said cheers to Charlie gave him a taster for sorting me out he gave me advice on keeping my big trap shut and keeping a low profile and I paid no heed to any of that whatsoever and off I trundled to go find some barbiturates to add to my now growing collection of drugs.

Well as luck would have it I found the very man. A slight gent aged around forty, long hair and a bit ratty looking and he was selling barbiturates cool. I bought the lot, a lovely big bag of mixed downers, pick n mix if ya like, if ya don't bollocks to ya! I had everything in their tuinol, nembutol, reds, secanol and a few other things that I thought might make me go pop in the middle of the night if I got a bit bored.

I took my newly bought for bounty back to my erm tent, well not really mine but someone had this shitty little fuckin' one man thing and said I could use it if I wanted. It done the job to sleep in but not much else apart from that I hadn't counted on doing a lot of sleeping as there were far too many girls, bands and drugs to be had and boy did I need a break from girls, bands and drugs??

So back in the tent I tried to get a hit but this proved tragic to say the least as the tent was much to small and fuckin' people kept walking by and stumbling onto my tent and I was getting fed up with shouting FUCK OFF to every other hippie that passed on by, so asked my mate with the van if I could go inside and have a bit of privacy, he was cool so in I went tied the tourniquet tight around my arm and lunged an orange spike deep into my vain pulling back on the syringe to see the blood rush into the works filling up my arm spanner then I pushed down on the syringe and sieved threw the liquid mixture of amphetamines and water... whoooosh... up I went bang dang twang shit fuck and bollocks up I went son of a whore this speed really did the fuckin' mamba in me old noggin, my arms were seething in detergent and the veins in my forehead felt like they would explode WHAAAP!!! Boom fuckin shanka, I was up, boy was I up, as Cheech would say "man was that some gooood shit!"

I left the van feeling like as though I was ten feet taller than when I had gone in and my hole entire body was now shivering and tingling from the speed running through my veins, (fuck did I used to love fixing up speed). I walked off into the distance, transfixed on everything, wanting to do everything, see everything, play every guitar known to man and shag every women known to somebody else's man (oop's).

I did eventually bump into an old friend who was playing in CONFLICT and he was having this little jam in the field so when I saw him he beckoned me over to him and asked if I wanted to play I said fuck yeah! I grabbed the guitar and got totally absorbed in guitar heaven, we must have played for around an hour or so and when it sort of came to an end, maybe because everyone else wasn't so bloody high I looked up from the guitar and sore to my amassment a decent sized crowd had formed around us and as we stopped they all applauded, SHIT HOT!

I met up with an ex girlfriend we chatted and walked around for a while until we came across a hippie bloke doing some very suspect tattooing on anyone that would let him for some drugs or money. I asked him if he would tattoo my wrists with a chain motif and he said in a stoned slurry voice, "yeah maaan". Against my better judgement I sat my arse down on the grass and Tracy the girlfriend sat next to me. Then the hippie began to tattoo this really dodgy bit of ink work into my flesh, god was this a rotten piece of home-grown needle gun for beginners or wot? But Hey, ya get's wot ya ask for and I asked for a chain around both my wrists and that's sort of wot I got.

I met up with these two young lady's sitting in their tent offering facial make up so I volunteered my boatrace for drawing on? They very kindly drew all over me boat I wanted a ALICE COOPER type effect and they did one and to be honest it looked fuckin' great especially with my eye's bulging from out of my speed riddled face. I arranged to meet them that night as NICK TURNIP was playing in some tent so we made a time to meet and off I went again on my travels.

On getting back to my tent and the Ealing in crowd, I bumped into a low life called ACTION MAN. He used to rob chemists, and on this day he in fact had just robbed an ambulance of it's stock and told he had some ADRENALIN, shit I didn't know wot that stuff did and so I asked him wot it was and he said it resembled speed, well I was now coming down a bit so I thought why waste mine if there's a freebee going. So I took one of the glass bottled ampules from him and retired back into the van once again following the same ritual as before but only this time it should be a lot cleaner and safer? After filling the syringe with the liquid I slowly injected it into my arm, wot a bad move... WwwooooossshhH straight out the back fuckin' door of the van I flew like a bullet from a gun only thing was I was going backwards CRACK... I hit the deck on my arse. People came rushing over to see wot I had done this time to my stupid self, well it was apparent that wot I had just injected had no resemblance to amphetamines at all and it was in fact told to me later on that day a drug that was to be used as a last ditch try to revive people that had just suffered from a heart attack, wot a cunt!

Later on that night, it was time to go to the gig, so I gathered up
me drugs, didn't have a change of clothes as wot I came in stayed
on for the whole two weeks (dirty little scum bag) and took off
to find my date for the night.
On arriving at the girl's tent she greeted me with a kiss and re-
done my Alice Cooper look make-up and off we went. By the
time we had actually got to the gig I was getting pretty much
worse for wear after smoking vast amounts of dope in pipes and
bongs and such plus my speed enhancing drug had been
upgraded a few times mixing all this up with a rather potent
potion of home brew scrumpy that some mook had brought...
I was to say the least pretty fucked up? We found a place to sit
our hammered arses down and enjoyed the first couple of bands
but my memory gets a bit blurred now as I can't remember wot
happened next, apart from I know I wasn't with the girl I went
with.

NICK TURNER asked me up to play, I did a complete repeat
performance of the CAMDEN PALACE fiasco only this time I
was given a fretless bass to play (wot the fuck do you do with
these) it was bad enough trying to play a normal guitar let alone
some cunt nicking all the frets? So I got up and died miserably
from a lack of musical knowledge and far too many drugs and
alcohol, but I do remember seeing the dancer and thinking to
myself that I wouldn't mind a piece of that so while stumbling
off the stage I picked the dancing girl up and flung her like a bag
of spuds over my shoulder real cave man like and proceeded to
walk through the crowd with NICK'S dancer draped casually
over my shoulder as if I wore wearing a human poncho. I do
remember however getting back to my tent but I don't think I
got up to anything as I woke up the very next morning with my
crusty old under pants still draped around my ankles and her

stinky hippie knickers on my head for some reason. Maybe she thought it funny who knows? Who bloody cares!

The next day, or whenever, oh I can't be specific or remember come to that and I don't for a second think you give a shit anyway. Well I went out for a stroll and met up with one of the hippies who used to squat in Ealing and then again in the Maida vale squat her name was Sue. She was now living with the convoy, a group of hippies that had bought a whole load of old buses and lorries and were trying to live on the road as some kind of twentieth century carnival come gypsy hippie troupe of basically thieves and drug dealers with some genuine alternative life styled hippies thrown in trying to keep it all peas and bugs. But it was all doomed for disaster and I'm not sure if any of that mob are still around I'm sure the old bill put a stop to them in the late nineties, who knows who cares yet again, well anyway, I met up with Sue we had a chat shared a joint or three and it was then that she asked me if I would in fact do her a favour (oh no, not that kind of a favour. Shame though, as she was quite a pretty little thang). I digress?

So Sue asked me if I would sit with a couple of geezers that she was doing a bit of biz with and she would see me alright if the deal went down ok, so I said yeah ok I've got nothing else to do so off we went .
We were now on the edge of the festival grounds and all there was around were convoy caravans and trucks n stuff then along came this fuckin' B.M.W. yes I thought that too, wot the fuck and inside there sat these two right dodgy looking old gangster types you know the sort all flat noses balding heads ill fitting suits and scars that showed they weren't the best fighters in the world so they must be tooled up! Great?

Well she said will you wait here with these two and ill be back in a few minutes. I said a disgruntled yes as I wasn't really into this; it all looked a bit shifty? So anyway she went over to the car and had a word and then said "bye" and was gone leaving me baby sitting the stone henge kray twins from hell, brilliant!

After a while one of the square headed grant Mitchells peered out from the window and asked how much longer was she gonna be. I turned to him and said I hadn't a clue as I had no idea wot was going down and that I was just asked to baby sit them for a few minutes. Well this meathead obviously didn't like wot he had just heard because I could see him fiddling with something inside of the car by the door (no it wasn't that! Fuck off; I'm trying to be serious). I looked over at him and asked wot he was doing and he replied, "stand six feet from the car and don't move", I asked why? And he just kept on repeating the same thing, "stand six feet away from the fuckin' motor son" he said in his East London gravelly voice. I asked wot was the fuckin problem and then he opened the car door and pointed to a small but very scary looking rifle at me head and repeated his favourite saying "stay six feet away from the car", (you can join in next time he says it) oh yeah, it changed this time as he said "stand six feet away from the car YOU CUNT!" Oh very nice language, I bet you don't kiss your mother with that dirty mouth do you I said? Wot! No I never said that, fuck please reader try and keep up and stop straying off from the fucking story.
Ok, well I did as I was told and tried conversing with them but they were having none of it, so I thought I'd best shut the fuck up and hold tight and pray the silly fuckin' bitch hadn't gone and stitched me up by running off with their money or something leaving me holding the fort and inevitably getting my noggin' blown off.

Oh no that wasn't to be the case as I was about to be rescued from a hippie in one of the caravans behind me, yes some old fuckin' nutter with a shot gun had witnessed the whole thing and was now trying in his own way to get me bleedin' head blown off by pointing his shot gun straight at these two retards heads from his caravan and saying to them if you wanna shoot him then I'm gonna shoot you?!

Great, cooool, cheers, thanks a fuckin' lot mate, that's all I needed, a well wishing hippie with a fuckin' gun on my side. SO there I stood two nutters with a gun facing me one way and behind me a hippie pointing a double barrelled shot gun straight past my head aiming at them, plus if he did fire the gun it would in fact hit me as I was in line of fire?

Well we all stayed in a stand off position for seemed to me to be a lifetime when the girl came back all happy holding whatever it was they were trading and she ran up to them and as if by magic like nothing had happened they said cheers to her said sorry for the misunderstanding to me she gave me a kiss on the cheek (like I really needed that) stuck a gram or two of Charlie into my hand the hippie in the van asked me in for a drink which I took him up on and everything went back to abnormal as usual! Fuck, shit scary bloody hippies ah?

That night I went to see HAWKWIND play as it was Solstice night and the DRUIDS where doing their thing up at the stones. So I ventured up there coz you could go up there then they stopped people the year after I think but any way up I went met a young lady got stoned and fucked her on one of the stones at midnight real magical it was too (not really, I did give her one but it wasn't magical, and we got told off by the Druids for spoiling their ceremony. Tuff, my balls needed a ceremony of their own, and it was an ancient act too! As I did her from behind, so as I could watch the Druids chanting).

After getting thrown out of the stones we went down the front of the stage and enjoyed Hawkwind do their thing.

The next night I had a musical moment of my own as I ventured into a tent around ten o'clock or sometime like that and there was a jam session going on so I joined in and played my little heart out only stopping now and again for a hit of speed that I had hidden behind one of the amps. So every now and 'gain I would let someone else play for an hour or so and I would go and have a fix then come and play, so cool. I did this from around ten until the early morning fucking great watching the sun come up while playing JIMI HENDRIX solo's and the smell of wood burning fires and food still on the stove from the night before, you never get them senses out of your head bloody magic maaaan!

The next day or so I was getting quite worse for wear and slept for two whole days and nights only waking as somebody was driving back to Ealing to sign on the dole and there was space for me if I wanted to go so I went.

I slept all the way there so by the time we arrived back in London I was still with my stone henge hat on (I mean as in, I was still dressed with all the Alice cooper make up on, I had my machete still stuck down the outside of my boots and a hand held axe hanging off of my trousers my hair hadn't seen a comb for a week and a half so I looked like a fuckin' cave man totally unaware of this I walked into Ealing dole office and everyone ran out as it must have looked as though I had come to start a war in there or something, ha,ha,ha I didn't even catch on as I was getting angry because nobody would let me sign on until one of our lot came up to me and calmed me down then told me how fuckin outrageous I looked...fuckin great!

We all got our money and went back to the festival where I had some great fun and stuff. Shagged a couple more birds, took more drugs, got into some ridiculous situations and basically had a fuckin' ball, then came home and slept for bloody ages.

A POEM
I WROTE THIS WHEN I WAS THIRTY FIVE
AND I WAS JUST ABOUT HALF WAY THROUGH
A BREAKDOWN.

KILL, KILL COUNCIL ESTATE.

Kill, kill council estate
Full of anger, full of hate
Kill, kill council estate
Spike a dead and rotting puppy on Iron Gate.

Four in the morning still awake
Neighbours on a curfew coz there's no four minute warning
Soon it'll be light, catch the ravers returning
Fear and loathing with a dash of psychosis

Prozac the neighbours, oh isn't it great

Used to be one of the chosen few
Looking all around me all I seem to see is frozen spew
Wot ever happened to the likely lads
Grew into junkies, straights and fags

Prozac the innocent bystanders, oh isn't it great

Kill, kill council estate
Full of anger, full of hate
Kill, kill council estate
Mug and rape your grandmother, then serve her up on a plate

It's really fun down here on the council funny farm
Marshmallow hypodermic keeps ya quiet and calm

Prozac attack
Aint no fun, I wanna shoot my G.P.
But they won't give me a gun

I really like the jacket
But the sleeves are much too long
So, give me back my drugs and let me finish righting this song
Charlie Manson   -
Where are you now
Coz every city's got one
Oh isn't it fun

Party, party council estate
Couldn't give a monkeys
Isn't it great!
Party, party council estate
Now they've taken my brain
Everything's great

FLICKNIVES AT DAWN

IT WAS THE ONLY WAY that Frenchy Gloder (of Flicknife Records infamy) and myself could have met.... In a police cell somewhere in the West End after both of us had been arrested for fighting (not each other). On release we walked back to Shepherds Bush and to Frenchy's house where he lived with Gina. They had 'Flicknife' Records up and running by then and of course we had quite a lot in common, parents of Mediterranean descent, music etc. He'd signed up all of the bands I was into at the time (wot a result!)...free records...clothes, basic black leathers and our own customising, something left over from hippie days, oh yeah... and yawwwn...MR BROWNSTONE. Yes, still chasing the fuckin' dragon (you would have thought I might have caught it by now). Sorry to go on and on about smack, it gets a little boring after a while, don't you think, reader?

SO WE SCORED of course, and a new friend and scoring partner was born. Many adventures can be told of our exploits and gigs. 'Alice in Wonderland' nightclub in Soho opened a short time later where we managed to shag all the girls (and in my case beat up so many undeserving arsehole 'musos' - you know who you are... a buncha fakers and fraudsters). Together we mourned the deaths of truly righteous friends and were at each other's first born (hi to Jesse James, Tyhge) and later on Frenchy's cash helped me try and get a project up and running. We'll talk of this later...

I *had* decided to wrap this collection of recollections up at around the age of 25-30, but here are a few snippets and highlights of events that were to follow in the future for me...

AROUND the age of 23, I formed a band with Wattie's brother (of The Exploited) Terry. The band was called SERIOUS DAMAGE and we were a 'crossover' punk-metal outfit, fitting in with others of that ilk such as G.B.H, Anti-Nowhere League etc. These were the bands that were 'flying the flag' and I loved it. After many rehearsals and auditions, finding members was so bleeding hard, they either looked the part but couldn't string two chords together, or played well but were total freaks of nature (ring any bells Garry?). Well I finally got a line-up together and we played a few gigs around London, one being a strange line-up of us (Serious Damage), The UK Subs, the Exploited and Crass, I think that was it. This all fell apart when I beat up the drummer, so back to old school friends...

I was frequenting a bar at this time called BUMBLES in Acton; the place was run by Mannie and his family. Now Bumbles was supposed to be a wine-bar, but unfortunately all of Mannie's mates and acquaintances used it (another book could be written of the exploits at this little 'harmless-looking from the outside' bar, with it's little bee above the sign outside) but Mannie had bands playing and there was a strong community of old that would gather there at the weekends (it was fuckin' brill). Well I formed a band with Derek Gibbs (of The Satellites as mentioned earlier); basically I was going back to 'school'.

The band was originally formed for a birthday party and the line-up consisted of myself, Derek, Skinhead Andy (Brutal attack) and Steve Brown on drums. Wot a bunch of misfits. I had a name hanging around so I called ourselves THE LONDON

LOSERS. We were ok and did quite a few gigs around London; the Clarendon Hotel in Hammersmith was a favourite, on the 'Klub Foot' nights, loads of girls, loads of speed, loads of fighting. Unfortunately we seemed to recapture our youth a bit too much and most gigs ended in a punch up. We made a demo but argued so much that we called it a day.

It was during the Bumbles time that Gaz and myself would get together again, as I got married there, well not there exactly, but 'round the corner in Acton Registry Office and Garry and Andy were best men. The wedding went ok even though we were coming to the end of our relationship (it was a last ditch), Lynne was pregnant with my boy Sonny, the only good thing to come of it all really.

I was now hanging out more and more with Frenchy, we would spend hours waiting for the 'man', in the backs of cars, sitting in pubs sharing half a lager for wot seemed like days, hanging on the telephone and waiting in some of the most ugliest and scariest squats in downtown London. Frenchy seemed to be quite versed in keeping it together and could get really shit-faced and you'd never know...hiding behind his John Lennon glasses. I was just a mess, running about, falling over, missing the point to everything...wot a nightmare...still.

I also would have a real problem in overdosing, I could overdose twice a week and more but none of these ever came to anything, but now I will tell the strangest of stories and you the reader can decide for yourselves...

FROM HERE TO ETERNITY
(AND BACK TO SHEPHERDS BUSH)

....Frenchy and myself had been out all day and scored a poxy little bag of brown. We went back to Frenchy's house and Lynne and Gina (Gina *never* took class 'A' drugs) were there. Gina I think was printing t-shirts or something and Lynne was waiting for a hit (no change there...) there wasn't enough to get smashed on but enough to keep the turkey at bay, stop the shivers and such...I had just got the needle in when I overdosed. Now I must stress that wot happened after is pretty weird and I have no explanations for it and two stories are to be told.

Frenchy, Gina and Lynne were left with me overdosed in the armchair, according to Frenchy my heart had stopped three times and I was out for at least an hour, blue lips, white face and the house in panic. As we were all now pretty well specialised in the art of bringing people 'round, while also knowing when you've got a goner on your hands, Frenchy was doing every trick in the book, mouth to mouth, banging my chest, throwing buckets of cold water over me and quite a panic had set in.

On the other hand, I was now on a very different trip altogether... now I can only tell it as it happened, I had injected a 'washout' (the last bit in the spoon) and immediately I was aware of standing in a room with no walls, no ceiling, no floor, but white....brilliant white.

I had no recollection of wot Frenchy was going through at this time. I was straight, not stoned and obviously fully aware as I can recall it all perfectly as I'm writing this. There was no panic, no fear, just confusion...I wanted to know where I was and wot was going on. I was swearing quite a lot and remember thinking that maybe I should tone it down...I asked, no, demanded to be told where the fuck I was and why I was brought here. Totally lucid, I started to suspect that this might be a whole lot scarier than just some weird dream I might be having. Then there was a very aware feeling of 'Oh shit, you've done it this time' and proceeded to ask for some answers (but not really wanting to know, as I had a good idea wot was happening). Anyway I asked to speak to (no way can you say the word 'God') someone...then there was a voice, not a spoken voice but a feeling...'who would I like to be representative?'

Well I didn't really know the bible, wouldn't recognise any of them anyway, so it would have be someone dead who I trusted...but who? I didn't know that many people that were dead, so I put whatever was going on, to the test (the cheek of it), I asked for Jimi Hendrix. Yes Jimi Hendrix (you can put the book down now if ya like, but I'm only telling it like it was, it seems just as ridiculous to me but...) well there he was, Jimi Hendrix, large as life (not a pun) standing in front of me, no smoke or mirrors just me and Jimi. I asked him wot the fuck was going on and he answered 'Behind me are all the people for you to meet....' I looked and I knew nobody, lots of faces, all merged together, and some looked really old and important but I hadn't a clue. I said with total clarity that I did not know these people and the reply was to look behind myself. On doing this I saw my wife, my daughter, Frenchy, a whole lot of friends and family all smiling and beckoning me over and one little boy standing out from the crowd. I had no idea who he was at the time but on reflection, he was near his sister.

The next thing I was asking to go home and as if by a flick of a second there was Frenchy standing over me, hitting me about the head, I was soaking wet, Lynne was crying and I started crying. I never told them of wot had happened for a good six months or more until I was watching the t.v and there was a programme about after-life experiences. Well I've never been religious and it never made me want to join any weird sect...There's no moral to any of this but..... four years later my unplanned son was born, I had given up heroin, my relationship with their mother was over and I fought in the courts for three whole years and finally won custody of my children and brought them up as a one-parent family.

A POEM...
(By S.Redman)

SWEET SWEET SUICIDE

Suicide, sweet, sweet suicide
Releasing me once and for all from this mortal coil
The ultimate dilemma
Should I stay or should I go
Could I or couldn't I
Is it bravery or is it a sin
Or if I do shall my fate be
To be reborn and do it all again
This time not as a man but a mouse
The mocking punishment for a cheating
Life.

Suicide, sweet, sweet suicide
You exist as a temptress
A warm and safe haven for lost souls and misguided lives
I sometimes yearn to be held in your arms
To fall asleep in the bosom of endless dreams

THE ULTIMATE EUPHORIC VALIUM MIND STATE

And sometimes I can't believe my very thoughts
Of cowardness and fear
Where is the fighter where is the lover where is the father

The cavalier
When life is high
And all is well
You disappear into the wind
The faded memory, of a man I know
Love, hate but ultimately fear.

MALICE IN BLUNDERLAND
OR-
A NIGHTMARE ON MEARD STREET, W.1.

As stated before in the chapter 'Flicknifes at dawn' Frenchy and I struck up quite a friendship and before long we started hanging out in ALICE IN WONDERLAND or GOSSIPS of Meard Street, across the road from the INTREPID FOX in Wardour Street W.1.

Frenchy was to play a big part of the club back then releasing an album of bands and stuff, he'll go on to tell you about this later, I on the other hand had a great time in 'Alice's', pulling girls on the back of ZODIAC MIND FUCKIN' WARP ! ! !

Northern prat....

He used to make tea for Chris Need's and Frenchy back in the day apparently a good cartoonist but when YOUTH got hold of him and put the band together I was right pissed off (gutted) as they all seemed to look like me ?

So everywhere I went for a good six months or so I was asked if I was this zodiac mind warp cunt.

No I fuckin wasn't, so when I met the man in question in the toilets of 'Alice's' one night it wasn't a very good reception for him, twat. He was having a piss and started talking to me in a fuckin' American accent 'plonker', it was then that I realised it was this zodiac geezer everybody was on about, well I turned to him and asked if he was in deed a bleeding yank and he replied no so I said why the fuck are you talking like one you stupid fuckin dick!?

He seemed bemused at my response and then reverted back to his native tongue of Mark Manning the fuckin' northerner, and I felt he was somewhat backward rowing as he obviously realised that I wasn't one of the regular dress up like a biker wear a bit of make up and look like a cunt for the night party brigade and I had a beef or could have one or as it happens was gagging to.

So when he started talking northern (eeeh uuuooop moooon, duuuaaaont yaa naa ooo I aaum leeek moon) or something like that I dunno I'm not a fuckin' real writer I'm making half this shit up as I go along! Ooop's that's let the cat out of the proverbial bag. Good, any hwoo mon I replied yes you? you must be that cunt zodiac car boot or whatever ya stupid name is and ya nicking my image that I've fought long and hard to perfect to this grandiose perfection of yobbery, and promptly goaded him to smack me in the jaw, (PRAT).
Yes you've guessed it (he pooped his pants) and I think I ear slapped him (can't swear to it as I was drunk, and my memories could come back to haunt me).
Ha, ha, ha!
Well he never did admit it when we became nearly associates on a couple of projects but who cares (sue me motherfucker) COBOLT STARGAZER or JEFF did help out on the CLUB BASTADOS E.P. and did a great job apart from getting all carried away with himself and as everyone else recorded it for me for pizza and speed he after the fact demanded payment to the ridiculous value of £200.00. Well apparently JOE my partner in crime with the club had offered it to him but he never told me about it so when I got a threatening letter from Cobolt (JEFF) demanding his £200.00 squid. I told him to go fuck himself. Later on I bumped into him with their new bass player at the ASTORIA THEATRE on one of the rock nights I think or

some cunt's press do, I forget, he bowled over to me all bold as brass and demanded his cash .... Ha, ha, ha. Are you sure? I wasn't having any of it as I was already pissed off with him sending me that stupid arse letter, well I saw red and told him in no uncertain terms to go fuck himself and he could have something on account if he'd like, he said "yes" ... SO I GAVE HIM AND THE BASS PLAYER A HEADBUTT. That seemed to do the trick; they both walked off holding their bruised bonces proclaiming that he was going to talk to Joe and tell him wot I did and wot a big bully that I was.

FFFFFUCK OOOFFF

BLOODY POSERS......

Having said all this, they did add, a few months later, an excellent twist to my sex life, (I slept with them all....).

Nooooooo, but I started to get girls thinking I was zodiac and as they were flavour of the day they wanted to sleep with him. Well even though I was peeved at the poser side of things I couldn't very well miss the fact that if I played along a bit, my sex life would get marginally better not that it was flagging in any way but hey if long haired leather wearing tattooed swastika badge and steel toe cap boots were in, bring it on.

CHEERS MAAATE.... A big thank you must go out to Mark Manning. So once again, nice one (maaaan), boy did I get laid! I never admitted to being zodie, even so most of the time they didn't seem to care FASHION BLOODY FASHION... oh well if ya can't beat them – beat them up. Ahaa no, join them that's it...

Oh while we're here Frenchy has got a few words he would like to be noted on said Mindwarp.

In the words of FRENCHY SIZZORHANDS, "I remember one night in particular Steve and myself were in the back bar of 'ALICE IN WONDERLAND' when up came the Mindwarp and for some reason was looking at my leather cut off gloves. Now the band had just had some success and were flaunting themselves unashamedly around the place as if they near fuckin' owned it. Well some people have very short memories and this night the said Zodiac found himself getting out of his depth when he asked, no demanded, that I hand over my gloves, wot a stupid question to ask; for one, I wouldn't have and for two, as he was about to recall Zodiac or Mark had been my fuckin' tea boy only a couple of years previous. So when confronted by this stupid question I answered him with like answer and told him that he obviously had not recognised me now that I had changed my appearance by having a dred lock hair do and was going through a very colourful time in my choice of clothing. Anyway as I reminded him of who I actually was he then looked quite sheepish as he remembered and apologised as a good tea boy should!!!"

Another memorable night I can remember was when the bloke from QUADRAPHENIA you know the mod, with the eye liner and stuff well I had a bit of charley for sale so in a back room behind the doctor's booth, he of DOCTOR AND THE MEDICS he used to do the DJ. Spot and sometimes we used it to take drugs in. Well on this occasion about five or so people gathered backstage and we all chipped in and scored a couple of grams of coke. After the deal was done we were having a line up and I designated my twenty pound note for the honours, well everyone had their snort and this geezer was last in the line so he had the twenty in his hand after having his snort.
Well instead of giving it back to yours truly he pocketed it himself the bastard and when I asked for it back he denied he had it. Well I wasn't having that (here we go again) so after asking him a few times he started to argue that he never took it and was getting really shitty about the whole matter and people

were now telling me to leave it out as if I was the one causing all the agro. I must say I had been very patient, as I really did think he thought he gave it back as why would he want to steal twenty squid from me, surely he wasn't that fuckin skint or maybe he was just that out of it but anyway he kept on and on saying that he never took the cash, the lying twat. So the tempers were getting high and I was to be honest pretty fucked up and finding it ever harder to keep a cool head, when suddenly one of his friends (actually it was the geezer in YOU RANG ME LORD. Won't say who!) spoke up.

So he in his infinite wisdom thought that by telling me that this arsehole was in a film that I should know would in someway detract from the matter in question and calm things down, (bollocks). It was like leading a gaggle of mods into a screwdriver gig .... Ha, ha, ha.....

I was told, did you know that he was the main bloke in QUADRAPHENIA and I said who was that then all casual like, and he said leading him straight into my trap.

THE MOD!!?

OH, I said, well if you haven't noticed I'm a fuckin' biker and weren't you if I'm not wrong the top mod or as they called you the FACE ...

Yes was the answer, wrong answer, as I told him well I might as well get my mod then as I'm here and you've stolen my twenty fuckin' pound note ya cunt

And with that (you've guessed it) I give him a boot in the nutzzzz... ha, ha, ha that told him he fell to the ground I was held off jumping on the wanker but I did reach into his top pocket and low and behold wot did I find there, yep you guessed it, my twenty fuckin' pound note, how did I know it was mine well it had traces of Charlie on it..

GOT ME MY MOD AS WELL ....

BACK OFF BOOGALOO.

Apart from the 'Alice in Wonderland' club, I used to frequent all the others at the time too, THE WAG, THE HIPPODROME, THE LIMELIGHT, THE SAN MORITZ. AND THE SLIME-LIGHT and a host of others. One of my fave friends at this time would be RINGO STAR'S DAUGHTER... LEE STARKY. I met her one night at the Hippodrome in the West End and struck up quite a good friendship (I must say now, as she'll have the fuckin' dogs out looking for me if I don't tell's ya the truth. Lee was a mate, a bloody good one actually for around four years, and so with her and a crowd of others that I will no doubt tell you of later we had some great fun times and it was a pleasure knowing her, but I have to state clear she was never my girlfriend and unfortunately for her (snigger) ! I NEVER GOT TO SINK THE PINK ... ok LEE.

I even wrote a bleedin' song about her called, SHE SAID NO!

Ya know the way it goes boys ....if we did I would lose my respect for ya?

I don't want to spoil our friendship, Blah, blah, blah.

Why didn't she just say you're a good laugh but I don't want that thing near me!

Well we had some good times together and I will and still do treasure them warmly, unfortunately as like most of the other people that I've named in the book I can't really go into too much stuff nor can I go into any detail of any kind (shame, you'd love it..) for fear of libel and stuff as I've mentioned her name but we had some brilliant fun and boy could that little girl put some booze away (I can say that, cant I?). She would still be standing or at least conscious well after the rest of us were asleep or in a state of fluffy cloud slumber. We used to go to the HARD ROCK CAFÉ in Marble Arch or is it Hyde Park, who knows it was cool as she'd been going there ever since she could remember so we never queued up and got in straight away plus we got free drinks and stuff. I had some great times there. I remember one night standing at the bar and these two solid burly looking guerrilla sized blokes were staring me out so I cautiously strutted my cock sure self over to where they stood and asked them wot they were staring at? The reply was, in a heavy American accent, "you maaan we thought you might be an English hells angel", (ha, ha.) "Not really big enough, or regimental enough to be honest really gov".

But as I supposedly dressed the part, did look like a biker (and I was, a little later in an M.C. CLUB) but I would have thought that the lack of a patch saying Hells Angel would have given the game away?

Anyway, we got talking and one of them was ok but the other was a real PIG and I didn't take to him at all well. It turns out that they had to take some time out as they were involved in the L.A. riots and were waiting for things to cool down as they were two of the cops that had been a bit too eager to smash the skull in of that black geezer (can't remember his name, don't really care) and all hell was breaking loose back home and well I think they were due for a white boy lynching so here they were in old blighty keeping a low profile, cool, (wot goes around, comes around, ah boys).

So I had a few drinks with them and then they wanted to have their photo taken with me. Ok so I stood in-between the both of them and Lee took the pic's, I think I do however remember doin' the rabbit ear sign behind the mouthy one's big fat stupid Neanderthal like head.

When they had finally finished posing with me, I really wanted to wind them up so I asked politely if I could in fact see their badges. They showed them to me and at this point while being full of mud slider drinks vodies and orange with more than a

snifter of Charlie the Cocaine Kid up me nose flute, I had the brilliant idea of running off with one of their badges and tried to secure a plot as to how I could get out of the hard rock without them catching hold of me. Well the plan was just sorted and I managed to get one of them to let me hold the badge when Lee got wind of what was about to happen and pulled me to one side and gave me a grilling lecture etc. about how everybody knew her bla,bla,bla, but she was right like always. So there's no great ending to this story, shame though as I would have really liked to have robbed one of the coppers that was in that riot, would have made better reading (sorry).
And a small fortune on ebay.

EVER SEEN A NIGGER WITH A BLACK EYE!

Now hears a story involving me, Lee Starky, Joe Devlin, Bella and Smithy.

ASTORIA THEATRE.
Scene is set, there was a lack of Billy Wizz around at the time and this was when 'loadsa money' the character played by Harry Enfield was all the rage and funnily enough we were loaded pretty much of the time due to our alternative lifestyle and currency adventures, but with no amphetamines in our blood we all got pissed real quick and well you know where that leads don't ya, yes (BANG IN TROUBLE). Well we were having it large at the Astoria on this particular night but there was a strange mood to the evening not the usual fun stuff and it all felt a bit heavy and stuff.

Everything seemed to be going ok for a while then Smithy decided to start getting stroppy and as usual picked on the smallest bloke he could find (Smithy was a roadie to everyone at the time and thought he was a bit of a chap, Pratt if you ask me, you're not, sorry oh well, I'll say it anyway prat, prat, prat, bully, enough!).

So on picking on this smaller half-caste geezer who was a face that we knew but never really talked to, he found that this particular bloke in question wasn't such an easy pushover. So when Smithy tried bullying him, this guy gave him a right hander that shook old Smithy boy and he realized that he may have been a bit to hasty as to have picked on this particular individual, so he went and got the security that we all knew and tried to get him thrown out. But by this time this particular geezer wasn't having any of it and stood his ground (great I thought, as Smithy turned to me for back up and I told him where he could stick it), as he had started it then he should finish it but the poo was already starting to show and he was making a big fuss instead of getting on with the fight which I must say I was fuelling by saying go on hit him, you started it!!!
SHIT STIRRING I THINK IT'S CALLED good, plonker, well it all got out of hand and everybody started to fight, it was great, the bouncers didn't know what to do and it was just going off all night everywhere. I can't remember where Smithy went as the row had now gone from the initial dude to now Joe who was not listening to me and was helping his old buddy Smithy, unfortunately for Joe Devlin.
Description….. Joe was half caste, stood around six foot four quite heavily built, lovely bloke but could have it if the need be. Well this small individual was all over him and to tell the truth I think Joe was gutted that such a short arse could do so much damage but he give as good as he got and fought for ages. I was off fighting other people I have no idea who or for what, it was great, a real free for all….
Yeeeeeeee, haaa.

What I do remember is that Lee and Bella were getting frightened and wanted out of there and as I was covered in blood 'n' stuff they grabbed hold of my arms and told me in no uncertain terms to stop it and go with them out the back door as the police were being called, so off we went. Once outside we were waiting for a cab when the nightclub doors flung open like some wild west film and flew this geezer with Joe still trying to put an end to it but this particular bloke was as tuff as old boots and so as our cab arrived just in time we managed to bundle Joe in the back and off we sped with everyone else including the hard nut getting quizzed by Mr Plod and Co.

Back at Lee's Mum's house Maureen (RINGOS FIRST WIFE) and great lady r.i.p. we all went there to get over the night's adventure and clean up, so funny as the chapter name suggests. On opening the door to their Hyde Park mansion type thing house with a million security cameras and such stuff, Maureen stood there stunned looking at the spectacles in front of her. All of us covered in blood (none of it I must say, ours) apart from I had a few small cuts and bruises but Joe had the best one liner greeting that I've ever heard especially as Maureen had never met Joe before and there stood this six foot plus black man covered in blood being held up by her daughter and friend Bella and with no hesitation Joe say's, "HI, BET YOU'VE NEVER SEEN A NIGGER WITH A BLACK EYE!".
Fucking class, well we went inside and Maureen made us dinner and patched up Joe's bloody face and we all had a good laugh, and carried on drinking until the early hours or at least until they got bored of me still holding my can of Pils lager from the Astoria as she asked at one point in the evening why have you still got that can of beer as she had gone down into the cellar and brought up a case of fuck off expensive wine and didn't notice

me drinking any of it. I put the final nail in me social coffin by telling her I had infact been topping up my beer with the said Beaujolais bleeding 190 wot ever fuckin' year it was (totally wasted on me) so on hearing this she calmly called me an uncouth ill mannered piece of shit, laughed, got up from her chaiselonge bid us good night and promptly went off to bed.......

HELL FIRE AND DAMNATION, IN OLD AMSTERDAM... HORACE AND ME...

Ok let me begin this story with a bit of background, IT all started with DAVE (LUSH) who at the time was playing with a band called the HELL FIRE CLUB. This was a band made up from some guitarist of popular fame although I never knew who he was, apparently he was supposed to
play for or have something to do with the PSYCHADELIC FURS or some shit like that. Then there was RAVEN from KILLING JOKE a blinding geezer who could party till you dropped, (most excellent) RAT SCABIES of the DAMNED and BRIAN JAMES, and I think at the very start they had that annoying bloke from Thin Lizzy, BRIAN ROBERTSON but he left and so did the two DAMNED PLAYERS and so in stepped STEVE HOLLAND a local boy on drums (he joined F.T.W. later and TRASH from ZODIAC on bass, replacing RAVEN, oh yeah and TRASH later helped out on the CLUB BASTADOS E.P. that I made for me night club, CLUB BASTADOS (I'll give myself a mention there). Well they had great things mentioned for them and a few deals and such were being mused at in the pipe line. Enough of them, now on to me and Horace, a very much better story. Ha, ha, ha.

I was playing in my own band of drug taking misfits the LONDON LOSERS and having a great time at that, when Dave and HELL FIRE CLUB got this gig in Holland just outside of

AMSTERDAM coooool, now, everyone wanted to go. There must have been around twenty or so that initially put there names up for going to Amsterdam for the crack... (Speed, coke, puff, etc) hum, hum, staring at naked women in glass rooms and generally doing all the usual things you do in Amsterdam. Well as per usual the list was getting marginally less in number as the gig was approaching, more and more people were now pleading poverty not being able to get time off work, not being able to raise adequate funds, their girlfriends would not let them go to Amsterdam on their own, and the like.

Well it whittled it's way down to me and Horace, now Horace and myself knew of each other but had never actually spoken wot with people saying he was a nutter and the same about my good self and us both having a particular acquaintance known to us both and not best liked or really needed in our lives (we didn't want him nor his bloody gaggle of motorcycle enthusiasts there, none the less we was all in fact a part of the same large circle of friends and that was that). Only trouble was I thought that Horace was creeping up this individual's arse and not known to me he in fact thought the same of me and so we decided not to really get acquainted with each other, until this gig arrived on our doorsteps and was now clear that we were going to be the only two (fans) for a better word...... that were now left going, so something had to be done!

I think it was myself that asked for Horace's phone number and we talked and came to the decision that we would go together and to hell with everyone else. Only trouble was I was one of the people without sufficient funds so a cunning plan arose where I had a motorcycle for sale and Horace knew of someone gullible enough to buy it!

You can see a pattern emerging already can't you reader. Horace brought this guy round to my house and between the both of us managed to convince this bloke that this was the bike he was looking for and that at the price I was selling it for he would be indeed insane, if he didn't take it on the spot, one chance only, I've got someone else coming round in a moment that will definitely buy it, so the special price that was on offer, a poultry four hundred quid (just wot I needed as it happens to go to Amsterdam), well as you already must have realized MUG he bought it, and the next day we were off.

Now the band Hell Fire Club had no funds as such to get there so they decided to drive and catch the ferry (bollocks to that). Horace and me went by air on the Friday morning, the band left on the Saturday morning, I think to get there for the afternoon and then get onstage in the evening as they were topping the bill as this great new rock act from London, mmmmmmmmm.
Funny thing happened at the airport I recall, as Horace was wearing a flack jacket (you know the ones, they have a million and one pockets in them, all zips and secret compartments).
Well when we eventually arrived at the departure lounge and finally got to passport control, the woman on the desk asked for our tickets and passports and so as we were handing them over the woman asked if we had anything in our pockets that should go through the scanner act!
Bollocks, big mouth here thought it was his cue to make a stupid arse joke about Horace having stashed a lump of dope in one of the pockets, why, why, why, can't I just shut my big fuckin' mouth.
Because I can't? And so they in turn decided to go through every single pocket, zip, secret stash place you name it they searched it, oh well it was all done in good humour, or at least I was laughing (dick head).
So after this slight setback we eventually boarded the plane and I kept my mouth shut just in case.

When we eventually arrived, oh yes, I must get back to the original story and fill you in on why we hadn't been so eager to meet before now as you know it was all down to our mutual non-friend so when we both had time it became abundantly clear as we spoke of the matter and had a lengthy in-depth warble with each other and realized we both in fact thought he was a complete and utter prat..

So now that was over, everything else was plain sailing, so we went forth to enjoy our first morning in Amsterdam. When we arrived we decided to catch a cab as we were determined to be as decadent as we could and train travel was definitely out, so on our arrival in the central city we paid the cab driver and got out of the cab when Horace turned to me and asked, "Do you know where we can score some coke?" I replied by saying that I had been there just a few months before and I knew of only one person and on saying this as if by some unforeseen divine interventative act of chance there stood standing but only a roach throw away from us was the very man in question!

Bloody bollocks I couldn't believe my luck plus it made me look cool and great especially as we approached him and he remembered me and asked how I was, so I told him of our dilemma and he said to our surprise that he had in fact got just two grams of the finest flaky stuff from somewhere I don't know nor do or did I care, where it came from just let me give you money and we'll be off, and so it was!

After scoring we decided to find some digs, that was easy enough, the first place we asked had a room cheap enough and seedy enough for our needs so we were in. We unpacked then we racked out a line of the Peruvian sansquach south American gypsy mountain people food, that hit the fuckin spot ZZZZZ-WWWACK and off we went in search of space (oh, no that's a hawkwind record?).

Anyway we eventually came to a bar that looked ok; it was in fact the Hell's Angel bar THE OTHER PLACE. In we went, ordered a beer each asked for their puff menu and scored some paki black and some skunk I think. Then there was this sailor sitting next to us that was worse for wear and really being a fuckin' nuisance. We tried our best at avoiding his unrepentant abuse and neither of us wanted to get into a fight especially in the angels gaff, and especially as we'd just got there, but this cunt just wouldn't shut the fuck up and after a while I asked the gov'ner, some big old angel if it was all right to put an end to his abuse and I think it came just in time as everyone was getting fucked off with him, so we hit him with the ashtray, said something to the sound of, "Fuck off cunt or you'll get a proper pasting", you know the sort of stuff and the angel agreed and so he was tossed out and we carried on drinking our drink .

Now we left there and decided to go to another bar where we felt safe and could go quite freely to the bog and have a line when it suited us, as you know in Amsterdam dope's cool but they get uptight if ya caught with powder up ya nose, but here they seemed to turn a blind eye. Well we stayed for a while then decided to go and find another bar to frequent. On walking around for a while we saw a place that looked real friendly like so in we went, cool, all the people were so very inviting they said "hi" and got us a beer, they seemed to know just what we wanted and everything so we stayed then we went off on another journey but everywhere seemed a bit miserable apart from this other drinking hole that seemed so very welcoming just like the last two so in we ventured and sure enough it was the same greeting and everything, it was in fact then that it dawned upon us mainly as the barmaid was now looking very familiar and knew exactly what we wanted that it all became clear.

WE HAD BEEN WALKING ROUND THE FUCKIN' BLOCK
There weren't loads of bars with these people in that were so
welcoming at all, it was in fact the same fuckin' bar.....!!! Wot a
couple of prize arseholes...

Ha, ha, ha, how we laughed. Not?

Next, stupid thing that was to happen that was not on the
agenda was the whole saga of my ring! No not wot ya thinking,
I'm talking about a ring that you wear on you're finger ok.

It was the smallest ring on the pinkie, yes just to make matters
more camp and outwardly stupid looking, I had worn all my
skull rings from the GREAT FROG but unfortunately my little
finger decided to swell up thus wedging the ring and fixing it on
tight. Now this may sound pathetic and all in all it sort of was,
apart from the fact that I couldn't get the bleeding thing off, I
tried everything I could even asked the landlord if he had a file
no, and he pointed me in the direction of the police station, so
off we went, found the cop shop went in asked for the desk
sergeant and bashfully waved my pinkie at him telling him how
it hurt and where could we find the hospital to which he replied
"FUCK OFF", yep now how's that for tourist information
"FUCK OFF AND GO AWAY" was the next thing he said in a
broad Dutch miserable piggish voice, so off we fucked..... My
hand by now was starting to swell up and it was now not becoming such a joke as it was really fuckin' hurting. There was a bar
SUSIE'S SALOON another biker bar so we went in for a beer
and to try to find out where the hospital was, once inside we
were talking to each other when a barmaid overheard us and
said she may be able to help, cool, she came back with one of
the Dutch angels. He must have stood six foot four plus and
weighed twenty stone. I thought he'd have taken one look and
laughed at my predicament and walk off to tell about this dick
in the bar with the swollen finger but surprising as it was he was
a fuckin' cool dude and said that he could have it off in a couple

of seconds (I knew he wasn't talking about his sex life and I didn't make one of my stupid little innuendo jokes, as this was definitely not the time nor place for such witterings) he actually led us out back and into their garage where he placed my swollen finger into a vice and produced a file, not just any old file this bastard was around two foot long and comparing it to my little finger then comparing it to him the scale was most definitely well out of proportion (shit and pants, spring to mind). But this guy couldn't have been more professional if he'd tried and with just a couple of smooth strokes he managed to saw the offending jewellery off, thus letting my blood run free once more and all was ok.

After this, we ventured inside where HE bought us both a drink and we had a bit of a joke about my predicament and that was that. Then a Dutch police officer came into the bar, I thought oh well here we again. This time judging him on the first old bill we'd encountered in the police station but nothing could be further from the truth as this guy sat next to me as I was about to roll a joint, now I know you can roll joints in Amsterdam but I still get itchy doing it in front of plod but this particular officer seemed to enjoy the awkward feeling that must have been so obvious to everyone and so he turned his head and asked if we was indeed tourists. Well Horace and I looked at each other then at him still cocked up by the way and feeling quite paranoid and said "yes", with this the officer pulled out from his jacket a block of wot seemed like red seal dope and asked if we had bought our dope from the coffee house. I said we had and he said that I should skin up from his stash as it was far better than anything we would be able to buy in the coffee shops!!! COOOOL, BIZARRE, and so I did and as I lit the joint it was apparent that he was not talking shit and that his shit definitely shit all over our shit and so with that he left, leaving both me and Horace shit faced.

That night is a bit of a blur to me and to Horace as we've tried recalling the night time activities and we can't fuckin' remember a whole lot apart from us going into a rather posh restaurant in the early evening and ordering a bit of dinner. Everything seemed ok until it started getting dark outside and the restaurant went into evening mode with the dimming of lights and this old cunt came out and started fucking around with this piano in the corner of the restaurant. We both made some childish jibes and mutterings about the place being empty and wouldn't it be funny if the piano player asked us if we would like a song played ......oh shit.

You know wot's coming now don't you, yes you've guessed it, the manager came over first and lit a candle on our table mmmmmm thanks, then he asked if everything was ok (like they do) so now it was getting quite romantic apart from the fact that there was only me and Horace in the whole fuckin' restaurant, so when the piano player got of up off his stool and walked towards us it wasn't such a funny joke when we said I bet he asks us what song we'd like him to play, bollocks and piss!

He did.... "Hallo", he said in this slarmy dagoish slightly gay voice, "how are you both this evening?" we both stared at each other then looked back at him and said all deep throatily,

"Yeah mate, we're all right, why?" Then he did it the bastard, I still don't know if they were taking the piss or wot but the fuckin' little wanker asked us,

"Is there a song you would both like to hear, a little something special maybe?"

I replied I thought in quite quick wit, "Yes, do you know FUCK OFF AND GO AWAY!!"

After that we both went on a journey of more drugs, I was after scoring a bag of smack but I knew Horace wasn't into that stuff but I said it and put it up as an option as we were both here together out of the realms of anything that was going on back home and to my surprise he said "yeah why not never did it, let's get some and see what all the fuss is about". We searched the back streets for a while until we finally came upon some horrible looking dodgy little black dude. He was standing in the shadows and as we passed by he stepped out and said in a wisped voice, "hey, would you like to buy some heroin?"

"Yes", we said and followed him down some dark alley way where he produced a small bag of brown powder, well I don't know if he was ripping us off or not so we took a chance and scored the twenty pound bag and went off back to our hotel room where we sprinkled some of the brown powder into a joint, then we added healthy spattering of cocaine and with that added some skunk and a bit of paki black hash, sheeeeeiit , this was gonna be one hell of a headfuckin' joint and surprise, surprise it was, damn did it take off so much so that I can't reveal anything that happened only that we ate much too much, we ended up in all sorts of bars and clubs but finally woke in the morning still in one piece and still holding our cash and we wasn't beaten nor raped and pillaged by the local rampaging gangs of dodgy biker types dressed in leather clad, chain dangling, wearing them stupid little leather caps that only dodgy old poof's would wear, thus luckily giving them away ...

The next day, this was now Saturday morning and the day of the gig in this park somewhere in the outskirts of AMSTERDAM. We had a map and so we made our way to the bus stop where we caught a bus straight there (I think). On our arrival we were met at an iron gate by some security, we introduced ourselves as being a part of the HELL FIRE CLUB entourage. Wot a stroke of luck that was as they knew all about us and this geezer came over and welcomed us both thinking we were in fact part of the band, so who were we to disagree and so we told him that we was indeed the HELL FIRE CLUB and with that he offers us this young guy to be our host and all round personal gofer for the day? (Fuckin cooool or wot!)

This bloke led us to our portakabin where we were both introduced to the mini bar that was stacked full to the brim with drink, wot a stroke of luck so we told him to fuck off and come back in an hour or so. Well on him leaving, we skinned up a couple of joints and racked out a few lines of our now very small wrap of Charlie, not to worry though as we were now getting pissed good and proper, only trouble was the promoters were getting quite annoying as it was getting late and the rest of the band hadn't arrived yet and we had no answers for them so we carried on getting drunk.

Around six o' clock in the evening the band arrived they were due to go on at seven o'clock, the door burst open and in they fell, all in a panic as they were caught in a ferry strike or something, I can't remember and I don't really care!

But they were all rock 'n' roll, agitated and where's our stuff and where's the rider drinks gone and who's been sleeping in my bed and who's been wearing my lipstick, and who's got my skirt, (you know the one, you do! It's pink and it's got frills with little kittens on .... Mmmmm). Oh, and who's - eaten all the fairy cakes, moan, moan, fuckin' moan.

And just to rub it in a bit more both Horace and myself turned to Dave and said, "hey man, we've left you a fuckin' line of coke maaaan, a light shone for a second in Dave's eyes as just for a second, just one that is, as he thought he could see maybe a glimmering twinkle of light at the end of this really gloomy looking saga of shit events.

And so with no hesitation we both looked at him straight in the eye and pronounced that the line of Charlie was infact UNDERNEATH HIS FUCKIN' HAND ALL THE FUCKIN BASTARDING TIME and he had wiped it clean off the table, ha,ha,ha, - hee, hee,hee – ho, ho fuckin' ho.
We laughed!
Wot a couple of cunts...

NEXT on the agenda was their gig, oh dear, what a disappointment. They went down like a sack of limp wristed half arsed, so far up their proverbial bum holeyoe with no stage presence and the crowd, wot was left of them booing, while Horace and me sat at the side of the stage finishing off the last of the beer in the two remaining crates, and having a right old chortle to our nasty selfish drug taking, beer stealing selves. Ha.
After the agonising performance was over they had to carry their own equipment back to the van as Horace and myself where in no fit state to barely walk let alone carry anything. After their van was filled it happened that the management had organized a meal or after show party for all the bands and security staff etc, so obviously Horace and myself invited ourselves along. Well after all that drinking and drug taking we needed some food in our bellies!
Now, everything seemed to go pretty well until I noticed that some of the security staff where eyeing Horace up and down and things seemed to get a little edgy, I asked 'round the table if anything was amiss but people were just saying that my mate with the rap around glasses, bowler hat and weighing around seventeen stone and looking real menacing was staring them all out and they thought he was gonna do something quite violent. I ventured over to him and asked Horace wot the beef was all about but he just sat there, blank faced and I must say fuckin' scary looking!!! (I was glad he was on my side, actually!) well I

was doing my surveillance thing and keeping a breast of things and was in ever more wonder as to what he was gonna do or come to that what it was that was pissing him off.

So I decided not to think about it anymore and get ready to back my now new friend that was turning in front of my very eyes into the local psychopath but hey I was with him, as I felt I should back him up best I could. So I collected a small arsenal of ammunition to help out when the shit hit the proverbial fan! Crap there was loads of them and at one point somebody said that all the security were off-work police officers, oh fuckin' great, that's all I needed not only a punch up that I knew we couldn't win but they were all pigs at that. FUCK, SHIT AND BOLLOCKS... cheer's Horace mate!!!

After a while, it was getting quite clear that the tension between them and us was getting well out of order and finally one of the security officers came over and asked me what was the problem with my friend and why would he not stop looking at em?

I decided to back him up by saying, in a ridiculous, trying my bestist to sound hard as I could voice, "I DON'T KNOW, WHY WOT'S THE FUCKIN' PROBLEM WITH YOU LOT". Pratt! Well as soon as I said this I nudged Horace and low and befuckin' hold......

HIS GLASSES FELL OFF ...... ARSE!!!

And we could all see that he was in fact all the time, fast a fuckin' bastard sleep!!!!! Mmmm aahhhrrr....

Nice one maaate. I looked a complete prat, but fortunately everyone else had thought the same thing (not that I looked like a Prat!) and we all had a big relieving laugh, then Horace woke up and I think he asked if there was anything else to eat.

After that fiasco, we were all by now worse for wear in one way or another and bed-ways was right-ways now and to my amusement I discovered that their management in their infinite wisdom had ordered them a Cadillac to pick them up from the gig and deliver them to a hotel for the night, cooool. Horace and me jumped into the limo leaving the band to argue who was getting in and who had to get a cab. We were both asleep and nobody was gonna kick us out, not with our day's incredible track record, so off we went to the hotel, cant remember anything about getting there but I do remember waking up the next day and staring into Horace's eyes and wondering wot the fuck he was doing in my bed, then I looked down and there was only me and Horace in the fuckin' bed and as for the band they were asleep and scattered all around the bed and floor with only Horace and myself bogarting their bed, as like a final piss take.

WELL I THOUGHT IT FUN TO FIT IN A SONG I WROTE MAYBE NOT THE MOST POLITICALLY CORRECT ...
BUT HEY!
(I actually stole the title from a single HORACE had released)

CHARLIE IS MY BEST MATE!

Charlie is my best friend Charlie is me mate
Charlie wants ya baby, gonna nail it to your gate
He's on a helter-skelter, going up and down
He's brought his family with him
And they're coming to your town

CHORUS

CHARLIE, CHARLIE, CHARLIE.
HE'S MY MATE …

VERSE 2
Sharon, Sharon, Sharon Tate, where is ya baby,
OH
He's hanging on the gate.
Charlie likes acid, getting out his head
Charlie won't be happy, until, we're all fucking dead

CHORUS

VERSE 3
Sitting in his prison cell, shaved off all his head
Who the fuck's he think he is
RIGHT SAID FRED?

He knows he's there for ever, does he really care
Sitting all alone, without no fuckin' hair

CHORUS. END.

HOPE YOU ENJOYED THAT LITTLE BIT OF FUN
AND NONSENCE!

I'M OUT A HERE ….THE ALTERED STATES OF UNITED EUPHORIA …

WHERE MICKY MOUSE IS KING
AND THE STATUE OF BIGOTRY IS QUEEN

1990 and I was now hanging out with Joe and a guy named LEE, (MARINE LEE) R.I.P.

Yep another one bites the dust; the SONS OF SATAN were re-patching the Club. I was in nightclub heaven while going for custody of my two kidz, at this time I was hanging out with two girls living in Portobello road, going out with one and occasionally shagging the other plus there were a couple of other girls on the scene (blowing my own crumpet I mean trumpet, and why not, YOU would too if it was your book so fuck off calling me a bragging wanker). Well back to the story, Joe and myself were making a good few bob at this and that and as I was about to get my kids and settle down (yeah, right) we thought we would get out of town and go on a fuck off holiday with all our ill gotten gains. I was at the time playing with my band of the time THE CHOSEN ONES and Frenchy yet again had put us into the studio and we had just cut the single with LES WARNER from the cult on drums, with BRAD and JOHN from BLAH on drums and vocals DAVE LUSH was supposed to be on vocals to but we had an argument and he went home. I can't remember wot it was about so who gives a shit!

The very next morning it was all very rock 'n' roll. Joe came round bright and early while SHAUN from the SCREAMING

MARIONETTES gave us a lift to the airport, we arrived and checked ourselves in. Now I must go back a bit, we booked our flights on a whim to LOS ANGELES and as we had loadsa money we booked shit hot apartments in the HOLIDAY INN in the centre of HOOLYWOOD cooool dude and pre-ordered a brand new BUICK motor to drive around in. Well all was good at the airport as I was flying not only on a jet to the states but on three grammes of Billy Whizzzz and four cans of Tenants Stupor, all this at seven in the morning, yes I know stupid cunt but I thought it was all good rock 'n' roll plus I thought it was only a four hour flight to L.A. X. (wot a big Prat). So we boarded the plane I had my brand new cut of our record on tape that we had only just finished the night before and I was now really pumped!!

I should have guessed that something was amiss as when I asked Joe if he too would like a couple of grams of speed he declined the offer (this wasn't the usual Joe) but I just thought he was being over cautious and a bit of a wimp, so when we finally strapped ourselves in and the old rumble of engines had died down and we were now flying over Scotland you can imagine my surprise, shock, awe, horror and disbelief, when the captain decided to inform the passengers that we would be touching down at L.A. .X. in eleven hours time ...... nnnoooooooo oh nooo!

So I had to spend eleven hours sat in a chair full of throttle juice and only my record (great as it was) as my only entertainment, Bollocks! I turned to Joe who was laughing his black arse off, wanker! He knew all the time and thought it funny most properly as you do about now, that I was gonna go fuckin' mad sat in a chair plus to add to my frustration he in his sadistic sense of humour had taken a handful of sleeping pills and was already telling me that he was about to crash out for oh lets say eleven hours or so CUNT.... Big fat wanker.

So I was left annoying every bastard that was stupid enough to listen to my tape. It was then that I decided to listen to the on line radio fffffuckkk in heeeellll!!! All there was, was the life story of MADONNA for fucks sake, could it get any worse?

Yes it could!! As I listened to it, about seven fuckin' times, I could now answer questions on her life story!

Well we eventually landed and of course there was a delay in 'off boarding'. Great, I was now a fuckin' wreck I'd had no sleep in three days and I was fit to drop. Well we finally got to the customs desk (oh yes I must tell you that it was Independence Day and we thought it would be great fun to wear great British t-shirts). So there we were, Joe had this old black dude at his desk and as Joe is a bit on the dark side himself being six foot four and weighing around nineteen stone then, and was in fact half caste (can you call people that, now days?) well he was anyway, he jokingly held his hand out and gave the old bloke a righteous "yo bro!" Fuckin' stupid hand slap. Well I wasn't having it so I got this lovely old Hispanic women and I jokingly said, "Hi ya darling" in a very inoffensive way. Well WOT A COW she turned out to be, she asked me why I had that particular shirt on and I replied in good jest and humour, "I've come to take my country back" and she promptly told me that she had heard of our British football hooligans and preceded to get re-enforcements by calling the security guards as I was a threat to the UNITED STATES OF HAMBURGER, wot a bitch. I was taken with Joe, both of us fuming at our predicament to the customs office and deportation quarters in the airport, how very dare they?

I was beginning to get very fuckin' angry at this point as there was this short arsed airport cop giving me the evil eye while holding fast to his stupid little gun, I wanted to get that fuckin' gun and shove it up his arse and funnily enough I decided to tell him this, by the way it didn't go in my favour very well and we all started to have a bit of a shouting match. After a while I was told in no uncertain terms that if I didn't shut the fuck up I was on the next plane home, (shut up, boooo!!) As it turns out though, luckily in my favour and as if by magic the airport customs police were watching the football on the TV and as it was the year of the World Cup they were cheering ITALY on, now this was to be a godsend for me as I started up a conversation with the cops and found that they were all of Italian descendants. Well wot a stroke of luck as I had just come back from ROME with my Mum, Sister and Daughter and we were there for the opening match (that's a whole different story), so on this remark all of a sudden I was everybody's friend and they asked me questions about ITALY as they had never been there. So I was now this fountain of knowledge and a fuckin' big liar as I told them that I was in fact at the very first match and saw with my very own two eyes ITALY score the first goal of the tournament, wot a load of bollocks, but hey ya have to do wot ya's have to do.

We got released from the customs with honours and were now set free to roam the streets of LA, LA, LAND…
After picking up the hire car we drove off with Joe heading into the traffic and his seat so high the top of his head was bent over from the roof of the car it was bloody hysterical wot with cars coming at us and Joe having to do a 'u' turn in the middle of some big interjection type thing, actually it was scary as hell.
We eventually found our hotel after giving some old guy a lift and he in return showed us where we were going as the map

they had given me was no use at all, all fucking squares and boxes. Once inside we checked in and was taken to our room by this very wired and funny black guy who kept asking if there was, "ANYTHANG, I MEAN, ANYYYY THANG ...MAN, AAANYTHANG YA NEEDS MUVER FUKER, DUDE I'M YOR MAAAN, NIGGER, DAWG, ETC,ETC!?" Ok mate, I thought keep ya bloody monkey suit on geezer. Our room was very nice indeed and you could look out over the whole of L.A. wot a sight, real cool, and at night you went to bed and slept to the sound of V, EIGHTS chugging away, fuck you know you're in another country when all ya hear is Harley's and V Eight engines all night, fuckin great.

That night even though I was particularly tired out of my tiny mind, we went out for a walk, to check out exactly where we were as neither of us really knew anything about the States let alone where we were, sad in'it. So after walking about aimlessly for an hour or two we decided to walk across the road to a bar that looked interesting, well I had no sooner set foot in the road when around the corner came about ten or so Harley's with full patch members riding them, they stopped in front of me in the middle of the road. I thought, oh no not already, here we go I've only been here two minutes and everybody wants to kill me! But no, they asked if we were new to the country, I said yes and that we had just arrived. The guy at the front then decided to tell me in great detail that I can't cross the road where I liked, it's J walking (I thought that meant you had a spliff in ya mouth) and I was to put my shirt back on as this was an offence in L.A. Men naked from the waist up is offensive... ok. Plus I had a bottle of beer with no paper bag, oh yes and it must be a brown paper bag, (wot the fuck). All this information given from the local M.C. club! Cool dude, if not a bit weird, any who, we said cheers for the advice and went on our way.

On crossing the road we opened the door to the bar that we had spied from our hotel room, and went in, well... knock me down with a proverbial feather, slap my arse and call me Judy... if we didn't know most of the crowd inside, a real mix of BILLY IDOLS old band the TWENTY FLIGHT ROCKERS, a few roadies I knew from back home and a host of people all eager to meet with our acquaintance. Wot a result! We straight away put five hundred quid behind the bar and thus securing our arrival in the heart of L.A.

WE HAD ARRIVED!!!

If you have ever been to L.A. well then you will know wot I mean when I say it all feels like you've been there before, as everything has been filmed time and time again until when you see it for yourself it's as if you're in some weird deja-vu-esque type of place where everyone and everything is a fuckin' film, even the people act as if they're in a bleeding movie (very strange, indeedee).

We went to one bar and I swear to god (or any other false idol thing) that we saw the FURRY FREAK BROTHERS in this place, yes we did, there they were, sat, all of them PHINEAS, FAT FREDD, and FREEWHEELING FRANKLING and no the cat was not there! I'm not a total space cadet. Wankers!

You know wot I mean, anyway, Joe and me were in hysterics until they turned 'round but unfortunately these guys were not in their manner anything like the cuddly hippie fun lovin' peas 'n' bugs type in the cartoon books, as they quickly responded to our giggling with, "Hey motherfuckers are yous twos laughing at us boys over here?".

"Erm no!"

We left that bar (funnily enough) and went back to our regular haunt where we knew our enemy if there was going to be one. Well it didn't take long before we made an impression on the locals, see as we had put cash behind the bar we automatically gave ourselves the right of way to after hours. Now this didn't go down well with one of the regulars. This particular guy decided that who the fuck did the two brits with the flash cash and gob to match think they were and as time was being called and he was asked to leave he decided to tell everyone that he was not going anywhere while these two fuckin' nobodies, like who the fuck do they think they are just turning up and getting preferential treatment over and above a regular punter?

Fine, but I was pissed by now and thought I would add to the question...

Well he was not amused at my comment, that being,

"Go blow it out ya fuckin' arse, and wot ya gonna do about it anyway you American wanker!?"

I stood in front of him and said all this and then he stood up, SHEEEIT! He must have been about six foot seven built like a hamburger factory with extra gristle, apparently was an Indian chief or something (we found out later) anyway he was fuckin' huge!

The barman told him to calm down and just go mmmm, this he was not going to entertain as it was quite apparent to me and everyone else that he wanted to knock seven shades of shit out of my then scrawny tattooed not so bleeding hard now are ya? ...body, and well, he went for it. I bottled him and he just looked at me, then a couple of punters grabbed at him and I ended up hanging onto his back (why or how I got there I don't know) but this seemed a good place to be as he couldn't reach me even though we must have looked freakishly like a human merry go round wot with him gyrating round and round with my legs flapping in the air plus it seemed everyone else was hitting him and trying to get the fucking giant mutant Indian hulk freak show thing out into the street. I remember JOE whacking him hard and this monster of a man shrugged that off too. Bugger, I would have been asleep if he had hit me like that, but hey we all eventually battered him until he left the bar.

After all the commotion had died down we all had another drink and were laughing at the matter, when a loud banging was heard out the back of the bar, a couple of people went to see what all the fuss was about but we could hear for ourselves as soon as the door was open, yes you've guessed it, it was the incredible hulk again, this time he had come back with his rifle and was now threatening to shoot my arse?

Great I thought, I haven't been in the States one full day and night and somebody wants to shoot me, apart from the police tosser at the airport, so that makes two, not bad going ah!

Eventually a couple of the regular girls went out and calmed him down and he eventually went home, we met up with him a few days later and it was all done and dusted. We bought him a couple of drinks, shared a few stories and he didn't eat my head ....

There was quite a lot of trouble in that particular bar but it was all in-house. As I recall, one particular evening, the sharing of jovial banter and drunken misadventures had come to an end and while everybody was getting themselves ready to go to their beds or stagger off to an all night drinking establishment, the door opened with a crash as it slammed against the brick wall and in ran these three young black dudes with masks covering their faces and carrying lumps of wood held as makeshift batons of sorts. Well these three dumb arse amigos from the projects obviously hadn't done any homework as in surveillancing the premises or come to that even popping their ugly little mugs round the door to see who exactly the clientele were inside, before going in, all guns blazing as it were. One of the boys in the 'hood' shouted out in his L.A. drawl street voice, "HEY MAN, GIVE UP DE CASH IN DE TILL MON". (That's

sort of West Indian in'it, oh well, fuck it. You knows wot I mean)
NIGGER, DAWG, MUVER FUKER. (Is that more like it?).

As soon as he opened his mouth it seemed that everyone knew
exactly what needed to be done and the whole god damn place
set themselves upon the task in hand of ridding the bar room of
the THREE STOOGES of bar room robbing .

Giving them an array of glass smashing bottle throwing, GARY
the owner pulled a proper baton from behind the bar and
proceeded to bash the living shit out of this one poor unfortunate's head until he ran screaming out the door from whence he
came, the remaining two stupidly tried for a second or two to
barter with the clientele by shouting out loud and clear to
anyone that would listen (erm, nobody) "Hey, man, stop, stop,
stop, fuckin' hitting us dude, erm we're sorry, fuck it's hurting,
erm, no more please son of a bitch . Ouch!!!". Etc, etc ....
Blah, blah, blah.

Needless to say they left licking their wounds with their non
street cred gangster handbag snatching mother of a limp wristed
shit cow tails behind them. As quick as they had come in, infact
the whole scene only lasted a few seconds it almost seemed as
if it were a very well rehearsed and choreographed stage fight
as the timing was so fuckin' spot on and may I say staggeringly
fookin cool. BISH, BASH, BOSH. While being made honour-
able members of the bar we had now made some new and influ-
ential friends, one of these was a man called DAN. Now Dan
was one fuck of a scary character, as in everyone told us not to
hang out with him as he was not the full shilling and had a bad
reputation?

I nicked named him DAN, DAN, THE PSYCHO MAN!

Sounds interesting? And he was, he and his wife STACY I'll
call her as she is an actress and I'm not in touch with them so a
changing of name is called for, well now Dan and Stacy had

taken a shine to us and decided that they would be our unofficial tour guides for the duration of our holiday, fuckin' cool
man!

The first story I can remember is Dan calling in on us around
seven in the morning about the third day of us arriving in LA.
We had this fuck off brand new Buick motor rented for two
weeks and as we couldn't find our own home with maps or even
pieces of cheese laid down as a trail to find our way home the
fact that someone wanted to drive us about really appealed to
both Joe and myself. We started off by doing the HOLLY-
WOOD thang, and driving up the Hill's to where all the Celebs
stay BORING! We looked at a few houses with guards outside,
we looked at that stupid HOLLYWOOD sign. I got hungry, so
we drove to BARNEY'S BEANERY oh, yeah like really cool (I
think not). We ordered food and the service was interesting to
say the least as everything you order comes with a waitress with
a ridiculous half arsed mocking smile and the immortal words,
"ARE YOU READY TO ORDER (SIR" ? !). Everything has a
fuckin' 'Sir' on the end, best is they don't even have any 'Sir's' and
stuff over there it's just crap, oh yeah and the best saying ever
"HAVE A NICE DAY", everywhere you bloody well go "HAVE
A NICE DAY, HAVE A NICE DAY, HAVE A NICE DAY"..
..Fuckin annoying innit?
Trying to order isn't much more brain tantalisingly informative
as you can't just have eggs and ham with toast. Oh no, this
turned out to be a crash course in culinary food ordering, all I
wanted was food on a plate, but how would you like your eggs?
Answer… on a plate! No siiiir, would you like them fried,
poached, boiled, sunny side up, runny, splattered up ya arse
with tomato ketchup or maybe siphoned through a straw and
injected straight into your bleeding cortex !!! While the dumb
bitch tries to force feed ya piss weak beers and French fries

(chip's, don't ask for chips, they think you're mad or you have just made the fuckin' word up?) TOAST, sounds easy, doesn't it, no, no, no, sir, fuckin' bleeding SIR how would you like you're toast? NOT BURNT, BITCH!

Add to that the most arguably worsest ever insult you could ever, ever, ever want to hear from a yank to well just about anybody really, now I'm not overly patriotic to the united condom or anything but when you keep getting miss fuckin' staken for a bleeding AUSTRALIAN cunt ! The cheek of it, of all the cunt trees in all the world and they think you're a fuckin OZZY, well bollocks to that, I had quite a few run-ins over that particular one, excuse me SIR I don't understand you're language? Now that's a classic isn't it, I can't understand you're fuckin'... bloody... it's our's... we gave it to you... you dumb son of a premenstrual dingo minge eating, arse jabbing bunch of wankers!

GOD, TAKE ME NOW ..... Why is it that Americans just sound like Americans to us but they can't understand or grasp in any way shape or form us for some dumb reason and insist on likening our accent to anywhere but where we actually come from, really didn't want to say this but they asked for it GREAT BRITAIN there you are. TOSSERS and there's another word you wont know?!

And while I'm here wot about dick van fucking dyke?..... (That's it, just wot about DICK-VAN-DYKE!!!

Chin chimminy chin chimminy chin chim churoo, FUCK OFF! YOU CUNT...

Back to the story,

Another day we all got packed, rolled up our bathing costumes, sun tan oil (Joe didn't need any? Ooooh cheap arse racsist joke, ha, ha, ha) swimming hat and sandals, (not) and decided to trundle merrily off to the seaside, mmmm.

VENICE BEACH actually, wot a dump! Naaaa, not really I'm not going to slag everything off but "wot a dump". I never realized how big Hollywood was , you really do need to have a motor to get around as everything is so damn far apart, it took us near on an hour or so to get to the beach but on our arrival it never let us down, all palm trees, bars, roller skating bimbos, skate boarding teenagers aged around thirty or so, more fucking boys in 'da hood' moochin around like anyone fuckin' cared if they lived or got run over by a crack addicted ice cream van driver (oop's) ok. People selling shit, t-shirts, shades, towels, crap marijuana and the usual bollocks. One particular t-shirt I bought that I then noticed everyone seemed to be wearing after I had purchased mine was FUCK IT'S 115 DEGREES! Still, cool, oh yeah and the old favourite LIFES A BEACH excellent.

We hung out on the beach for most of that afternoon and it was as the t-shirt said 100 degrees. I felt like I was stuck in a sauna with a fat bastard sitting on my face, jeez it was hot, hot, hot. After a while we decided to go eat (yeah) on the pier their was this restaurant that specialized in just steak and lobster, mmmmm, and again mmmmm, I love steak, I love lobster, I really love, steak and lobster, all on the same fuckin' huge plate with a side order of fries (not chips) and a huge, not really needed but ya got it anyway salad. Well the steak was a frightening monster sized lump of cow meat I'm sure they just quartered the poor fuckin' beast out back and slung it straight on the old barbeque, WOW now I can eat and JOE wasn't shy in the old food department neither but man this was choice… I've never had a lobster like it neither, then nor since, wot a treat. It took a good couple of hours to finish and I scoffed the remainders of Joe's down too (fat pig) well 'waist' not want not!
After the dinner from heaven we all squeezed our fat and hurting lard arses back into the Buick and drove off up the motor-

way coast line to MALIBU.   Not a lot going on there, surfers and stuff I personally wasn't too impressed but as I don't swim and not into trying to surf especially with nothing but a plank of wood or is it fibreglass oh, I don't know nor do I fuckin' care very much! under ya feet and trying to put a smile on ya face saying "shiiit I'm not scared, look at me Mum, plus adding a mile of water underneath ya gonads, and don't they have sharks over there? Any way's I kept to spotting girls in G string's mmmmm G strings, and seriously trying my best to not spot the over zeal-ous men in thongs? Wot the fuck are they about? Plus there was a rocking biker bar behind us that looked real mean unt hard-core motherfucker, but I didn't want to go inside as I had broke my steel toe capped RANGER boots when kicking a wall (stupid story, i wont be telling) so I had trainers on and I was sporting Joe's bloody surfer shorts, that I had worn that morning for a dare as he was twice the size of me and they looked stupid, plus I had on my ENGLAND shirt complete with UNION JACK. Now I didn't mind looking a cunt in front of the innocent bystanders but there was no way I was going in that biker bar looking like a representative for BRITISH ARSE HOLES "R" US, and knowing my luck a camera toting reporter for BACK-STREET HEROES or some other biker mag there with a much too happy trigger finger and so there I would be immortalised forever in the pages of biker history as the cunt from London dressed as the cunt from London. So I watched from the self appointed hiding place (in the bloody backseat of the car) Joe on the other hand revelling in my humiliation of dress sense decided to get on the roof of our Buick and as a small group of leather clad bad to the bone looking every bit (bastards) the part, while mockingly rumbled their thundering steeds of steel (enough, we get it. motorbikes !) past us he gave them the bird, or as we say the finger, well two actually, he outstretched both hands and gave two birds the flick off !

They in turn gave him a similar birdie straight back, so there we sat, me in the back of a Buick looking like a long haired version of Billy the fish and Joe on the roof giving the local M.C. CLUB the fucking bird while Dan and his wife stood outside laughing at the whole scenario.

We eventually decided to go back to the hotel, but not before popping back into the steak 'n' lobster restaurant, (fuck) the manager came out this time as he recognised us from the afternoon and wanted to congratulate me on my amazing feat for stuffing one's face full to gill's, he then was stunned and amazed and called the flippin' chef when he was told of my hunger and that I just had to have another steak 'n' lobster surprise, ha, the surprise was that the chef was so knocked out by my ability to put away so much cow and fish that he set me a task; that of being that if I could infact eat another whole steak 'n' lobster (without the fries/chips 'n' salad, of course) I could have it for free! I tried but I couldn't get the whole lot in, I was in fact hurting, my belly was full to the brim but he was still impressed and we had such fun they even sat down with us and shared a joke or two and yes they gave me the benefit of the doubt and let me go home well fed and free of any cost, cheer's.

The next day we went on a journey to TIAWANA, MEXICO, not a lot to say about the whole event as most of the time was spent in the car on the road, sharing stories and stuff.
One story that we were told made both JOE and myself feel very much as though we had definitely come to another country and that not all of HOLLYWOOD was based around film scores and the like. We were on the long road to SAN DIAGO as you need to pass through it to get to MEXICO and Stacy started telling us about the time they had when one day they found themselves bored and on the road, so decided to have a

little fun! Oh boy! Stacy started to tell how they had a MAGNUM loaded and ready for action in the car, so being bored with a couple of hundred miles of freeway in front of them they decided that the course of hilarity would be to in fact shoot out the tyres of a passing juggernaught ! Yep, we thought so too!

Apparently they did shoot out the tyres of a very large juggernaught and sent it spinning and smashing into everything on the freeway completely wiping out that stretch of road, mad eh!

When we got to Mexico, we done all the usual tourist stuff and was coming home when it grew dark and Tiawana is a very different place then as all the tourist stuff was taken inside and some of the local street gangs were beginning to emerge onto the main drag, you could taste the atmosphere change as the food was being cooked outside now and the smell of violence could be felt tingling the hairs on your and up your spine.   I didn't feel very safe as them low-rider cars were starting to be seen bouncing up and down in front of each other while the occupants could be quite clearly seen carrying baseball bats and the like inside of the cars, different patches could be seen worn in a number of ways that being a tourist myself didn't know and wouldn't know where to begin to differentiate between them so I left it all up to DAN!

Dan was a cool dude and led us around pointing out the local do's and don'ts in down town TIAWANA gangland territory. We passed by the evening with no trouble though, only a couple of 'calls over' by short stocky slick back hair cut off jean jackets and dialogue that sounded like they had been watching far to many Cheech and Chong films. The main reason of street questioning was my tattoos as I had full sleeves and the fact that tattoos in the States or Mexico come to that, cost a hell of a lot more there so I was pretty much paid up, but fortunately once hailed over and asked what gang I was in my accent gave me away and as soon as I announced that I was in fact a biker from London on holiday they were cool and to be honest quite respectful, not too sure how it would have gone down if I were in fact batting for a local team without my team mates around as these boy's looked as if they meant business.

On leaving Mexico we finally reached our hotel where we scored a few rocks of crack and a couple grammes of Charlie and proceeded to get high and talk shit for hours on end. By the morning I was feeling pretty much twisted by now and wanted to do stuff? Oh no!
I asked Dan if he had any guns. Stupid question (do bears shit in the woods?) Dan said he did (of course) so what would I like to shoot? I dunno! Well Dan said we can go back out onto the freeway and pick up a couple of CHICANOS or WETBACKS take em out into the desert and shoot em up a bit!
WWWWWHHHOOOOO HOLD ON A MINUTE.
I asked Dan to repeat wot he had just said and so he did, "Yeah dude, all we do is, see, ride about for a while, find a Mexican hitch hiker at the side of the road, offer him a lift and take the motherfucker out into the desert and let him go, give the fuck five minutes to run and hide then go find him and shoot him up a bit!" A bit? "Yeah, a leg, an arm wotever, just shoot the dum son of a bitch". Jeez, boy did I ever feel like the green son of a Londoner, well Joe looked at me and I looked at Joe and for a second we thought he just might be messing with our heads and stuff but when he then looked at us with a puzzled look on his face we thought shit this guy's for real and to make sure that he brought the scenario right home to us both smack bang then and there he looked at us both in the eyes, as if we were the two most greenest pricks on the block and said "HEY, DON'T YOU

GUY'S GO SHOOTIN NIGGERS BACK IN LONDON OR WOT!"
Answer... "ERM, NO! ACTUALLY, I said in a very posh sort of way for some reason?

Well we never did go 'coon' shooting especially as Joe was half black himself (dear me) but I did go looking for whores with him and he made sure we took this fuckin' great machete with us (just in case) mmmmmm.

The next couple of days were spent drinking the twenty litres of Mescal and Tequila we had brought back from Mexico. We only drank ten litres though but this was enough for me to have a man period as blood was coming out of my arse every time I had a shit, great fun ah!

I remember one day asking if I could score some weed and Dan obliged by going out and then coming back the next morning with Joe gone out for a couple of hours, leaving me in bed with one hell of a hangover. Well the door bell rang and I answered it and there stood Dan and Stacy. Dan said that he had scored some weed and that he was gonna show me how they smoked weed in Hollywood as I had been taking the piss out off them silly little skinny roll up things you see on all them teen American films. So he sat down on the edge of the bed and Stacy took off her coat to reveal that she was in fact wearing the shortest mini leather skirt, and a see through black lacy affair that held nothing to the imagination and with her very big in fact huge tit's poking through and fishnet stockings she was dressed to thrill, shiiiiit, I couldn't keep my eye's off of her tit's and she sat with her legs crossing and uncrossing by the edge of the bed so as I could get a quick glance of her knickers. Only thing was, she wasn't wearing any knickers so it was like that scene in BASIC INSTINCT... only thing different was that Dan was there, and Dan was getting off on it and I was thinking oh no suppose Dan changes his mind or maybe worse he might want to join in and have a threesome, oh my god, and maybe Dan's bisexual and he might want me as well and he's one big hard son of a bulldozer of a man so a fight is not gonna happen, plus I was naked under my now stuck to me like glue, sheets. I kept making small talk and wishing Joe the fuckin' big wanker would hurry up and come home but he never did and Dan kept saying that, "ya know Steve, Stacy always gets wot Stacy wants? If yas know wot I mean!". Yeah, mate only too fuckin' well, but kept shtum and made out that I was dumb to the whole situation, I must have been in bed with them two playing head games for about an hour, thing is Stacy was one fit looking bird she'd done a cover for PLAYBOY back in the day and had starred in them 'B' film horror flicks and well I did fancy the shit out of her and most probably would have done the dirty deed but with Dan looking??

Eventually it was apparent that I wasn't going to play ball? And they left so I could get up and meet them across the road in the bar, and that's exactly wot happened (sorry if you were waiting to read some juicy sex scenes or in fact me getting raped by Mr big while his girlfriend gets herself off by having a quick flick 'n' twiddle while watching, sorry about that!)

ARSEHOLES!

Talking of arseholes, as it happens one afternoon Joe and myself managed to score a bag of magic beans… nah, not really, we actually scored eight QUALUDES and thought we'd take them that night as a mate was doin' security on the doors to some night club and we could get in free, plus if we got into any trouble it would be cool as we were with the door men.

So on the night in question we got a cab and gave the address to the driver and off we went. On arrival we met Gary our friend and as promised he was on the door and we did get in for free, now I must state here and now that when we arrived the club was almost empty as we were obviously early so we ventured to the back of the night club were we found that they did in fact have a rather large garden, cool, we thought, so we went outside found a table in the corner sat down a waiter come barman came over and took our orders (nice one squirrel) excellent as we didn't even have to go to the bar. So we sat there, dropped four QUALUDES or as there called in blighty MANDIES and waited to get fucked up!

Well that didn't take very long, and as we were ordering more drinks and having a laugh I noticed that the clientele was a bit gay and there seemed to be a shortage of female flesh hanging around. I mentioned this to Joe who just looked at me and told me to stop getting paranoid and being homophobic, well as the night drew on it did look very suspect indeedy as more and more over dressed and over hair styled people where turning up and nobody had a bird, I tried to take no notice but eventually I needed to take a piss so off I ventured inside, once I opened the door from the garden to the club inside it became more than apparent wot kind of a place it was?

OH MY GOD!

Camper than a big camp of campers pitching up their big camp pink sparkly tents in Dolly Parton's big camp park for camp campers !

More gay's, queers, queens, fags, transvestites than you could shake a big fluffy camp stick at!

Gayer than all your campest Xmases coming at once, (and I certainly wasn't going to go picking up any loose change off the floor, ha, ha, ha, fner, fner. Cheap arse queer joke thrown in).

So now I've established that it was in fact a gay club, phew! I went to the bog, had a piss and returned to where Joe was sat. After explaining to Joe just wot sort of club it was we decided to go inside and sit by the front door and stay out the way, as I and Joe are not homophobic but we're not queer and we had nowhere else to go so we thought we would keep a low profile and stay with the doormen (nice boy's they were, dressed in very tight fitting white T-shirts and you could see they had been working out? All them taught muscles when they flexed their biceps) OI! STOP IT!

We managed to find a quiet table by the door and so we sat down and ordered a drink. Everything seemed to be going ok until this young guy came over and through the fuckin' loud rave music asked me by whispering in my ear, "Would your friend like to dance?"
HALLO!
I started to laugh but I didn't want to tell Joe in case he took it offensively and start a fight. So I tried to suggest to the young man that I didn't think he would, now you'd think this would be sufficient but oh no, there's always one isn't there, and he wouldn't go away, "please ask him oh please", I was getting pretty fed up with this idiot and Joe was now asking me wot the fuckin' idiot wanted. I told him not to worry and I'll get rid of him so I told this bloke to piss off he wasn't interested, and he did, so that was that. BOLLOCKS was it, about five minutes later this bar fly fairy fag came mincing back over with a look of determination on his face, sat down next to me again and said,
"Look will you ask your friend if he wants to dance coz I really dig him?" FUCK OFF I replied this time, I was getting pissed at this fucking nuisance, and Joe was now demanding to know wot this sparkling spanner was after, shit, fuck it, bollocks to it, so I told him. Joe I said, he wants to know if you want a dance!!!
Ha, ha, ha, the look on Joe's face was priceless, he didn't know whether to lump him one right there and then or head for the door and run like fuck. Totally hilarious, Joe infact was quite

eloquent about the matter in hand and said politely even though he had to shout because of the loud music,

"No I don't wanna dance and go away". So the young gun went off and I took the piss out of Joe as you do for around five minutes until the fucker came back, fuck me, why couldn't this tit take a 'no I don't want a pissing dance', well he couldn't and he came over and this time he was apologetic and said to me to pass on the message that he was sorry and didn't realize that it was obvious that Joe and myself where infact LOVERS and he didn't want to break us up or take my lover away so he was apologising?!

Joe, asked wot he had said to me, when I told him, Joe got uptight but not as uptight as me as I'm pretty okay with most people and I really do try and keep an open mind while I took the whole dancing thing with a pinch of snuff but hey don't say that "I'm in love with my mate Joe" if only to say that if I was a poof or a raving turd burglar, bum bandit etc, I certainly wouldn't be with bloody Joe anyway (sounds a bit suspect) anyway, with that I decided the only course of action was to SMACK the cunt in the gob! THWAAACK!

That did it, well it sort of did, as the cat was now out of the purse, I mean bag! Oooop's, my mate on the doors had gone off somewhere and all hell kicked off, we got out in one piece a few scratches but all in all it could have been a lot worse, ha, ha, ha, funny to think though that me and Joe could be lovers ha, ha, ha still makes me giggle if not squirm a bit too!

INSTANT WANKER?

Or M.D.M.A. or ESCTASY, take ya pick, we chose to rename the so called love drug to 'Instant Wanker' as on the day in question Joe and myself purchased a gram or two as it was still new to us and we wanted to know wot all the fuss was about, so on this day we indulged ourselves on the drug and decided to go to the hotel pool that was situated on the hotel roof, (cool) we got in the hotel lift and up we went to the roof where there lay the swimming pool with about ten or so people swimming around or laying about on sun loungers getting some rays in.

Joe and me looked a right couple of arses as we decided for a laugh to wear each others shorts, as he was six foot three or there abouts and I am five foot nine so his shorts were real tight and mine looked fuckin' ridiculous as they came down past my fuckin' knees looking a bit like surfer wear gone mad, plus I decided to keep my steel toe-cap RANGER boots on, mmmmm. That made me look fuckin' hard (not) anyway we grabbed ourselves a sun bed each and lay down waiting for the drug to start doing it's thang.

At the end of the pool I noticed a couple of likely looking females giving me the eye so with no haste I nudged Joe to tell of my discovery and yes he too was impressed, maybe too impressed as he sussed on straight away wot the coup was while leaving me in total confusion as they were quite good looking but seemed to be with these other two blokes and why was they interested in us anyway especially looking the way we did. Well it didn't take too much longer to get the picture as I beckoned one of the girls over and she strutted her stuff over to where we were sat, sat her pert little bum down next to me and asked us if we had any blow in our room? Fuckin' cool ah! No chatting up, straight in, I said no but we were looking to score a bit of personal and did she have any or know of somebody where we could score a bag, she said yes she could and would we like her to score a couple of grams and go back to our hotel room, shit yeah!

But a couple of grammes? Wot was she on about, I asked her the price and she quoted me thirty dollars a gram fuck off! That's about twenty quid for a couple of joints I answered all knowingly that just coz I'm a fuckin' tourist that she couldn't rip me off with some dumb arse price for a couple of meezly joints. Then she told me that I was all confused and blow was infact cocaine, so I then complemented her answer with, well in England blow is dope, marijuana, oh, she said and we laughed. She then said well do you wanna go have some of that? I said yeah but wot about the two guys with ya, she said they wouldn't mind and Joe started to laugh (wanker) I still hadn't fell in, the coin wasn't dropping like fuckin' deeerrr, I told her that ok fuck em let's go and asked Joe if he was coming too? He looked at me and laughed, then said you still don't get it do ya! Get wot? They're on the game! Nah, I said, and asked the young lady next to me if this was in fact the case, she looked at me and giggled then answered my question while looking over at her friend who was now laughing as well and said yes dum arse wot do yah think!?

We left the pool, me almost running with embarrassment followed by a belly hurting with laughter Joe (toss pot Devlin) cheers mate!

The ecstasy was now starting to creep up on us so for some reason we decided to get in our Buick and go through the manual. Well we was going for a drive but we found that we couldn't as we were too fuckin' out of it and the car was now made of jelly and looked for some reason rather sexy!!!

We sat in the car and played with the manual until Joe pressed a button that read retractable coat hanger then pressed the button and I was in the back and a sharp rod flicked out from the side of the car and nearly had me fuckin' eye out (Joe laughed). I then found a way of utilizing the buttons on the arms of the seats so as to make the seat move as if it were in fuckin' motion, so if I had had a girly on my lap I could in fact shag her without actually moving, cool.

This got boring and the drug was now coming on stronger so we ventured over to the bar. On going in we ordered our drinks, a combination of WILD TURKEY and BEER with shots of TEQUILA. We were drunk! Great, fuckin' cool dude, until the ecstasy finally kicked in good and proper reducing both Joe and myself into a couple of WANKERS as the drug overtook the effects of the booze and leaving us both feeling very bloody sexy? We stayed in the bar for a couple hours then decided it was much to freaky so we went up to our rooms and took a couple Quaaludes and fell asleep .

On waking we got dressed had a shower, oop's not in that order, and ventured once again back to the bar where I met a NATIVE AMERICAN or RED INDIAN to those of you with no under-standing of the struggles of the NATIVE AMERICANS? No I don't care either! A thought???
WHY DO PEOPLE LIVING IN THE WEST INSIST ON HAVING RED INDIAN (NATIVE AMERICAN) CHIEFS AND THE LIKE TATTOOED ON THEM?
AND YOU NEVER SEE AN INDIAN WITH A PICTURE OF ANY OF OUR GREAT CHIEFS.
For instance
MAGARET THATCHER, WINSTON CHURCHILL, or in fact ENOCH POWELL!
Ha, ha, ha.........
Sorry, just a stupid thought?
I digress, getting back to the bullshit, the Native American in questions name was STONE.... Quite appropriate as it turns out as he was (stoned that is) all the time we were there and I helped out in this department a couple of times too.
On this occasion however it was to be my first meeting with him or in fact with the first really real Indian I have actually ever met. We got on great, a bit too well it seemed for a while as we real-

ized as the night went on that we both had the same drug likings too, this manifested itself in him going out for a while and coming back with a couple of rocks of METHAMPHETAMINE or CRANK and he also was into using the old ARM SPANNER (syringe) so when he finally arrived back at the bar we scurried off to the bog to have a quick NICK COTTON (Nick cotton being the geezer in EASTENDERS at the time who was a junkie) so the name served well!

Shit, as soon as the rock's dissolved and I had shot the warm gluey liquid into my veins it felt like I was on a bleeding rocket WHOOOOSH...... jeezus, we three came out of the bar room bogs eye's blazing and looking like we were going through some kind of G-FORCE or something as it felt as if my facial skin was being torn, no ripped from my very face leaving my teeth gnarling and my eyes bulging, there was a giveaway sign of blood trickling down my arm too that wasn't such a good move as somebody noticed and requested we should leave the building?

We did eventually but not until we three had talked some proper crap to each other at a speed of liking to hundred fuckin' miles an hour and no one listening to a word the other person was saying nor even caring as the speed was so intense, shit, that was good gear made the stuff back home feel like watered down washout left overs from some sad old speed freaks party. Oh well, after rabbiting on and on and on and on at each other and everyone else for hours we did eventually leave and decided to mark the event the next day by having a TATTOO. Now Stone was nowhere to be found on the day so myself and Joe walked up and down SUNSET until we came across a Tattooist (ya can't move for them now!)

The shop was a clothes shop actually and there was this gothic type hippy geezer in the back doin' tattoos (badly) from wot I saw but hey all we wanted was a momentoe of our trip to LA, LA

LAND and that's wot we got, both of us had in the same place on our legs a tattoo with the immortal words of YO, L.A. FUCK OFF. Now the young Californian tattooist thought we were disin his homeland until we told him that the reason for the fuck off was that everything we had done and seen was fuck off good not the contrary, so with that established we went back to the bar to show off our new ink.

That night Stone came back into the bar and we obviously all got drunk and high again. I met another guy who was a REPO man, now I've never met a repo man before nor did I have a clue wot they in fact did? Until he filled me in, (no he never punched my lights out) as we all know now a repo man reposesses your motor if ya don't pay the instalments on it. Now all that on the surface seems ok until he told me that he in fact repossessed cars from the projects like down town COMPTON! Oh dear, now ya don't wanna go messin' with those mother-fuckers dude!

But he did and he showed me the nine bullet holes in his torso to prove it. Shit I said, is ya job worth it and he said he loved it as he was a joy rider as a kid and a thief so this was doin' wot he loved and getting paid for it and it was legal? But hey man, having fucked up crazy black and Mexican dudes chasing your arse with guns wasn't my idea of "aving a laff" but hey each to their own.

Getting back to Stone, at the end of this particular night I had, had a bit of a punch up with some mook in the bar earlier and as a way of relieving my frustration as both Stone and myself were both now very drunk and incapable I managed much to the disapproval of every one else to get him to give me a ride on his HARLEY up SUNSET, not a good idea but he was up for it and so off we both ventured outside into the hot L.A. night, sticky with sweat and booze, brains fried and still a hankering for more mischief, we were both in breach of all the stupid by laws, drunk, no shirts, bottles of beer with no bag, riding a motorcycle and being under the influence of numerous drugs. So he started up the mean growling monster of a machine and I straddled onto the back holding on tight to the sissy bar and off we went, bbbbrrroooom... up and down SUNSET BOULEVARD, I got him to mount the pavement as they do in all them old ANGEL films, and he did, how we never got nicked I'll never know but we didn't and we had such fun!!!

I would have stayed in L.A. as I had been asked to, by Stone and Dan and Stacy, plus I was offered a Harley on loan for as long as I needed plus a room was on offer with Jack, a roadie from hackney and Dan wanted me to go with him to reap in a marijuana harvest belonging to a well known film star that I can't mention and ride horses, go fishing and shooting for the winter on his ranch, shit and bollocks!

Trouble was that I had infect bigger fish to fry back in old Blighty, and was due in court for custody of my children and this was to be my last big adventure for a while as I was to begin a harder adventure as a one parent family!

Well there's not a lot more to write about on this trip, only to say that this particular holiday turned out to be so much more than just a holiday, it really was an eye opener in that I never really thought of Americans as being that much dissimilar from ourselves but shit they really are foreign?!

And I think that JOE DEVLIN and myself actually arrived at the end of an era for HOLLYWOOD sub culture, or white subculture anyway as the whole rapp thang took off shortly afterward and the authorities in their infinite wisdom shut the whole thing down, as I come to find on returning in 2000, this time around taking my fifteen year old son to L.A. and then onto SAN FRANSISCO giving him SONNY BARGERS life story to read on the trip, only to find yet another shit hole.

We stayed at Ashbury on Height, where all the hippy stuff went on, only to find no smoking bars cafes etc, vegetarian bloody food everywhere and a whole lot of Vietnam vets and black homeless everywhere and the place stank like a dustbin, fuckin' horrible.

I spent a week in L.A. trying to give the boy an education on all his rap music and take him to where exactly all the gangbangers lived and show him the grand alternative great american rock culture of L.A. with it's V.EIGHT engines rumbling on through the night and young rich white girls on Saturday nights coming down from Hollywood hills to slum it up cruising along sunset showing anyone who asked their tits, smoking fuckin' good home-grown scored from some Porto Rican shit shoveller on the corner of any bleeding street, I wanted to take him to where the FURY FREAK brothers lived, where CHEECH and CHONG got all there stories from but when we got there all that stuff had gone, only to find they've now put a stop to the Saturday cruise down Melrose and sunset strip, closed most of the biker bars while keeping homeless negros, Vietnam vets, bikers, stoners and junkies off the streets or at least hide them out of sight of tourists, keeping them in the back streets or confining them to their ghettoes or projects as there condescendingly called.

I did however get him his first tattoo, from a young tattooist who very kindly came to our place of residency and put some ink down on the boy!

Shame he wasn't older and that it's all gone a bit like London and everywhere else, this is part of the reason for writing this book, so there's a point of reference to show that we were here and that we were hard fuckin' drug taking rock 'n' rollin' headfuckers...

THE MAKING OF "THE, CLUB BASTADOS" E.P. AND THE OPENING OF THE LEGENDARY CLUB BASTADOS...

WELLY, WELLY, WELLY WORMS AND FLIES.

Here's the story of how the nightclub and EP came about, with the help of JOE DEVLIN (well known roadie, stage manager, larger than life figure and all round good-bad guy, my best friend and drinking/substance indulging partner in slime for five long, long years as we never slept!

Total nutter and lovable rogue). Also THE MAN WITH NO NAME or JOHN THE MONEY? (As he will be called due to libel reasons, plus I couldn't find him to ask his permission). He was infact nicknamed 'the money' as he put up the dosh in the first place, in return for playing guitar on the E.P. and being a silent partner in the night club mmmmmm....

So we three amigos clubbed together and conspired with others of similar ilk to gather an array of musicians, celebs, clowns, bikers, drug dealers, dog walkers and out of work anybodies, somebodies and nobodies together so as to help me create for the mere price of just BEER, PIZZA, AND LOVLEY DRUGS!

An E.P that I wrote the music for and most of the lyrics (apart from DAVE LUSH). I managed to get JOE to fix it for us to hire EASY HIRE STUDIOS for a fuckin' bargain price, while I convinced an old friend and ally DANNY, + HELEN from 'Graphic Entertainments' to design the artwork for the E.P. and my logo that I have used since, that of the BASTADO MAN (well, nicked from the Mexican day of the dead).

SO, a gathering of musos had to be found to actually play on this recording for the nightclub, luckily both Joe and I were on the London party circuit and who I didn't know Joe did, as he was stage manager for the Brixton Academy and well, basically knew everyone that needed knowing at the time.

It was Joe that got the recording studio sorted at the 'EASY HIRE STUDIOS' as we were partying there most weekends anyway, so they cut us a deal for a four day recording session, three days of which where actual recording and one day for mixing the whole thing down, cool. Joe managed to get COBOLT or JEFF to come in on the deal as a second guitarist to my god, oop's, I mean, good self and help out on the engineering (even though I've given him a bit of flack earlier in this book he did do a very good job and the whole thing would not have sounded as good and professional as it does without his input, so a big up to Coby, even though he did ask for £200.00 and got all out of his pram about it, ending in me head butting him and Zodiac Mindwarp's new bassist whose, name I can't remember at the ASTORIA THEATRE one night only to be told that Joe had in fact promised him a cash handout but failed to enlighten anybody else) nice one Joe!

Next on board would be DAVE LUSH who was with me in F.T.W. (unincorporated) I think at that time, he came down and put the finishing touches to my lyrics that I had written only two days before with the music.

Then we had TRASH from ZODIAC on bass, he was easy to get as he was going out with Dave's sister at the time and they all lived at Dave's Mum's house (all very rock 'n' roll). Next up was STEVE HOLLAND on drums, he was playing with everyone as a session drummer and actually joined F.T.W. for a while. We then go to SHAUN of the infamous SCREAMING MARI-ONETTES. He actually only got it together to come down for some backing vocals but he did however lend us his drummer PAUL another session player who came down to the recording session, heard the song he was to play on once, played it, had a beer and was never seen of again .

Next up was JERRY and ALLEN from popsters, JEESUS JONES. I knew Jerry from way back and we were all hanging around together for quite a while when JESUS JONES were at the top of their game, so they came down for the gig and contributed to some backing vocals that was hilarious as Jerry was so fuckin' out of his head on booze and coke every time it got to his part to sing he would vomit all over the sound proofed enclosure window, really funny, you had to be there.

Next I'd like to thank a young PHIL BAX who engineered the whole thing, jeesus he never knew wot he was letting himself in for but he did a grand job even though I was spiking his drinks with amphetamines the whole time.

LEE STARKY came down with BELLA (a model and friend at the time) plus everyone's bloody girlfriend, they all turned up to sing backing vocals on the song 'TOO LATE, I FOUND SOMEONE NEW SO FUCK OFF ARSE HOLE!' (A country and western song I wrote in fifteen minutes about a bloke who totally destroys his girlfriend's life, very funny) ha, ha, ha.

And then my kidz, ZIGGY and the boy wonder from hell SONNY, he was only about seven years old and a total night-mare (still is, sorry boy) and he was running amuck in the studio all the damn fucking time. It was like trying to record at home but on a bigger and more costly scale, he at one point managed to get into the electrical mains cupboard for the entire studio and shut the whole place down, yep all the lights, the mixing desks everything went off! Shit! Apparently PETER GABRIEL former ex genesis singer was next door and in the middle of mixing a song and we were very lucky it all didn't shoot out into space as the recording stopped midway through, shit we could have found ourselves paying for his recording costs (like yeah). Well the recording went spookily well, even though I had to sing the guitar parts to Steve Holland as my amp hadn't turned up and he wrote the musical score down from me humming the guitar and stuff, really bizarre but it worked and he put the drums down without actually having a written song as such to hear or jam too (fucking brilliant).

Then Coby came in on the session and put things in order and we got all the rhythm tracks down. Then we spent a day on Dave's vocals, he was fuckin' brilliant, the best singing I've ever heard him do and it didn't take him for ever (like usual, sorry Dave)!

Next up was the guitars. Mmmmmmm, I was in guitar heaven the best time I've ever spent, even though most of it wasn't used in the final mix and as I was so fucking pissed and out of it when it came to mixing day that I never got my two-pennaths worth in, but hey ho it all came out alright in the wash I suppose? (Damn, shit, bollocks, I wanted to be louder and Coby got a bit more of the solo side in as he did most of the mixing).

On the guitar solo day, Coby actually arrived with an eight pack of tenents super lager and a wrap of speed. This he thought was very rock 'n' roll but I arrived with a crate of tenents super or stupor as it was named by us all, and a rather fetching ounce or so of the white stuff. I took preference as soon as it was clear to and spiked Phil's drink, within minutes he was getting right into it and we played like demons for fuckin' hours, well over the time limit and on into the night (such fun) ah, memories.

So with the record finalized we then had t-shirts and sweatshirts made up (I still have them made once a year as popularity is still rife for them, I also use the logo BASTADO man for other shirts and merchandise that I sell, look out for it, sometimes you can find me advertising on web pages or lately on ebay).

Ha, ha, ha. A quick advertising ploy (why not) we also had flyers made up and Joe and myself went and gate-crashed KERRANG'S offices in Oxford street, and they gave us a write up and so did a few other papers just on the flyers alone. We released the twelve inch single named 'NEVER MIND THE PISTOLS THIS IS BOLLOCKS' written in Spanish, in keeping with the Mexican Spanish type of theme, the single got a rave review and MORAT gave it the single of the week in KERRANG and I later released it through FLICKNIFE.

THE CLUB

On the opening night of CLUB BASTADOS in the basement part of the ASTORIA we had managed to over compensate for the turnout and the place was awash with every fuckin' face in the SOHO scene at the time. I had got the singer from MAURNBLADE to host the D.J. spot and my old mate BRAD SIMS from 'SIMS TATTOO'S' (there ya go Brad a plug for ya) came down and was tattooing people. I think in fact, I know, Dave lush had a tattoo before coming on stage to sing the record live as we had done a couple of rehearsals and had managed to get a rough idea of how they all went, jeezus it was loose!

Also we managed to have five of the London biker clubs there THE HELLS ANGELS, THE SONS OF SATAN, THE OUTCASTS, and mcc clubs THICK AS THIEFS and THE EASILY LED.

The night went off without a hitch (fuck off!) Well it went off without a punch up is a better way of phrasing that particular statement, and everyone had a fuckin' jolly good time. We had strippers and everything even if one of the strippers done a runner as she confessed to having slept with most of the clientele and was sure to get a bucket load of flack if she had actually gone through with her dance act? True, very, very true.

After that particular night we once again got rave reviews for a great night out, we tried again the following week but missed

MY EX-WIFE AND MOTHER TO MY KIDS

I was with Lynne from the age of 19 going on 20 and then on and off up until the age of 24 going on 25. My daughter Ziggy was born in 1981 we then got married. Six years later with Lynne pregnant at the wedding (last ditch attempt at rekindling a burnt out manure heap of a relationship) with my son, Sonny. He was born in 1986. I must say here and now that I haven't entered her name in all of the stories that involve her, as our time together was very off and on while being extremely violent at times and as you all know there's two sides to every story and mine will obviously be bias in my favour so for the sake of my kidz, and grand kidz, not to mention any liable litigations, and just plain respect for someone who's not in my life and hasn't been for years!!! (Plus this book is neither about her, nor the kidz as such but dedicated to them none the less). Because of this, I'm not sure if Lynne would want to be associated with a lot of the story pieces, as this is about my past and not hers.
Lynne has made a new life for herself and I think it's only proper that I should respect this....mmmmm well!
Even though she was a complete nightmare, and oh yes I mustn't forget to say that, by the way Lynne or as she used to be known Dim or Evil Lynne (from the kids cartoon HE MAN).
I completely faked all my orgasms…
Ha, ha, ha. Mmmmmm!

O.K. THANK YOU'S N STUFF...

First I would like to thank ME for being such a star all the way through this book ha, ha, ha, well if I don't, no one else will.

Secondly I would like to say without all the bands, artists, various drug dealers, drug takers and other assorted mmmmm, people? that made up the scene be it cool dudes or arse holes including myself at times (ok more often than not) there would be no book for a bleeding nobody such as myself to write, so cheers to you all.

I would like to say a big up Môn to Gary for his contributions, thanks to Frenchy, Horace, Leo, for being themselves, and of course Kerry (double bubble) Andrews poor moo! she spent hours spell checking and proof reading this mindless drivel (so any spelling mistooks ya knoo how dud dem). Also I suppose I'll have to thank Danny unt Helen from GRAPHIC ENTERTAINMENTS even though they said they wanted no affiliation with the contents of my scribblings, but hey you designed the cover etc so you'll have to be named, and everyone else who found time to give in helping me jog a blurry memory while getting it together to find the time and patience to sit down for days and nights on end and finally getting round to putting all this shit down on paper.

No thanks to the wankers who were too scared, jealous or just down right above it all to get involved, heads stuck up there arses (yes you know who you are).

I have no regrets with my past and feel I must convey this in these my final notes as so many people seem to think that having been a junkie, a fighter, lover, artist, musician, poet, life analyst oh and a bit of a rogue (lovable I hope!)
and a single dad through a big chunk of this (for better or for worse) you'll have to ask my kids that one?
Our lives are what they are and you can't mask the past, nor can you pretend it never happened, so let's all rejoice in ourselves, have a good giggle about some very stupid situations, revel in the naughty bits while squirming in some of the more horrific but wouldn't change a thing if YOUR life depended on it times, so with too many names to mention, slander, and so on.
I won't!!

If ya interested in purchasing C.Ds or T-shirts try this website:

www.myspace.com/stevespeedmachine

Or I may have this site up and running by then:

www.bastadoschurch.com

DEDICATED TO MY KIDZ N GRAND KIDZ...
Ziggy, Sonny, Iziah, Micky.

AND ALL THE FORGOTTEN HEROES FROM
THE STREETS OF SUBCULTURE LONDON (circa)
1975 – 2006)
R. I. P.

A FINAL THOUGHT (don't know who wrote this but it's cool).

THE POSITIVE SIDE OF LIFE:

Living on Earth is expensive,
but it does include a free trip
around the sun every year.

How long a minute is
depends on what side of the
bathroom door you're on.

Birthdays are good for you;
the more you have,
the longer you live.

Happiness comes through doors you
didn't even know you left open.

Ever notice that the people who are late
are often much jollier
than the people who have to wait for them?

Most of us go to our grave
with our music still inside of us.

If supermarkets are lowering prices every day,
how come nothing is free yet?

You may be only one person in the world,
but you may also be the world to one person.

Some mistakes are too much fun
to only make once.

Don't cry because it's over;
smile because it happened.

We could learn a lot from crayons:
some are sharp, some are pretty,
some are dull, some have weird names,
and all are different colours....but
they all exist very nicely in the same box.

A truly happy person is one who
can enjoy the scenery on a detour.

AND A FINAL TATTOO ANECDOTE THOUGHT FOR
LIFE, THAT I WROTE:

STRIP A MAN OF HIS CLOTHES AND HE'LL STAND
NAKED AS THE NEXT MAN.
STRIP ME OF MY CLOTHES AND MY SKIN WILL
ALWAYS SHOW MY TRUE COLOURS...
(s.r.2005)

SO....... YOU CAN ALL GO
FUCK OFF NOW!
AND
DON'T LET THE DOOR HIT YOU ON THE ARSE ON
THE WAY OUT!

UP YA BUM
And
Remember,
DONT TAKE DRUGZ KIDZ

OH; GOES ON THEN!

FUCK THE SYSTEM,

FEAR THE REAPER?

TAKE SWEETS FROM STRANGERS

SPITTING IN THE WIND, COMES BACK AT YA TWICE AS HARD

IF IT'S NOT BROKE, DON'T FIX IT.

IF IT IS BROKE, THROW IT AWAY.

CHARLES MANSON, FOR BEING MY LIFE COACH?!

THE SOFTER THE CUSHION, THE SWEETER THE PUSHIN', BABY.

EVERYTHING THAT IS NOT, AND EVERYTHING THAT IS NOT IS WHAT IS NOT WAS.

DON'T LET THE BASTARDS GRIND YA DOWN,

DON'T TALK TO STRANGERS.

NEVER BUY A SECONDHAND CAR FROM A MAN IN A SUIT.

NEVER TRUST A HIPPIE.

THE FIRST BAG IS ALWAYS FREE?

AND TA, TA,

OH, AND JUST IN CASE.

THE OLD BOY'S STILL GOT IT!
I, JUST CAN'T REMEMBER WHERE I PUT IT?

And this little line of an I.C.U. song that I've always loved.

WE WERE BUTTERFLYS FLYING IN THE SKY,
ISNT IT A SIN,
NO ONE LET US
IN ....

I am currently working on some new projects, so keep a look
out for these top tittles

1). MARY'S MINNIE AND THE MAGIC WORM.

2). TERRY THE TURTLE HEAD. (And the brown nosed bog
turds from hell).

3). THE DIRTBOX COWBOYS.

4). CLITASAWRARSE.

5). THE X VILLAGE. (a story of a promiscuous little fucker
who spent his life lovin' 'n' leavin' a host of women and wakes
one morning in the arms of a lady of the night in a strange bed
in a strange village. Then while trying to escape he encoun-
ters a gaggle of his X wives, goul fiends, and assorted strumpets
all seeking their scathing revenge on his arse!)

Neeyha, ha, ha!

PROJECTS THAT I HAVE ACTUALLY DONE!

CHAIN AND SPROCKET
(A comedy c.d. made with a mate (name check) Harley Pete cippa.)
Four songs, mainly about food?
Best song and inspiration behind the other three was
CHINESE CHICKEN FOR TEA...

MUZAK MAKING...

1). THE BORN AGAIN LOSERS

2). ANTI SOCIAL OLD BASTARDS

3). THE SCREAMING MIRKINS
4). THE LAUGHING KAHOONERS

Printed in the United Kingdom
by Lightning Source UK Ltd.
117538UKS00001B/7-36

the mark, and then John the money got itchy feet and done a runner never to be seen again leaving me holding the fucking bill, cheers mate!

So it faded away, well not for good I took charge of things while Joe gave up on it all and went back to roadying and I got the club up and running a few months later at GOSSIPS in MEARD STREET. Then again, in different places, bike club meets and the like.

I then went on to form my fave band F.T.W.(unincorporated) we made an album that took a year to do, never quite finished it as the record company changed their financial agreement halfway through recording and wanted me to tour all over the country to pay for the recording time (bollocks to that). So we had our differences and this all ended with me once again liberating my art from the studio and it stays sat in my cupboard until now!

I can't fall into the old record company ploy of, its them that are doing you a privileged type of favour in signing you up, then they want to bleed ya dry even before you've played a gig well FUCK OFF! I'll always be stubborn as I'm not ever gonna sell myself short just for recognition, there's enough faces out there who know me. I don't need to release a fuckin' record to be noticed thank you.

This is however one of the reasons why I have never "made it, maaaan" But hey I'm an artist and I would rather keep my art here and release it myself than sit back and watch some other cunt sunbathing their lily white arse on the beach of some Spanish holiday resort courtesy of all my hard labours.

Another project came from the F.T.W. line up. I dismembered them and formed a punk version of it called THE LONDON LOSERS a name that was used before but I've always had a soft spot for it. So I put a band together around the name and we gigged but I was getting worse for wear on the amphetamine side of life so it disintegrated into the dust.

I then formed a bike club called THE LOSERS a money making venture that turned to shit as we got busted inbetween a war for territory by two of the biggest outlaw M.C. clubs, that tried using me as a middle man punch bag. So I got out of that by the skin of my teeth even though I managed to get a kick in the pants for blowing their cover?

I later went on to resurrect the CLUB BASTADOS thing and it's still an ongoing thing but I had a breakdown a while after so not much has happened since as far as these types of adventures go. In fact the whole scene died for a while and as I was going through my own troubles it seemed everyone else was too. It must be one of those times, an end of another drug fuelled era.

I stayed at home for a while and got a really bad speed, D.F118, valium, ten pints of tenents a day and a shit load of dope a day, habit. My daughter had gone off the rails too (she's doin great now though). I joined the BLOOD, made a video, played a bit, got into art and made some cash from selling picture frames made from cavity wall filler, sounds crap but they really looked fuckin' great and I made more money from that than I ever did out of music or clubs!

I then got into the whole FETISH scene, as it was a real laugh to begin with but I was so fucked up that I had to put myself on hold as I was also getting in trouble with biker gangs and all sorts of shit. I had another breakdown for a couple of years and now I have changed address and I am starting a new life at the age of forty six, I'm writing this book, releasing a book of poetry and lyrics and I've started a comic, so all's well that ends well, mmmmm we'll see ah!!!???